Praise for Getting to Know the Church Fathers

"This book is a treasure—an exposition of the writings of the early church fathers without an agenda to prove that they support either evangelical or Catholic theology, but rather to simply understand what they wrote and believed! This book fills a gap in evangelical theology, reminding us that every century of church history has something to teach us, including those early centuries when seeds were planted that later grew to have a profound impact on the Christian church. I recommend this book to all who care about doctrine and the progress of history from the early apostles onward. Here is a rudder to guide us, not an anchor to weigh us down."

—**Erwin W. Lutzer**, Moody Church

"Bryan Litfin's book not only introduces ten key figures of the early church but also shows why the study of the church fathers is still beneficial for Christians today. This is an excellent primer to the life, faith, and writings of these pillars of the church. Litfin leads us smoothly from the age of persecution and martyrdom to the period of division and doctrinal controversy, always showing how Christ and his gospel remained the central concern and strength of early believers."

—**Glen L. Thompson**, Wisconsin Lutheran College

"As they say, 'It's not what you know, it's who you know!' And in this case, knowing the church fathers will enrich what you know with confidence and fresh insight. A big thanks to my friend Bryan Litfin for getting us reacquainted in an understandable and stimulating way."

—**Joseph M. Stowell**, Harvest Bible Chapel;
former president, Moody Bible Institute

"*Getting to Know the Church Fathers* offers a clear and engaging introduction to the lives of some of the most significant Christians of the early church. Bryan Litfin has managed to take a subject that is often tedious and remote and transform it instead into one that sparkles with personal interest and contemporary relevance. The questions and bibliographies that end each chapter provide opportunities for further reflection and study, and the brief selections from these early Christian writers offer a glimpse into the hearts and minds of these key figures. Litfin's work offers a superb introduction to the formative Christian leaders of the church, one that is eminently readable and enjoyable."

—**Bruce A. Ware**, Southern Baptist Theological Seminary

GETTING TO KNOW THE CHURCH FATHERS

An Evangelical Introduction

BRYAN M. LITFIN

BrazosPress
Grand Rapids, Michigan

© 2007 by Bryan M. Litfin

Published by Brazos Press
a division of Baker Publishing Group
P.O. Box 6287, Grand Rapids, MI 49516-6287
www.brazospress.com

Second printing, April 2008

Printed in the United States of America

Library of Congress Cataloging-in-Publication Data
Litfin, Bryan M., 1970–
    Getting to know the church fathers : an evangelical introduction / Bryan M. Litfin.
       p. cm.
    Includes bibliographical references.
    ISBN 10: 1-58743-196-3 (pbk.)
    ISBN 978-1-58743-196-8 (pbk.)
    1. Fathers of the church. I. Title.
BR67.L58 2007
270.1—dc22   2007008647

CONTENTS

Acknowledgments

I owe an immeasurable debt to my teachers:
my father, Dr. A. Duane Litfin,
who taught me to think like a Christian;
Drs. Stephen R. Spencer and D. Jeffrey Bingham,
who taught me to think like a scholar;
and Dr. Robert Louis Wilken,
who taught me to think like a catholic.

In addition,

Dr. Jason R. Hubbard was an excellent traveling companion on a research trip to North Africa.

My friend Amy Rachel Peterson helped me understand Perpetua's spirituality as a woman.

I am also grateful to Moody Bible Institute for providing
an environment conducive to intellectual life. In particular I
acknowledge the help of Librarian Joseph Cataio,
who obtained many items for me through Interlibrary Loan.

But most of all, I am grateful for the support of my wife,
Carolyn Litfin,
whom I describe with the words Tertullian used of his own wife:
dilectissime mihi in Domino conserva.

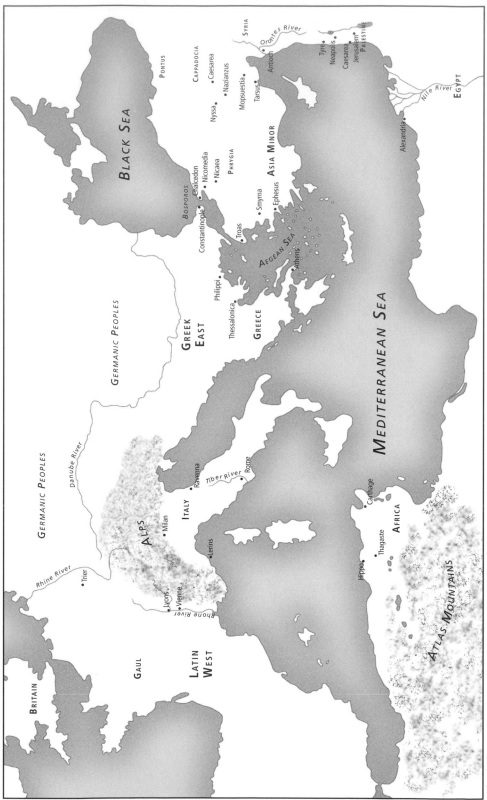

TIMELINE

BC

800	Founding of Carthage
753	Founding of Rome
658	Founding of Byzantium
347	Death of Plato
332	Alexander the Great's conquests; founding of Alexandria
322	Death of Aristotle
300	Founding of Antioch
52	Julius Caesar conquers Gaul
43	Founding of Lugdunum (Lyons)
27	Caesar Augustus becomes the first Roman emperor

The Birth of Christ
AD

30	Death and resurrection of Jesus Christ
30s–60s	Events of the Book of Acts
100–165	*Life of Justin Martyr*
100+	Gnostic heresy widely preached
115	*Ignatius of Antioch* travels to his martyrdom
130–202	*Life of Irenaeus of Lyons*
140	Marcion begins preaching heresy in Rome
156	*Polycarp of Smyrna* martyred
170–215	*Life of Tertullian of Carthage*
177	*Blandina, Sanctus, and companions* martyred at Lyons and Vienne
180	Martyrdom of the *Martyrs of Scilli*
186–251	*Life of Origen of Alexandria*

203	*Perpetua, Felicity, and companions* martyred; Origen's father *Leonides* martyred
250	Emperor Decius decrees a severe persecution of Christians
251–356	*Life of the monk Anthony of Egypt*
260–339	*Life of Eusebius of Caesarea*
299–373	*Life of Athanasius of Alexandria*
303	Emperor Diocletian initiates the Great Persecution
312	Emperor Constantine victorious at the Battle of the Milvian Bridge; Donatist schism erupts in North Africa
313	Emperor Constantine issues the Edict of Milan
318	Arius begins preaching heresy
325	Council of Nicaea defines the Trinity
330	Emperor Constantine refounds Byzantium as Constantinople
337	Death of Emperor Constantine
349–407	*Life of John Chrysostom*
350–428	*Life of Theodore of Mopsuestia*
354–430	*Life of Augustine of Hippo*
367	Easter Letter of Athanasius lists the biblical canon
378–444	*Life of Cyril of Alexandria*
381	Council of Constantinople supports the Nicene doctrine of the Trinity
387	Baptism of Augustine
390	*Death of Diodore of Tarsus*
402	Pelagius begins preaching heresy
410	Alaric the Goth invades Rome
428	Nestorius becomes bishop of Constantinople
431	Council of Ephesus condemns the doctrines of Pelagius and Nestorius
440–461	*Papacy of Leo the Great*
451	Council of Chalcedon defines orthodox Christology
476	Last Roman emperor in the West deposed by a barbarian lord
500	End of the Roman Empire and the Ancient Period; beginning of the Medieval Period

Church Fathers indicated with *italics*
Some lifespan dates are approximate

INTRODUCTION

When someone asks me what I do for a living, and I say I'm a professor whose academic expertise is the early church fathers, I've become accustomed to receiving a quizzical expression. If the person is a stranger, I often ask if he is a Roman Catholic, because Catholics have been exposed to the fathers of the church. But evangelical Christians haven't. "Would that be someone like Jonathan Edwards?" one friend asked me, referring to the colonial American theologian. "Earlier than that," I replied. "From the Roman Empire." Most Christians today haven't met the fathers. Perhaps they've heard of St. Augustine, but that's about it. If this is true in your case, I believe you're missing something valuable. For many readers of this book, this will be your first real encounter with the ancient Christian writers. And so you have embarked on a journey of *discovery*. To convey that sense of discovery to the students I teach, I use an illustration about a boy I call Billy.

Little Billy loved his grandmother very much. His childhood years were filled with visits to her house after school or on Sunday afternoons. Grandma always gave him something delicious for a snack: not the carrot sticks or yogurt Billy's mother insisted on at home, but a big slice of warm apple pie melting the ice cream on top, or Tollhouse cookies still gooey from the cooling rack. Grandma had a swing out back, an old-fashioned one, not so safe as modern plastic swing sets. It was just a frayed rope looped around a tree limb far above, running through a plain board seat down low. When you really got it going, it would swing in long stomach-churning arcs while the tree creaked ominously in protest. If while playing in the yard Billy happened to fall and scrape a knee, Grandma was there with some grandmotherly concoction to tend his wound—though her comforting words actually accomplished far more as a remedy. Billy just loved going to his Grandma's house. She always lavished care and concern on him, giving her undivided attention to whatever he might be interested in at the moment.

But as he became a teenager, Billy's visits to Grandma's house became less frequent. He had his driver's license now, and his schedule was filled with sports and activities. His friends, both male and female, demanded more and more of his time. Of course he still loved Grandma, and always dutifully wrote her a thank-you note for the birthday cards she insisted on filling with cash. Yet as the years went by, his visits to Grandma's house began to come only at Christmas, if at all. An occasional phone call kept him current with his "grandson responsibilities" and eased his conscience. But soon the young adult named Bill had a demanding career, a family, and a life of his own.

So it was that Grandma's death came as something of a shock to him. He hadn't really noticed her declining health—though he could have if he had paid closer attention. Her funeral service did not bring closure to him at all, but left him with many lingering questions. The responsibility fell to Bill to dispose of Grandma's possessions and to sell her house. The process caused him to reflect in new ways about his grandmother, and indeed his whole family line. "Who was this woman?" he wondered. "Where did she come from? What people and values shaped her world?" It dawned on Bill that while Grandma had shown great interest in every minor preoccupation of his life, he had never really known her as a person. He began to regret that in a profound way.

One day Bill was cleaning out his grandmother's attic. The door to the attic led from the guest room—the very room where he used to spend the night whenever his parents were out of town. He had seen that door many times, often imagining the fearsome monsters that might lurk behind it. But he had never done more than peek through the door frame (always in the light of day, of course). Now he opened the door for the first time with adult eyes. Dust particles swirled in the single shaft of sunlight coming from a small window. The air was musty and close. Bill's eyes fell on a large object in the far corner. It was a cedar hope chest, the type that, back in the old days, young women always received when they got married. Bill opened it with hushed expectation, like a pirate discovering lost treasure in the stories Grandma used to tell.

The chest was in fact filled with treasure—though not the kind made of silver and gold. Bill first picked up an old baseball glove, which smelled of rich leather and oil. His long-deceased grandfather's name was handwritten upon it. So Grandpa had been a baseball player? "One of the finest," his grandmother seemed to whisper to him. Next he examined a necklace with a finely-crafted ivory locket hanging from the chain. Inside were two small pictures of Grandma and Grandpa. On the back it was engraved with the words, "Until I return." But Grandpa had not returned from the war. A framed picture of Grandpa in his uniform reminded Bill of what a handsome fellow he had been in his day. In another portrait Bill wondered who this pretty girl might be—wait a minute—could it be Grandma? Bill was so used to her round, wrinkly face that it was startling to think of her as an attractive young woman with love interests of her own. A photo album of black-and-white pictures, now yellowed with age, told the whole story. It was a story filled with all the joys and sorrows, the light moments and memorable occasions, of lives lived in the real world.

At the bottom of the hope chest lay one more thing. It was a leather-bound family Bible with Grandma's name inscribed upon it. As Bill leafed through the delicate pages, he discovered marginal notes and scraps of paper brimming with her prayers, wise observations, and private spiritual longings. Moisture gathered in Bill's eyes as he remembered how Grandma had offered him some of these same Christian observations—but only rarely, for he had typically been disinterested in such matters, too quick to run off to the next game or activity. As he sat on his knees in front of the old hope chest, a single thought dominated Bill's mind: "Why didn't I take the time to explore this legacy when I had a chance? I never knew I had such a meaningful family heritage!"

The story of little Billy reminds us how easy it is to let the past be crowded out by the urgencies of the present and the opportunities of the future. This is true in many realms, church history among them. The church fathers often are treated as once-beloved ancestors who have been forgotten today. Their world is a vague memory, their presence an awareness we possess only in the most fleeting of ways. We know there were famous Christians who lived "back then," but we can't quite put a finger on who they were or what they did. Something about being thrown to the lions and the Romans and all that, right? Yet despite our indifference to their world, we are inextricably bound to the church fathers. They are our spiritual ancestors, for better or for worse. Just like the family tree we inherit, we are their descendants whether we like it or not. It is easy enough to go through life like Bill: with a vague awareness of the past, yet too busy with present responsibilities to think much about something as intangible as our "heritage." But like Bill, we would be missing some real treasures if we did not explore our Christian origins. To do that, we first need to realize that the opening actors in the Christian drama were flesh-and-blood people who lived their lives in God's presence just as we do today.

The Mighty Deeds of Christian History

Most Christians who have been exposed to the early church fathers probably have seen them marshaled as evidence for one theological argument or another. Too often a snippet from an ancient writer is yanked out of context to support a modern viewpoint. Such an approach is unfair to authors who never intended that their writings be excerpted out of their whole corpus to serve as ammunition in a modern-day war of words. Yet this misuse of the ancients is not even the biggest problem here. At a more basic level, it misses the very nature of the Christian faith itself—at least the faith as the church fathers understood it. For them, Christianity was not only about *doctrines*. That's not to say they ignored doctrines. Indeed, great theological struggles were waged over the doctrinal difference made by a single Greek letter. But, for the fathers, Christianity was not a collection of abstract ideas or secret wisdom which could be gathered in a manual and memorized. Instead it was a *story*, an account of things that have happened in the arena of human history on this earth. In his book *The Spirit of Early Christian Thought* (a book well worth reading for the interested newcomer to the church fathers), Robert Wilken writes,

> . . . I am convinced that the study of early Christian thought has been too preoccupied with ideas. The intellectual effort of the early church was at the service of a much loftier goal than giving conceptual form to Christian belief. Its mission was to win the hearts and minds of men and women and to change their lives.[1]

Wilken is saying that Christianity is a real-world, event-oriented religion. Why? Because its very epicenter is the God-Man who came to us in time and space, bridging the non-material and the material in himself. The Bible is replete with historical people and places and names, all of which give structure to its cosmic narrative of creation, fall, promise, redemption, and restoration. The Christian religion tells the story of what God does, and especially what he does in the Lord Jesus Christ as people come into relationship with him.

When Caesar Augustus rose to power as the first Roman emperor around the time of the birth of Christ, he wrote a work celebrating his exploits commonly called the *Res Gestae* (pronounced *race gest-aye*, meaning "acts" or "things accomplished"). Augustus's successor Tiberius caused the *Res Gestae* to be inscribed on buildings throughout the empire to proclaim the mighty achievements of his stepfather. In a similar way, the Christian religion recounted the earliest believers' own sort of divine *res gestae*.[2] Far more than a set of doctrinal propositions, Christianity gave an account of the mighty deeds accomplished by God through Jesus Christ in the power of the Holy Spirit. The Lord God has triumphed over the forces of evil, and is carrying human history to its conclusion just as he has been doing since the first day of creation. The ancient church was an eyewitness religion, attested by people who had seen and heard the great things God has done. Therefore, for those early believers, *people and events* mattered more than abstract ideas. Or, to put it differently: central Christian ideas were always tied to actual events that had transpired in our world. For that reason, this book will focus on several key church fathers as individual personalities. Many books have been written on the history of Christian doctrines or important themes in early church history. But in this book, I hope to introduce you in a more *personal* way to some of your spiritual ancestors. I want to help you get to know some folks who are part of your own spiritual legacy and heritage in the faith.

What is a "Church Father"?

Before we begin, let's clear something up. We will be calling the people we meet "the church fathers." What do we mean by this designation? In the realm of everyday experience, a father is by definition someone who came before us. A father's children are genetically linked to him as his descendants. No matter what our actual human fathers may have been like, most of us can grasp the concept of an ideal father figure. He is a man who, having walked the path of life already, guides his children in wisdom. This is the idea behind the term "church fathers." The fathers are a previous generation of believers who continue to guide their spiritual descendants in the Christian church today. The term "fathers" was even used in this sense by the later writers of the ancient period to refer to the earliest generations of believers. So it is a term with much antiquity behind it.

One immediate question might spring to mind: What about the church mothers? Were there no women who contributed anything to early Christianity? The truth is there were many great women in the ancient church. The early Christians often lauded the noble and heroic qualities of female saints, especially martyrs and virgins who lived consecrated lives before God. Yet we must remember that in ancient society, women rarely were taught to read and write, and certainly were not expected to produce an intellectual literary output. For this reason, few women's writings have come down to us today from the early church period. In this book we will use the term "church fathers" as a kind of standard designation, while remembering that many Christian "mothers" contributed greatly to church history as well. To help keep this in mind, we will be looking at one of the few surviving ancient texts actually penned by a woman: the account of the noblewoman Perpetua, who went to her death by martyrdom in the year AD 203.

Today the academic study of the ancient Christians is called "patristics" or "patrology," which comes from the Latin word for father (*pater*). One of the most influential systematizers of the modern study of ancient Christianity was Professor Johannes Quasten. In his four-volume work *Patrology*, which discusses every surviving Christian writer from the ancient period, Quasten defines the "fathers" as the Christian writers from New Testament times up until Isidore of Seville (AD 636) in the Latin world, and John of Damascus (AD 749) in the Greek world.[3] While such late writers certainly had much in common with their forebears in the Roman Empire, most historians would consider the AD 600s and 700s to be well into the period we would call "early medieval" or "Byzantine." In this book, we will be looking at ten writers who lived before the year AD 500, which is approximately the time of the fall of Rome and the end of the ancient period.

Are we correct in thinking of these ancient writers as our spiritual "fathers"? Perhaps this sounds like the Roman Catholic practice of referring to priests in this way. Or we may recall the words of Jesus, "And call no man your father on earth, for you have one Father, who is in heaven" (Matt. 23:9). It is important to understand what Jesus is saying here. In context he is discussing the hypocrisy and pride of the Pharisees, whose outward pretensions (such as receiving a greeting as an esteemed rabbinic father-figure) would *replace* heartfelt obedience to God. Note that Jesus also says we should not call someone our "teacher" or "instructor," yet we have no problem using those titles today. Obviously it was not the title that mattered to the Lord, but the way it was used in such hypocritical religion. There is no problem with referring to someone as our "father" if it is done in the right way. Indeed this is exactly what Paul did in 1 Corinthians 4:15 when he said, "For though you have countless guides in Christ, you do not have many fathers. For I became your father in Christ Jesus through the gospel." Both Paul and John frequently referred to their converts as their children.

The idea of one's spiritual mentor serving as a father figure was very common in the ancient world. The second-century Christian leader Irenaeus wrote, "For when any person has been taught from the mouth of another, he is termed the son of him who instructs him, and the latter [is called] his father."[4] Likewise the ancient church teacher Clement of Alexandria wrote, "Words are the progeny of the soul. Hence we call those who have instructed us, fathers."[5] A few lines later Clement adds, "Everyone who is instructed is, in respect of subjection, the son of his instructor." The early church historian Eusebius even took the title "son of Pamphilus" from the man who was his intimate friend and mentor.[6] In the same way, perhaps we can learn to think of the "church fathers" as those who came before us, still playing a guiding role in our lives.

It has become customary to delineate four main criteria to identify a "father of the church": they must be *ancient, orthodox in doctrine, holy in life,* and *approved by other Christians.*[7] Such a perspective can already be seen in a fifth-century writer named Vincent, a monk from Lérins, an island off the southern coast of France. Vincent wrote an influential treatise that attempted to define orthodoxy and distinguish it from heresy. His famous dictum advises us to accept "what has been believed everywhere, always, and by all."[8] Vincent saw the Christian faith as being held in trust by the "fathers" who have passed it down to posterity. He based this principle on Deuteronomy 32:7: "Remember the days of old; consider the years of many generations; ask your father, and he will show you, your elders, and they will tell you." Vincent described the church fathers as those "living and teaching with holiness, wisdom, and constancy,"[9] and "who, each in his own time and place, remaining in the unity of communion and of the faith, were accepted as approved masters."[10] How unfitting it would be for us, he says, to reap weeds today where our forefathers had planted wheat! With eloquence Vincent wrote,

> Therefore, whatever has been sown by the fidelity of the Fathers in this husbandry of God's Church, the same ought to be cultivated and taken care of by the industry of their children, the same ought to flourish and ripen, the same ought to advance and go forward to perfection. For it is right that those ancient doctrines of heavenly philosophy should, as time goes on, be cared for, smoothed, polished; but not that they should be changed, not that they should be maimed, not that they should be mutilated.[11]

Along with Vincent of Lérins, perhaps we can now define the "church fathers" as those who lived righteously and passed down to later generations the core tenets of the Christian faith that they themselves had received from the apostles.[12] In other words, the church fathers and mothers are those men and women whose beliefs and lifestyles were consistent with what is recorded as the apostolic teaching found in the scriptures. Thus, the ancient fathers provide us with the first links of continuity to our Christian past.

Misconceptions about the Church Fathers

As we get acquainted with some of our spiritual ancestors, I would like to address a few common misconceptions that many evangelical Christians have. These are some of the most prevalent errors I have run into as I talk with other believers about the church fathers.

Misconception #1: The church fathers were not biblical. Many Protestants today associate the sayings of the church fathers with the nebulous concept of "tradition." Patristic teachings and creeds are sometimes referred to as "the doctrines of men," as opposed to the divine revelation given in scripture. Now it is certainly true that the writings of the fathers are susceptible to error, while the Bible alone is the inspired, inerrant Word of God. But even though the fathers are fallible human beings, this does not mean everything they wrote is therefore wrong. They may well have had some wise and profitable insights which square nicely with biblical revelation. The problem comes when we view everything through the lens of the Reformation era, when "Scripture" and "Tradition" became two competing entities. At that time, to embrace "Tradition" was to embrace a Roman Catholic viewpoint. The Council of Trent said in 1546 that the Bible and the traditions of the Roman Catholic Church are each to be venerated "with like feeling of piety and reverence."[13] This came to be known as a "two-source" theory in which "Scripture" and "Tradition" were viewed as separate fountains of revelation. "Tradition" (as found primarily in the teachings of the bishops) was said to possess equal authority alongside the Bible. Although the Second Vatican Council of the 1960s acknowledged a much closer unity between "Scripture" and "Tradition" than had previously been expressed in official Catholic decrees,[14] Protestants today still remain leery of church tradition.

Obviously, to read such perspectives back onto the church fathers is to do them an injustice. The fathers could not have conceived of "tradition" (that which is handed down) as being contradictory to the Bible, since all the church's truth ultimately came from God himself.[15] The Father sent Jesus to reveal divine truth, and Jesus shared this truth with the apostles. The apostles then preached the gospel to the world verbally, and wrote about the Christian faith in the inspired scriptures. This entire apostolic deposit of faith is exactly what the early fathers intended to embrace in their churches. So "tradition" was not a term opposed to scripture. In fact, it was the very possession of scripture and tradition that distinguished the orthodox from the heretics, who could not trace themselves back to the faith handed down since the apostolic times.

The truth of the matter is the church fathers loved the scriptures immensely. You cannot read the fathers without immediately noticing how the pages of their writings reverberate with scriptural quotations and themes. Scripture was in the very air they breathed; it was what nourished their souls. Athanasius, the fourth-century bishop at Alexandria in Egypt, listed the books of the Bible and then said about them, "These are the fountains of salvation, that they who thirst may be satisfied with the living words they contain. In these alone is proclaimed the doctrine of godliness. Let no man add to these, neither let him take [anything away] from these."[16] Origen, who also lived at Alexandria about a century earlier, was so devoted to scriptural study that he produced by dictation more than 2,000 written works, including commentaries, sermons, theological treatises, and a scholarly edition of various biblical manuscripts. For this task Origen is said to have needed more than seven scribes working together and relieving each other in shifts to keep up with their master's prodigious output.[17] Many of the fathers' writings are so full of scripture you can scarcely read a single paragraph without coming across a biblical citation or allusion. To keep track of it all, modern scholars use a multi-volume reference work called *Biblia Patristica*, which is filled with page after page of small-print Bible

verse references found in various early church writings.[18] Robert
Wilken sums up his lifetime of patristic study this way:

> [W]hat has impressed me most is the omnipresence of the Bible in
> early Christian writings. Early Christian thought is biblical, and one
> of the lasting accomplishments of the patristic period was to forge
> a way of thinking, scriptural in language and inspiration, that gave
> to the church and to Western civilization a unified and coherent
> interpretation of the Bible as a whole.[19]

While the church fathers' interpretive principles and worldview may
have been different than ours, we certainly cannot accuse them of
being ignorant of the scriptures.

Misconception #2: The church fathers were Roman Catholics. Once
again, we commit the error of anachronism if we read our later concept of "Roman Catholic" back onto the church fathers. Instead, we
should understand what they meant when they called themselves
"catholic." I am convinced many Christians today are being robbed
of their ancient heritage precisely because they have equated the word
"catholic" with being "Roman Catholic." Too often the terms get
confused, but they do not mean the same thing. In a course I teach
on church history, we begin each class hour by reciting the Apostles'
Creed together. This creed includes a confession of belief in "the holy
catholic church." One time a student told me that when she reported
this to her father, he became upset because of the word "catholic" in
the creed. The student's father was not alone in his misunderstand-
ing. No doubt this same confusion is reflected in the fundamentalist
churches which reject the Apostles' Creed because of this supposedly
contaminating word. Even those churches which use the creed (such
as the non-denominational Bible church of which I am a member)
raise a few eyebrows in doing so. Instead of being frightened of this
term, I suggest we try to understand what it actually denotes. The
word "catholic" comes from the Greek word *katholicos* which literally
means "pertaining to the whole" or "universal." When it was used
to describe the Christian church in the patristic period, it referred

to the unified community of all true believers in the world: those whose loyalty was given to the risen Christ, whose doctrine was orthodox, and whose faith was identical to the eyewitness testimony proclaimed by the apostles.

Historically speaking, we must differentiate between "lowercase-c" catholic Christianity and "capital-C" Roman Catholic Christianity. When did Roman Catholicism come into being? The Roman Catholic Church is an ever-evolving communion, so it is obviously difficult to pinpoint its precise origins. There is no question it has many continuous lines of development dating right back to the time of the apostles. That is to say, there are numerous doctrines and practices in the Roman Church which are found in the Bible itself and in first-century Christianity.[20] At the same time, the Roman Catholicism of today is not precisely the Roman Catholicism of the medieval or Reformation periods. To identify its origins, we need to define what we're talking about.

If we were to articulate some necessary elements of a "Roman Catholic Church," we would certainly need to include a developed doctrine that the pope is the heir of St. Peter and bears an ongoing ministry in Peter's name. We might also include the idea that the church at Rome should be the pre-eminent seat of Christianity in the whole Latin world. With these criteria in mind, we can perhaps identify an approximate time of origin for the Roman Catholic Church. As we will see in chapter 10, the historical circumstances of the AD 400s created a change in the church at Rome. Because of unprecedented turmoil and the weakening of the imperial government, the bishops found themselves forced to take on increasing civic responsibilities—a situation which continued to be the case in the medieval papacy. The Latin West was severed from the Greek East by the barbarian invasions. At this time, the bishop of Rome (or pope, as he began to be called) became the sole leader of the Latin church, claiming to be the living voice of Peter. These developments, coupled with the longstanding prestige of Rome and the people's habitual instinct to defer to the capital city, made the Roman pontiff the natural spiritual authority for all of Western Europe during the chaos of the early Middle Ages. Based on these considerations, we can date the emergence of Roman Catholicism to sometime around AD 500.

What about "lowercase-c" catholic Christianity? We must recognize that catholic Christianity predated the emergence of its later namesake. It was established long before the Roman Catholic Church ever came into being as such. In an essay entitled "Why All Christians are Catholics," D. H. Williams writes that "'catholicism' is not a shorthand way of saying Roman Catholicism or acknowledging the office of the papacy. It is much older than both and more expansive in meaning."[21] To be catholic is simply to be part of the worldwide body of Christ. Catholicity entails a sense of the universality of the Christian church. This universality is not manifested in a kind of watered-down ecumenism which says nothing in particular and holds to no definite truths. Just the opposite: catholicity is manifested in specific doctrinal content that is held and protected by all who are truly catholic. This means it necessarily excludes alternate versions of the faith—which is what the church fathers usually had in mind when they referred to themselves as *katholicos*. We must therefore understand that catholicity is a noble and worthy goal for every believer. It "operates on the understanding that there exist true doctrines and practices, an understanding which is meant to distinguish the Christian church from theological or moral corruption."[22] In other words, to be a catholic is to join with all who "contend for the faith that was once for all delivered to the saints" (Jude 3). Such was the catholicism of the early church fathers.

Misconception #3: The church fathers represent the "fall" of Christianity. It seems there is a certain historiography (or way of viewing history) subtly being transmitted among many evangelicals today. It goes something like this. The New Testament era was "good," and for a century or two the church was "pure." But then the subsequent generations started perverting the apostolic truth. By the Middle Ages, the perversion of the church—doctrinal, ritual, and moral—was ubiquitous. Only with the advent of the Protestant reformers was apostolic Christianity finally recovered. Thus it becomes necessary to span the ancient and medieval periods with a kind of Protestant bridge. We must leapfrog over the intervening centuries to get back to the early church of the New Testament period, or maybe of the first two or three centuries of the Christian era. During the dark ages after the "fall" of the church, there was a faithful remnant who followed true Christianity in an underground community. Often this historiography employs the vivid image of a "trail of blood" which is said to have been left by the persecuted yet faithful Christians who lived in opposition to the evil institutional church.[23] I know this historiography is being taught today because I have encountered it many times in my students.[24]

What are the origins of this notion of Christianity's "fall" and subsequent recovery?[25] Most of the criticism has hinged upon a particularly significant point in church history: the conversion of Emperor Constantine in the fourth century. The historical circumstances surrounding this event could hardly have been more dramatic. Because of an imperial decree in the year AD 303, the church was experiencing its most intense period of persecution. Many martyrs for the faith were being made amid unspeakable tortures. At this climactic moment, a new potential emperor began vying for power against his enemies. The ancient accounts tell us that young Constantine had a dream in which Christ appeared to him and told him to fashion a Christian symbol into a magnificent banner inlaid with jewels and covered in gold. Sometime earlier, he had seen a vision of the cross in the sky across the midday sun, with a message that read "Conquer by this."[26] Guided by these portentous omens, Constantine defeated his enemy and became emperor. He immediately granted toleration to the Christians and embarked upon a program of imperial support for the faith. However, according to the historical interpretation assumed by many evangelicals, along with Christianity's imperial acceptance came its corruption. Soon the masses clamored to join the religion of the emperor, which he is said to have embraced only for political reasons. The former dedication of the martyrs under persecution could no longer be found. The church was watered down by the uncommitted hordes who joined it in name only, without having true faith. Constantine's conversion was therefore an unmitigated disaster. The church had fallen. Unfortunately, many Protestants today operate with more or less this perspective. It is found especially in the Free Church wing of the Reformation and in Baptist circles, as well as in many of today's non-denominational Bible churches.

The "fall" historiography described above is *not* the viewpoint taken in this book, for several reasons. First of all, I find it to be an overly simplistic way of doing history. It is problematic to force the historical and demographic changes ushered in by Constantine into black-and-white categories of good and bad. History tends to be messy, not easily lending itself to portrayals which make absolute statements about positives and negatives. That is to say, Constantine could just as easily be viewed as a great plus for the church instead of a minus. If you were living in the time of Constantine, you probably would have viewed Christianity as "rising" not "falling"—because now the authorities were no longer planning to put your eyes out for being a Christian! My point is that we must always be careful in handing out white hats and black hats.

Another problem with the "fall" historiography is that it does not square with what many of the Protestant reformers believed about the early church fathers. The reformers often used the ancient church as an exemplar, the very thing to which they were trying to return. Of course, figures such as Martin Luther did view the Protestant movement as the "true church" whose suffering at the hands of the Roman Catholics finds parallels throughout church history. The reformers understood pristine original Christianity to have been tarnished by centuries of papal abuse. So the idea of a "fall" in this sense was a natural part of Protestant argumentation in the sixteenth century, when the balance of power weighed heavily in favor of the Roman Catholic Church. Such a perspective finds its most extreme expression in the Radical Reformation of the Anabaptists.[27] Yet this does not mean all the Protestants regarded the ancient church as the enemy. Rather, it was late medieval Roman Catholicism against which they directed their reforming efforts.

The reformers generally considered the early church fathers (especially Augustine) to be their allies. Martin Luther warmly embraced the church fathers whenever their comments dovetailed with scripture. Luther's biblical commentaries are full of patristic citations. He tells us he had thoroughly studied the fathers, and even endorsed the ideal of a reformation based upon their writings and the ancient creeds (though he thought this would be impossible to achieve).[28] Similarly, John Calvin considered himself and the other reformers to be more faithful to the early church fathers than the Roman Church was.[29] Against a Roman Catholic opponent, Calvin wrote that "all we have attempted has been to renew that ancient form of the Church" which had been sullied by the pope and his followers.[30] Calvin offered not just the church of the apostles, but also that of the ancient fathers, as a model against which the degradations of the Roman Church of his day stood in contrast. On many points of theology, "the ancient Church is clearly on our side, and opposes you."[31] Thus we see that most of the reformers did not consider the patristic period to be the era of a "fall." Rather, the fathers were judged as having retained scriptural teaching in most respects.

But here is the most basic reason I differ from the "fall" historiography: it robs contemporary believers of vast portions of their historical legacy. It is my desire that every Christian be free to embrace his or her continuous heritage in the faith. This means *all* the centuries of Christian history are your rightful possession. At the same time, we must always recognize that there are particular elements in each generation which we will not want to embrace, for they do not meet the scriptural standard of truth. Like the family tree we inevitably inherit, we must take the good along with the bad, the respected patriarchs as well as the black sheep. We should always keep a critical eye out, submitting every doctrine to the penetrating light of the Word of God. Armed with this sword, we need not fear to make all of church history our own. It is one of the richest aspects of our Christian inheritance. Even if we must sometimes separate the true currency from the counterfeit bills, we shouldn't hesitate to take the good stuff to the bank!

So Why Study the Church Fathers?

What benefit can we expect to gain from studying our forefathers in the faith? I have devoted a lot of thought to how I should answer this question for my students. One common reason given for studying history is to "learn from the mistakes of the past."[32] But I do not think this viewpoint makes much sense. Most historical situations are different enough from our own to make direct comparisons impossible. Another reason to study the church fathers might be to use them as ammunition in a debate. I have already criticized this misuse of the fathers. While I do think it's a superb idea to consult the historic view of the Christian church on a given matter, debates cannot be won simply by claiming "I have more church father quotes on my side than you do." If we are to derive a benefit from studying the ancients, it must lie somewhere other than their usefulness as moral lessons or as proof texts in modern argumentation.

I have found that the greatest benefit from getting to know the church fathers comes to us in this way: the fathers help us get in touch with the general thrust of the Christian faith. By "thrust of the Christian faith" I mean two things. First of all, there is the *doctrinal* thrust. The ancients give us insight into what historic, orthodox Christianity is all about. Their understanding of the overall message of scripture provides us with exegetical guideposts outside of which we dare not venture. They also have bequeathed to us some of the terminology we must use to do theology (such as the word "trinity," for example). Of course, on some interpretive details we will differ substantially from the fathers. But when it comes to the general thrust of Christian doctrine, we must stand alongside them if we want to be considered orthodox. There is a "mere Christianity" which defines the very essence of the Christian faith. This is where the church fathers have collectively blazed the trail for us. It is of vital importance that every Christian believer be found traveling along the same path of historic orthodoxy that the ancient believers first labored to create.

But as I have said above, Christianity cannot simply be reduced to a set of doctrines. Our faith is vitally concerned with real people, and with events that transpired on the world's stage as part of God's drama of salvation. Therefore my phrase "thrust of the Christian faith" also necessarily includes a *communal* aspect. When we get to know the church fathers as individuals, we will begin to understand something of the grandeur of the community to which we belong—what the Apostles' Creed calls the "communion of saints." We begin to feel connected to those believers who passionately followed Jesus Christ in their own eras, just as we do today. We become aware that there is a thrust or a movement of the church over time. Our study of the Christian past should therefore energize us to ministry and exhort us to faithfulness. It should give us a sense that we are not alone, that we are part of something grand and magnificent, that we must fight the good fight in our own generation like those who went before us.

I find Hebrews 12:1–2 to provide a relevant parallel here. Just as the steadfast witness of the Old Testament heroes described in Hebrews 11 could encourage the first-century Christians to stand firm, so we need the exhortation today: "since we are surrounded by so great a cloud of witnesses, let us also lay aside every weight, and sin which clings so closely, and let us run with endurance the race that is set before us." I don't know about you, but I don't want to go down in history as part of a sloppy, decadent generation of Christians. I want to live up to the example of those who have gone before, so that together we might look "to Jesus, the founder and perfecter of our faith." As you read this book, I sincerely pray that the lives of the ancient Christians will encourage you to finish the race they've already run so well.

Provocative Questions

1. Have you ever experienced a profound sense of your own family heritage? What were some of the feelings generated in that moment? Do you think it is possible to have those same feelings toward your "spiritual ancestors"? Why or why not?

2. Do you have any problems with thinking of the ancient Christians as your spiritual forefathers? What does the word "father" mean to you? How does that affect your view of the first generations of believers?

3. Read Deuteronomy 32:7. Does Moses's instruction for the Israelites to reflect upon their historical beginnings apply to modern-day Christians as well? Are we instructed by scripture to look to the foundational figures of our Christian faith?

4. Read Hebrews 12:1–2. Who makes up the "cloud of witnesses"? Why are they mentioned in the original setting of the epistle? In other words, what are they supposed to do for the Christian? How would the biblical principle given here function in the church today?

5. What would it look like to profess Christianity, but to be outside the general "thrust" of the orthodox Christian faith? Do you know anyone like this? Are you outside the historic thrust of the faith in any way?

Good Books to Dig Deeper

Ramsey, Boniface. *Beginning to Read the Fathers*. Mahwah, NJ: Paulist Press, 1985.

Wilken, Robert Louis. *The Spirit of Early Christian Thought: Seeking the Face of God*. New Haven: Yale Press, 2003.

Williams, D. H. *Retrieving the Tradition and Renewing Evangelicalism: A Primer for Suspicious Protestants*. Grand Rapids: Eerdmans, 1999.

1

IGNATIUS OF ANTIOCH

What will a condemned man say in the final days of his life? Much will depend on the spiritual fiber of the man. On May 19, 2005, Richard Cartwright was executed in Texas for a 1996 murder. According to the formal charges against him, he and some accomplices lured thirty-seven-year-old Nick Moraida to a remote park in Corpus Christi, where they robbed him of his wallet, money, and a watch. Cartwright delivered a fatal shot to the victim's back with a .38 caliber pistol. The criminals then used the stolen money to buy drugs.[1]

While awaiting execution on Death Row, Cartwright became known for posting his periodic musings on the Web. His posts reveal a man still battling internal demons. Instead of expressing remorse for his crime, he claimed someone else committed the murder, so he stood falsely accused. Such deferral of guilt caused Cartwright to seethe with fury at his wrongful imprisonment. He directed his rage toward an ever-present enemy: the guards who tormented him in jail. Life in the maximum security facility degenerated into a cesspool of vitriolic anger, tragic self-pity, and cold, cruel loneliness. All of

these emotions emerged through Cartwright's Internet outlet. Here
is an example of his pain:

> *December 24, 2004, 3:35 a.m.*—I'm pacing my cage, 1, 2, 3, turn, 1,
> 2, 3, turn. It's Christmas Eve and I pace. My emotions alternate from
> love to hate, pain to rage, hurt to confused. I pace trying to outrun
> the BEAST WITHIN. The beast made of my pain and hurt. There is
> no room for pity or sadness in here. No understanding of love from
> the powers to be . . . just pace my cage on Christmas Eve and keep
> my demons away. I'm at a breaking point. I don't know when I will
> fight, but fight back I must. One can only be pushed and cornered
> for so long. You either snap back and fight or break. I will not let
> them break me.[2]

There is something deeply sad here. Cartwright's bitterness, anguish,
rebellion, and despair seep from his words. He has lost his humanity.
He has become an animal. This is the way a man faces death when
he has no redemptive hope, no higher meaning to lend significance
to the prospect of his execution.

Much different was the profoundly Christian response of Ignatius of Antioch, whom we meet under similar circumstances of impending execution. We know virtually nothing of Ignatius's life until
we discover him through seven letters he wrote around AD 115 as
he was taken in chains to be martyred in Rome for his Christian
faith. Ignatius displayed none of the anger and hopelessness we see
in Richard Cartwright. In his brief appearance to us in his letters,
Ignatius is like a shooting star streaking suddenly across the sky, only
to disappear in a blaze of glory.[3] Truly he possessed a burning desire
to "reach God." A few centuries later, another preacher in Antioch,
John Chrysostom, rightly referred to his predecessor as "a soul boiling with passionate divine love."[4]

When we actually take time to meet the church fathers, we find them
to be exceedingly relevant. They are Christians who faced struggles
not so unlike our own. Ignatius of Antioch is no exception. Though
he lived long ago, the contours of his spiritual life form a shape we can

recognize today. And where he differs from us we have the opportunity to gain a new perspective on the Christian life. As we get to know Ignatius, the picture will emerge of a dedicated pastor who hoped to protect his flock by dying for the true faith. His church was infiltrated by heretics and plagued with legalism. Many enemies questioned his pastoral authority. To understand Ignatius in context, let's take a brief look at the Christian congregation he had inherited.

Earliest Christianity in Antioch

When we think of the great cities of antiquity, perhaps names such as Rome, Athens, or Alexandria come to mind more quickly than Antioch. But Antioch surely deserves to be named among the foremost cities of the ancient world. The Jewish historian Josephus claimed that after Rome and Alexandria, "without dispute [Antioch] deserves the place of the third city in the habitable earth that was under the Roman Empire, both in magnitude and other marks of prosperity."[5] Antioch was founded as a Greek city in 300 BC in the wake of Alexander the Great's conquests. In Ignatius's era, four hundred years later, it was the capital of the Roman province of Syria, with about half a million residents. Antioch was an affluent, cosmopolitan place with broad ethnic and religious diversity—including an established and influential population of Jews. The city's site was strategic: nestled between the Orontes River and the flanks of Mt. Silpius, it could be easily defended. At the same time, it was widely accessible. The city had a port on the Mediterranean Sea only sixteen miles down the river, and it was centered at a major crossroads between Asia Minor to the west, Mesopotamia to the east, and Palestine and Egypt to the south. Antioch was famous for its long central avenue with marble pavement and a colonnaded pedestrian walkway on either side. Ignatius often referred to himself as the "bishop from Syria," apparently taking no small civic pride in the prominence of his home town and region.

If Antioch ranks with Rome as an important imperial city, it ranks with Jerusalem as an important city for the origins of Christianity. Indeed, it was at Antioch that the followers of Jesus were first called "Christians" (Acts 11:26). As recorded in the Book of Acts, the Antiochene church quickly recognized the legitimacy of mission work among the Gentiles. The city is first mentioned in Acts 11 immediately after Peter received a vision telling him that certain ritually unclean animals were now allowed as food. "Do not call anything impure that God has made clean," the heavenly voice told Peter, implying that the Gentiles had been made acceptable. We then learn that some disciples went to Antioch and began to preach there, not just to fellow Jews, but to Gentiles as well. The hand of the Lord greatly blessed this ministry. However, some skeptics in Jerusalem grew concerned, so they dispatched Barnabas to check things out. By the Spirit's guidance he immediately recognized the work among the Gentiles as the grace of God. He then went up the road to Tarsus (along the same road which Ignatius would travel to martyrdom a few decades later) to bring Paul down to Antioch. Paul and Barnabas met with the church there and taught the believers for a year. Eventually the Holy Spirit commanded the Antiochene church, "Set apart for me Barnabas and Saul for the work to which I have called them" (Acts 13:2). It was from Antioch that Paul and his companions set out on their missionary journeys with the good news of God's grace for Jew and Gentile alike.

Many scholars argue that Matthew's Gospel was composed at Antioch.[6] This would explain some distinctive themes which Matthew records in his narrative. On the one hand, the Gospel of Matthew is recognized as the most "Jewish" Gospel. It presents Jesus as the fulfillment of Jewish prophecies (3:3; 4:14) and as a new Moses who expounds upon the law (5:17–18). On the other hand, Matthew's Gospel argues that the message which came to Israel had been rejected by the Jews, so it has now been extended to Gentiles instead (8:11–12; 21:43). It is no coincidence that the full language of the Great Commission, in which the disciples are commanded to "make disciples of all nations," is recalled only by Matthew (28:19). The author's special concerns reveal to us that his church community had strong Jewish roots, yet had embraced a mission to the Gentiles, and so was struggling with conservative Jewish Christians who wanted to keep the law intact. This description fits perfectly with what we know about the Antiochene believers.

The conflict about the place of the law in Christian life can be seen in a dramatic incident which played out at Antioch. The church there was accustomed to close fellowship between Jews and Gentiles, including the practice of eating at a common table. But then some men from Jerusalem arrived who argued that Christians should follow the Jewish law. This meant Jewish and Gentile believers must keep separate from one another. Paul vehemently opposed such legalism. His epistle to the Galatians was written from Antioch around this time to counteract this dangerous theology. Adherence to ritual works is so tempting, Paul says, that it's easy to be "bewitched" into abandoning the gospel of grace. The legalists who were afflicting the Galatian churches were also advocating the same sort of legalism at Antioch. Even Peter and Barnabas fell prey to their error (Gal. 2:11–21). When Peter had first come to Antioch, he willingly joined in the Antiochene church's acceptance of Gentiles by eating at the table with them. But when the legalists from Jerusalem arrived, Peter was intimidated and withdrew from fellowship with Gentile Christians. This caused the Apostle Paul to oppose Peter to his face. When even stalwarts like Peter and Barnabas get confused on this issue, we can see it was no small dilemma in the early church. The gospel of grace was not easy to establish. It required all-out effort from its most vigorous exponent, the Apostle Paul.

Barnabas eventually came around to Paul's position, and the two went out on their first missionary journey. Acts 14:26–27 records how they returned to Antioch rejoicing that God had blessed their ministry among the Gentiles. But the legalists were still up to their old tricks. After some heated arguments, the Antiochene church sent Paul and Barnabas to Jerusalem for an authoritative decision on the matter (Acts 15). Peter delivered a speech at the meeting which shows he had finally endorsed the Christian's freedom from the requirements of the law. The council decreed that circumcision was not required for salvation (despite the protests from the former Pharisees who led the legalistic party). The Antiochene Gentile believers were greatly encouraged when Paul and Barnabas returned home from Jerusalem with a letter that described them as "brothers who are of the Gentiles."

What does all this have to do with Ignatius? Understanding this background helps clarify the issues he was facing in Antioch sixty years later. Who knows? Perhaps Ignatius watched these events unfold as a young boy. In any case, Ignatius the mature bishop was a devoted disciple of Paul, teaching that faith in Jesus Christ did not require adherence to the Jewish law. But the legalists were still disturbing the church in Antioch, along with another group of heretics we will soon meet. The very future of the Christian religion was at stake—and Ignatius viewed the truth as something worth dying for.

Ignatius's Dual Opponents

The seven letters of Ignatius were written to various churches in Asia Minor, but many scholars believe the topics he addressed also reflected his own pastoral concerns in Antioch. If this is true, the letters reveal that Ignatius faced opposition in his home church on two main fronts.[7] One of these (as we have seen) was a legalistic Jewish expression of the faith whose roots go back to the very beginnings of Christianity in Antioch. The other was Gnosticism, which we will look at in a moment.

The city of Antioch had possessed a Jewish population since its founding in 300 BC.[8] Normally the Jews were allowed to live in peace under the Greek kings. The later Roman governors continued this policy of tolerance (with a few exceptions). Therefore, in AD 115

Ignatius's Christian church was co-existing beside a longstanding and well-established Jewish community, located primarily in the southern part of the city. In fact, it was precisely this respected Jewish population that had made the earliest Christian evangelism of Antiochene Gentiles so successful. Josephus records that the Jews in Antioch had already "made proselytes of a great many of the Greeks perpetually, and . . . brought them to be a portion of their own body."[9] Obviously, many Gentiles were intrigued by monotheism and were interested in converting to the God of Israel. So when Pauline Christianity came on the scene, offering a more "user-friendly" access to the one true God without the strict requirements of the law such as circumcision or kosher food prohibitions, it was a natural fit for many God-seeking Gentiles.

But the very thing that had first attracted Gentile converts to the Christian faith—its Jewishness—soon turned into one of the Antiochene church's biggest problems. Conservative elements within the community warned that the ritual law could not be so easily abandoned. Even many Gentile believers in Antioch viewed Judaism as a venerable religion with fascinating rites and customs that ought to be retained in the Christian church.[10] In opposition to this Judaizing tendency, Ignatius urged:

> let us learn to live according to the principles of Christianity. For whosoever is called by any other name besides this is not of God. Lay aside, therefore, the evil, the old, the sour leaven, and be changed into the new leaven, which is Jesus Christ . . . It is absurd to profess Christ Jesus, and to Judaize.[11]

For Ignatius, to "Judaize" meant to live by the law without recognizing that it points inevitably to Jesus Christ as the center of human history.[12] To keep the law as the basis of salvation was to deny the gospel of grace and to reject the essence of Christianity. Ignatius believed that "if we still live according to the Jewish law, we acknowledge that we have not received grace."[13] This is exactly what the Apostle

Paul had said in Galatians 5:2–4 when he wrote, "if you accept circumcision, Christ will be of no advantage to you . . . You are severed
from Christ, you who would be justified by the law; you have fallen
away from grace."

Ignatius realized it was vitally important for the early church to
distance itself from legalism. He was trying hard to establish Christian freedom at Antioch in the Pauline tradition. Since Christianity
developed out of Judaism, there was always a tendency to fall back
upon the law for salvation. Ignatius stood guard against this temptation in Antioch. At the same time, we should note that Antioch
served the church well by preserving a certain Jewish flavor within
Christianity—particularly against those who would give too much
space to Greek philosophy in Christian theology. This will be an
important point to keep in mind when we look at the christological
controversies in chapter 10.

The Jewish legalists were not the only source of opposition to
Ignatius. He faced another major opponent in Antioch as well: the
Gnostics. The term "Gnostic" is derived from the Greek word for
knowledge, *gnosis*. Gnosticism was not a coherent or uniform set
of beliefs. Rather, it was an array of movements that shared many
common tendencies and features. Central to Gnosticism is the belief that the sect's sacred texts and teachers could provide access to
secret "knowledge" about how the universe really operates. We will
have the chance to look at Gnostic doctrines in more detail later in
this book, when we meet some Christian apologists such as Irenaeus
who opposed Gnosticism. For now, let's simply note the one aspect
of Gnosticism which most bothered Ignatius: its teaching known
as "docetism." Docetism is the belief (held by virtually all Gnostics)
that Jesus did not really come to us in true flesh, but only "seemed"
to come in a physical body. His flesh was actually a ghostly appari-
tion (Greek *dokein* = to seem, and *dokesis* = a phantom). We can see
docetism beginning to emerge even in the New Testament period.
The Apostle John opposed it when he wrote, "Many deceivers have
gone out into the world, those who do not confess the coming of

Jesus Christ in the flesh. Such a one is the deceiver and the antichrist" (2 John 1:7; cf. 1 John 4:2).

The roots of the Gnostic heresy in Antioch go back to the earliest days of the church there. In Acts 6:5 we read of an Antiochene Gentile named Nicolaus who had converted to Judaism and then to Christianity. Some early church fathers testified that Nicolaus did not remain in the true faith, for he is reported to be the founder of the immoral sect mentioned in Revelation 2:6, 14–15 called the Nicolaitans. The practices of the Nicolaitans included eating meat sacrificed to idols and indulging in loose sexual standards, evidently in an attempt to make Christianity more appealing to the masses and to reconcile it with pagan culture. (There's a church growth strategy for you!) The Nicolaitans were seen as forerunners of Gnosticism. The fathers viewed both groups as attempts to liberalize the Christian faith into a more enlightened religious cult that would appeal to a wider audience.

The early church fathers frequently described the origins of various heresies, sometimes based on hearsay, but often on good authority. Several Gnostic teachers were connected with Antioch, such as Menander, Saturninus, Basilides, and Cerdo.[14] The fathers claimed the Gnostics derived their doctrines from the itinerant prophet Simon Magus, described in Acts 8 as a charlatan who wanted to gain magical powers from the apostles in exchange for money. Later patristic accounts exaggerate Simon's role as the founder of virtually all heresies and as the archenemy of the original apostles. While this cannot be taken at face value, often there is a nucleus of truth in such depictions. The evidence from the ancient Christian writers strongly suggests that organized Gnostic doctrines were being vigorously propagated in Ignatius's Antioch by very capable teachers.

Therefore, when we meet Ignatius on the road to martyrdom, we should understand him as an embattled bishop whose home congregation was being pulled and enticed by a dual threat. On the one hand, libertine Gnostics denied the reality of the incarnation and advocated a Christianity that meshed all too well with the cultural assumptions of the day. On the other hand, overly zealous Jewish Christians were calling for adherence to the law of Moses for salvation. And in between was Ignatius: snatched from his congregation by the pagan authorities and headed for an ignominious defeat through public execution—unless, perhaps, there might be a hidden opportunity here? Ignatius apparently thought so. He had resolved to make his death count for eternity.

The Road to Martyrdom

We do not know exactly why Ignatius was sentenced to execution by the Romans. It may be that an earthquake in AD 115 caused a popular uprising against the Christians for supposedly angering the gods, and in the backlash Bishop Ignatius became the scapegoat.[15] But in those days, just bearing the "name" of Christ was already enough to warrant the death penalty.[16] This is Ignatius's own explanation for his persecution: "I came bound from Syria for the common name and hope."[17] Whatever the official reason may have been, Ignatius was taken in chains from Antioch through what is today southern Turkey. Rome was his final destination. Interestingly, his route followed almost exactly the same path as the Apostle Paul's third missionary journey as far as Philippi (you can look at a map printed in the back of many Bibles to trace it out). Even though some of Ignatius's friends offered bribes to the guards to be kind to him, his treatment at their hands was rough:

> From Syria even unto Rome I fight with beasts, both by land and sea, both by night and day, being bound to ten leopards, I mean a band of soldiers, who, even when they receive benefits, show themselves all the worse. But I am the more instructed by their injuries [to act as a disciple of Christ]; "yet I am not thereby justified."[18]

Note that while Ignatius wanted to express the growth in meekness and humility he was gaining through his guards' persecution, he quoted 1 Corinthians 4:4 to remind his readers that no one is saved by righteous living. Here is a man on his guard against works salvation!

When Ignatius arrived in the city of Smyrna on the Aegean coast of Asia Minor, the military detachment decided to pause for a while with their prisoner. This respite during the hot summer month of August allowed Ignatius to receive encouragement from the bishop of that city, the noble Polycarp, who later went to his own dramatic martyrdom at the age of 86. In addition, several representatives from the neighboring churches of Ephesus, Magnesia, and Tralles made visits to encourage their Christian brother in chains (including a bishop named Onesimus who may have been the very slave on whose behalf Paul wrote to Philemon).[19] We should note something important about these visits: they would have required a certain amount of foresight, planning, and effort. Messengers had to be dispatched ahead, even as far as Rome, to let the churches know Ignatius was coming. At considerable expense, some of the congregations in Asia Minor paid for a deacon to accompany Ignatius when his journey resumed. Ignatius's letters continually accentuate the honor he was receiving along his route by all the faithful churches. He even urged them to write their own letters or to send representatives back to Antioch. It is quite apparent from all this stagecraft that Ignatius wanted his heroic martyrdom to serve as an emphatic statement of his principles. He hoped to win a moral victory by making the ultimate sacrifice on behalf of the version of Christianity he embraced, over against the legalists and Gnostics.[20]

From Smyrna, Ignatius wrote four letters: three to the churches that had sent representatives to visit him, and one ahead to Rome. The Letter to the Romans stands apart in its central theme. It is an appeal to the Christian community there not to interfere with his martyrdom in any way. Death for the name of Jesus was something Ignatius greatly desired. The other three letters are very similar to one another. They repeatedly emphasize one of the most important ideas we discover in Ignatius of Antioch: the role of the single bishop as the guarantee of unity within the church. Let us now look at that concept; for it very quickly became the fundamental structure of the ancient church.

Ignatius owns the distinction of being the first advocate of the *monepiscopacy*, in which a single bishop serves the entire Christian community in a city. The *episkopos* (= bishop or overseer) became the senior pastor of the whole urban area, assisted by elders called *presbyteroi*. This is a refinement of New Testament terminology, where *episkopos* could be substituted interchangeably with *presbyteros* to designate the elders of a congregation. But for Ignatius, the biblical offices of bishop, presbyter, and deacon have now been arranged in a specific way. The one bishop in each city shepherded his flock with the help of a council of presbyters, aided by deacons.

Why did Ignatius make this adaptation? If we were to view it as a "Roman Catholic" move to invest bishops with fancy robes and autocratic power over the laity, we would be greatly mistaken. Ignatius's letters clarify the reason for his move: the early church had been seriously undermined by disunity and false doctrine. Single bishops were the proposed solution. Ignatius viewed the harmony that exists between Christians who love and obey their bishop, and the bishop who exercises selfless pastoral concern for his flock, as a reflection of the harmony between the Heavenly Father and his obedient Son. Over and over, Ignatius celebrated church unity as a depiction of divine unity. Commending the church at Ephesus, he wrote:

> It is fitting that you should run together in accordance with the will of your bishop, as you already do. For your justly renowned presbyters, worthy of God, are fitted as exactly to the bishop as the strings are to the harp. Therefore in your concord and harmonious love, Jesus Christ is sung. You should become a choir, so that being harmonious in love, and taking up the song of God in unison, you may with one voice sing to the Father through Jesus Christ, so that He may both hear you and perceive by your works that you are indeed the members of His Son. It is profitable, therefore, that you should live in blameless unity, so that you may always enjoy communion with God.[21]

Ignatius obviously valued harmony in the Christian church as an expression of proper worship. Love within the body of Christ creates a beautiful song to God. Ignatius viewed the bishop as a picture of God's presence within a congregation. This is indeed a high view of the pastoral calling!

Furthermore, the monepiscopacy functioned as a strategic means of ensuring that the actual message of the Lord Jesus would be safeguarded against competing versions of the faith. Remember that other heretical teachers were claiming to represent true Christianity at Antioch. How could a new convert know who was legitimate? Ignatius regarded the bishop as a trustworthy figure who could serve as a focal point of the truth. We do this today as well. Most of our churches have a senior pastor—the acknowledged leader whom we all trust. Imagine you are advising a new believer who is moving to a distant city. In that city, you happen to know a godly Christian pastor. Though you don't know much about his church, you might well tell your friend, "Go to Pastor X's church. You can be sure the Word of God will be preached there." In the same way, Ignatius advised the Christians of his day to view the apostolic bishops as the guardians of the true faith. The monepiscopacy was such an effective strategy for safeguarding doctrine that the whole ancient church organized itself in this fashion.

Eventually Ignatius's time of comfort with his fellow bishops came to an end as the soldiers decided to move on. Leaving Smyrna, he was brought to the port town of Troas. There he received some good news from a member of his congregation who had followed him all the way from Antioch: the church back home was now "at peace." Modern scholars usually take this to mean that the divisions in the Antiochene community had been healed by the bold statement Ignatius was making through his noble death.[22] In any case, Ignatius took advantage of the stop at Troas to write a letter back to the church at Philadelphia, where he had briefly stayed along the way. He also wrote to the Smyrnaeans, who had recently provided such great comfort to him. Along with that letter, Ignatius penned a personal note to

Polycarp in which—passing the torch, so to speak—the bishop on his way to death offered specific pointers to his younger friend about godly pastoral ministry (including such advice as, "Have church more often!"). Ignatius's letters continued to emphasize his central themes: opposition to Judaizing tendencies and Gnostic docetism, the centrality of the bishop, Christian love and harmony, and the desire to gain God's crown of victory through martyrdom.

After Ignatius was taken from Troas to Philippi by sea, we lose contact with him. But according to Irenaeus (who spent time in Rome not long after these events took place) Ignatius did in fact meet his end by being torn apart by wild animals for the amusement of the Roman masses, probably in the infamous Colosseum. The crowd there that day would have viewed the spectacle as a crushing defeat of this meek man's Christian religion. But Ignatius understood his death to be a shout of victory. Today a Christian cross stands in the Colosseum of Rome with a plaque that reads, "The amphitheater, once consecrated to triumphs, entertainments, and the impious worship of pagan gods, is now dedicated to the sufferings of the martyrs, purified from impious superstitions." Ignatius of Antioch bolstered the true teaching of Christianity against his opponents by laying down his life as a witness for the name of Jesus.

Reflections on Ignatius of Antioch

Observers of the Christian scene today might suggest there are two main ways in which believers tend to relate to one another. On the one hand, some are zealous for the truth. These Christians have fixed doctrinal lines and well-developed theological systems. They know with confidence where the boundaries of truth are drawn—and they are not afraid to tell you when you have overstepped the limits! On the other hand, there are those who emphasize loving unity in the church. They will accept whatever doctrine you want to believe, without passing judgment even on the most unbiblical of ideas.

At times you wonder if they believe anything at all, beyond having some warm fuzzy feelings toward Jesus. These two approaches are sometimes symbolized by the "head" and the "heart." Most churches tend to follow one or the other pattern.

In contrast, Ignatius of Antioch shows us that passionate zeal for truth and desire for loving harmony are not mutually exclusive. Unity is a divine gift, granted precisely to those who are bound together by shared truth. Of course this means there will be people who do not hold to the truth, and so are excluded from the community. Where, then, should the dividing line be drawn? For Ignatius, the dividing line centered on *the meaning of the Lord Jesus Christ*.

The argument in Antioch was about Christology. The Gnostics denied that Jesus's body was real, so they gave no prominence to what he had accomplished in our world. They certainly did not like the idea of his suffering and death on the cross. Jesus was instead a revealer of mystical sayings about the supernatural realm. The divine *res gestae* was meaningless for them; God's actions in history counted for nothing. The Jewish legalists had a different problem with the work of Christ. They failed to realize how ultimate and final his sacrifice on the cross really was. They wanted to retain vestiges of the old way of doing things, rather than embrace the radical change ushered in when Messiah Jesus rose from the dead. Both of these christological errors had harmful consequences: they located salvation somewhere other than the cross. And so the immature believers were caught in the middle, pulled this way by docetists and that way by legalists. The church in Antioch lacked the unity that comes from a true understanding of Christ's person and work.

In trying to find a solution to this pastoral dilemma, Ignatius went to the Bible. In particular, he went to the writings and theology of the Apostle Paul. We cannot help but hear the impassioned tone of the Epistle to the Galatians coming through in Ignatius's own writings on some of the same issues. Read Galatians 5 and you will discover the absolute antithesis between the grace of Christ and works-based salvation. But Galatians 5:13–15 forms an important transition: "Do not use your freedom as an opportunity for the flesh, but through love serve one another." The freedom of divine grace must inevitably produce loving service within the body. It is from this perspective that Paul launches into his discussion of the fruit of the Spirit. So here is a biblical principle: understanding the doctrine of grace inevitably yields gracious people. Truth leads to action. Whenever you encounter accurate Christology, you will find people moved to replicate the spirit of Christian unity in their lives and churches. Ignatius of Antioch obviously had reflected deeply on these themes. He exemplified the patristic consensus that theology always goes hand-in-hand with piety. To know God is to love him and his creation. The "head" and the "heart" belong together!

Another key insight Ignatius received from Paul was that an orderly, well-led church can best hold on to the truth. The Pastoral Epistles, for example, elevate the church's leaders as the primary bulwark against false teaching. One of the qualifications of the bishop listed in the Epistle to Titus is "to give instruction in sound doctrine and also to rebuke those who contradict it. For there are many who are insubordinate, empty talkers and deceivers, especially those of the circumcision party. They must be silenced . . ." (1:9–11). In 1 Timothy, Paul's flow of thought is the same: the qualifications of church leaders are listed, and then the dangers of erroneous theology are immediately presented (chs. 3–4). Paul placed a high value on order in the communities. They were to be administered under authoritative shepherds.

Among the designated leaders of the first-century churches, certain ones always possessed greater prominence or authority than others. Titus, for example, was instructed to administer the churches of Crete and to appoint elders there (Titus 1:5). When we come to Ignatius's idea of the monepiscopacy, what we have essentially is a "formalizing" of this previously informal leadership. It is not that Ignatius denied a plurality of leaders in the congregations, for he often mentioned the godly presbyters in his letters. It is simply that, because of the threats facing the church, the single bishop necessarily became the focal point of unity among the orthodox believers in a given city. The early Christians adapted their church structures to the needs of their day, just as we do in our own context.

Why would Ignatius be willing to die for ideas such as the monepiscopacy, the reality of the incarnation, or grace-based salvation? The truth of the matter is, Ignatius did not die for an idea but for his Lord. The Jesus he knew did not come to earth only to give us mystical sayings, or to leave us enslaved to the rituals of the law. The man in whose name Ignatius died offered a communal experience of love through faith in him. Zeal for true doctrine certainly characterized Ignatius. A martyr ground up by the fangs of savage beasts like wheat in a flour mill cannot be accused of failing to make truth claims; his death is the ultimate witness to truth. But for Ignatius, zeal for the truth was not at odds with loving harmony—at least not within his own flock. While truth claims certainly divided the heretics from the true believers, Ignatius envisioned a level of unity among his people to which we rarely aspire today. He called for a Christian unity that would reflect the inner life of the Godhead—the kind of unity Jesus had in mind when he prayed "that they may all be one, just as you, Father, are in me, and I in you, that they also may be in us" (John 17:21).

In Ignatius of Antioch, these themes come together: church unity against threats to true Christology, the monepiscopacy, and martyrdom. By his death Ignatius believed he could bolster his view that a loving community under the leadership of the trusted bishop would best reflect the principles of the Lord Jesus. It was the radical strategy of a dedicated pastor protecting his flock in tenuous times. Perhaps we will come away from our study of Ignatius convinced that he was worthy of his nickname: "Theophorus," the bearer of God.

Provocative Questions

1. Read Galatians 5. While our issues today probably don't revolve around circumcision, legalism is still a problem in the church.

Have you ever been the target of someone else's legalism? Have you ever imposed legalistic standards on someone else? What are some issues about which Christians are legalistic? What is the difference between true legalism and maintaining high standards in the church? Why does Paul discuss the fruit of the Spirit in this context?

2. Docetism denies that Jesus came in the flesh, and so makes his work on the cross unimportant. The Gnostics emphasized instead Jesus's role as a teacher of wise sayings. Where do we hear this idea being propagated today?

3. What is the true meaning of the work of Christ? Is this doctrine central or peripheral? Would you leave a church over it? Would you marry someone with a different view on it? What would you be willing to do to defend it? When is the last time you discussed it with an unbeliever?

4. Read Ephesians 2:1–22 and 4:1–6. What is the biblical basis for unity in the body? Why does scripture make unity so important? How is it achieved, practically speaking? Ignatius emphasized that Christian unity must be visible and outward (by being in communion with the bishop). What visible signs in your church reveal your unity? What else could be done to show it?

5. Read Titus 1:5–16. In verse 7 the bishop (or overseer) is called "God's steward" of the church. How do pastors and elders perform this function today? Do you believe you should submit to your appointed church leaders? How much authority should pastors be given? If you could achieve Ignatius's vision of harmonious love between the pastor and the congregation, what would it look like in your particular church setting?

Good Books to Dig Deeper

The seven letters of Ignatius may be found in either of these translations with good introductions:

Holmes, Michael. *The Apostolic Fathers: Greek Texts and English Translations of Their Writings.* Grand Rapids: Baker, 1992.

Richardson, Cyril C. *Early Christian Fathers.* Philadelphia: Westminster, 1953.

Some comprehensive overviews of Ignatius and his setting are:

Schoedel, William R. *Ignatius of Antioch: A Commentary on the Letters of Ignatius of Antioch.* Philadelphia: Fortress, 1985.

Corwin, Virginia. *St. Ignatius and Christianity in Antioch.* New Haven: Yale, 1960.

Trevett, Christine. *A Study of Ignatius of Antioch in Syria and Asia.* Lewiston, NY: Edwin Mellen, 1992.

A Taste of Ignatius of Antioch

Letter to the Romans 2–6

Ignatius wrote ahead to the church at Rome asking them not to attempt to prevent his death. In his passionate desire for martyrdom, we sense the bishop's wish to make his final act count for eternity. If we are sensitive here, we can also read between the lines to find a man struggling with fear: fear of the pain that awaits him, and fear that he will not measure up to what is expected in his moment of trial. Ignatius describes to the Romans the man he hopes to be. It's as if he is steeling himself for what lies ahead. The letter reminds us that this was no superhuman saint, but a humble Christian trying to set his eyes on Jesus rather than the things of the world.

I'll never again have an opportunity like this to reach God. Nor will you Romans ever again have such a chance to be credited with a finer accomplishment—provided you remain silent. For if you quietly refrain from interfering with me, I will become a crystal-clear message from God. But if you love my earthly body too much, I'll only be an incomprehensible noise. I ask you to grant me nothing but this: that my blood should be poured out as an offering to God while I still have an altar available to me. In your love, you can become the accompanying choir for my sacrifice. You will sing praises to the Father in Jesus Christ because God has deemed me, the bishop of Syria, worthy to be summoned from the East to the West. Oh how good it is to be like the sun now setting on this world—for that means I will soon rise up into the presence of God! . . .

I do have one prayer request. Pray that I'll have strength in my soul and in my physical body, so that I won't just give lip service to martyrdom but will actually desire to go through with it. I don't want to merely call myself a Christian—I want to back it up when it counts. For if I can back up my words, then I will be worthy of the name of Christian. I will be known as a man of faith even when the world can't see me anymore. It's not the things you can see that have true value. For example, our God Jesus Christ revealed his glory even more clearly when he ascended back to the Father and disappeared. Nothing is really achieved by trying to persuade people. Christianity's true power is discovered only when it is hated by the world.

I'm writing letters to all the churches so I can proclaim clearly to everyone that I'm totally willing to die for God. But I can only do that if you won't interfere. I beg you, don't try to show me a "kindness" that I don't really want. Allow me to serve as food for those savage animals—for through them I can reach God! I like to think of myself as God's own wheat. I must be ground up into flour by the teeth of those beasts so I can be baked into a pure loaf of bread for Him. Instead of interfering, it would be far better for you to urge those animals on! Let them become my tomb and completely devour me. I don't want to burden you with having to collect my remains after I have died. Only then will I be a disciple of Jesus Christ in the fullest sense: when the world can no longer see my physical body. So pray to the Lord for me! Ask that by means of these animals I might become a sacrifice to God.

Please understand, I'm not giving you orders as if I were Peter or Paul. They were apostles, but I'm just a condemned criminal. They were free, but even at this very moment I'm chained up like a slave. But I know if I suffer, I'll be freed by Jesus Christ. United with Him, I will be raised to eternal freedom!

Right now, though, I'm a prisoner learning what it means to put aside my desires. From Syria to Rome, I'm already battling with wild beasts. By land and sea, night and day, I'm chained to ten leopards: the soldiers who have me in custody. When they are treated kindly, they only become more cruel to me. However, through their mistreatment I am becoming a better disciple—not that this earns me any credit with God.

Oh may I rejoice in those wild beasts awaiting me! I do pray they will be done with me very quickly. In fact, I will coax them to come eat me up right away. I hope they won't behave timidly like they sometimes do, lacking the fierceness even to touch the people thrown in the arena. And if when I'm ready for the great moment the animals are holding back, I'll force them to take me! Please bear with me here, friends. I really do know what is best for me. I am only now beginning to understand what it means to be a disciple.

I pray that the events in that arena, and the unseen forces of wickedness behind them, will not conspire against me out of envy and prevent me from reaching Jesus Christ. Bring on the fire, bring on the cross, bring on the hordes of wild animals! Let them wrench my bones out of socket and mangle my limbs and grind up my whole body! Bring on all the hideous tortures from the Devil! Just let me get to Jesus Christ. Nothing on this wide earth matters to me anymore. The kingdoms of this world are entirely meaningless. I am at the point where I would rather die for Jesus Christ than rule over the whole earth. He alone is the one I seek—the one who died for us! It is Jesus that I long for—the one who for our sake rose again from the dead!

2

JUSTIN MARTYR

I sometimes visit a cabin at a Christian camp called Honey Rock. It sits on a lake in the northwoods of Wisconsin, which is a great place to get away from the summer heat in Chicago where I live. But if you don't mind subzero temperatures and deep snow, the northern wilderness is a great place to be in the winter too. One Christmas I was at the cabin with my extended family. We decided to go on a short hike to a remote lake nestled in an evergreen forest. As we got out of our vehicle and headed off, I enthusiastically led the way ahead. Wading in snow up to my thighs, I forged a path through the pristine white landscape all around me. Yet despite the chill, it wasn't long before I broke into a sweat. Trudging through that deep snow was hard work! My family members were glad to walk behind me in the broad swath I had created. My trail in the snow made it a little easier for them to reach our goal on that crisp December day.

Justin Martyr was a church father who performed the hard work of breaking trail for future generations of Christians. He was among the first to engage the broader Greco-Roman culture with the Christian message. His predecessors, such as Ignatius of Antioch, had

53

proclaimed the simple essence of the gospel with great boldness. But they did not seriously attempt to correlate the claims of Jesus or the scriptures with the philosophical principles of their times. Justin Martyr was a man who did this, and so he can be considered the first Christian philosopher in church history. The writings he has left us are not warm pastoral letters like those of Ignatius, but the serious attempt of an intellectual to make a reasoned defense of the faith. Justin forged a path many later Christian apologists would follow. Think how hard it must have been to do that for the first time! We owe Justin a great debt.

For the gospel to be understood today, it has to be put into terms a modern audience can comprehend. The distance between the culture of Jesus of Nazareth and our own culture is vast. Some kind of connection point has to be created between the teachings of a first-century Jewish rabbi and the twenty-first-century seeker who is considering his eternal claims. Christianity doesn't always make sense to people right away. Many have picked up a Gideon Bible in a hotel room looking for spiritual truth, only to be left scratching their heads. Of course, I am not trying to discount the supernatural work of the Holy Spirit or the innate power of God's Word. Some conversions occur through direct religious experience, unmediated by any human evangelist. But more often than not, the message of salvation is carried by willing messengers. Therefore it must be expressed in persuasive words communicated by the message-bearer. As Paul said in Romans 10:14–15, "How are they to believe in him of whom they have never heard? And how are they to hear without someone preaching? . . . 'How beautiful are the feet of those who preach the good news!' " It is one of the believer's greatest privileges to engage unsaved people in oral and written communication that urges them to receive Christ. To do this we must put the gospel into some kind of meaningful contextualized expression.

Effective evangelists have learned that they can make the gospel message come alive by appealing to concepts the seeker can understand. A classic example of such relationality is the evangelistic tract known as *The Four Spiritual Laws*. There have been innumerable ways to present the gospel throughout Christian history, but none is more quintessentially American than the method devised by Dr. Bill Bright in the early years of Campus Crusade for Christ. Bright relates how the idea for what would become *The Four Spiritual Laws* was suggested to him in 1956 by a Christian speaker who was an "outstanding sales consultant."[1] Borrowing from the repertoire of an expert salesman, Bright realized that a focused and appealing gospel presentation was needed. He wrote an outline that "explains simply and specifically how an individual can arrive at a desired goal," namely, to become a Christian. The four laws state that "God loves you and has a wonderful plan for your life," but only by turning to Jesus can you achieve God's intended happiness. What are we to make of this? Certainly, a life with the fullest divine approval and blessing is possible only through Christ. At the same time, we can ask: what could be more all-American than striving for the goal, finding the wonderful plan, and attaining the greatest blessing from a loving God? It is a spiritual version of the American Dream. Dr. Bright had found a way to present the gospel in terms that matched our modern, goal-oriented, happiness-seeking mind-set. From a human perspective, that is one of the reasons his tract has been so successful.

The ancient church father Justin Martyr created the mold for later apologists to use. He sought to win a pagan audience by shaping the Christian message to conform to existing intellectual or cultural concepts. He found connection points between the church's proclamation and the thought-world into which he was taking the gospel. Yet he did so without compromising the faith like the many heretical sects. To understand Justin's apologetic techniques, we must investigate his intended audience. He was trying to reach an educated Greco-Roman populace whose basic presuppositions we will look at in a moment. But first, let's hear Justin Martyr describe his conversion from secular philosophy to the Christian faith.

The Only "Safe and Profitable" Philosophy

In Acts 1:8 Jesus told his disciples, "You will be my witnesses in Jerusalem and in all Judea and Samaria, and to the end of the earth." Justin Martyr followed the same pattern of evangelistic expansion: born in Samaria around the year AD 100, he boldly took the gospel to faraway lands. His hometown was Flavia Neapolis, a pagan city built near the ruins of Shechem where Jesus had met the woman at the well in John 4. But Justin seems not to have belonged to the Samaritan religious or cultural heritage, for he had a Latin name, was uncircumcised, and received a Greek education. Probably his parents had only recently immigrated to the new city. Young Justin was a lover of philosophy, so around AD 130 he made his way to a major metropolis where he could study under different philosophical teachers. This city was likely Ephesus, for the church historian Eusebius locates Justin there.[2] Could it be that Justin, as a Christian convert residing in Ephesus, was taught the heroic story of Ignatius of Antioch who had passed nearby fifteen years earlier? We do not know this for sure, but the suggestion is not improbable.[3]

Before his conversion to Christianity, Justin experimented with several different schools of thought.[4] His first teacher represented the Stoic philosophy. Justin devoted himself to this teacher for an extended time. But eventually he grew disillusioned with Stoicism, for the teacher appeared to have no personal knowledge of God, and even said such knowledge was completely unnecessary. This contrasted with Justin's own view that it is "truly the duty of philosophy to investigate the Deity."[5] We can see that Justin's quest was a spiritual one, not merely intellectual. He wanted to find absolute truth, and this meant investigating divine things. Justin left the Stoic teacher and sat under a follower of Aristotle with prideful intellectual pretensions. But soon Justin discerned the would-be mentor's real preoccupation when he started figuring out how much tuition money Justin would have to pay him. This seemed to be unworthy of a person truly devoted to wisdom. So Justin next tried a prominent

Pythagorean teacher, who once again was puffed up with his own knowledge. When Justin approached him to become his disciple, he scolded Justin for not being educated in music, astronomy, and geometry. Justin was deeply discouraged to learn that finding God meant spending so much time studying these preliminary matters. Finally he decided to try a teacher who was highly respected by the Platonists. At last Justin's philosophical education began to take flight. Platonism emphasized finding the highest spiritual ideals which transcend the physical world. Justin found himself mesmerized by this quest. He imagined he had become a wise man, and was expecting to receive a vision of God very soon.

It was in this expectant frame of mind that Justin went one day to a lonely spot by the sea to contemplate Plato's philosophy. Soon he realized he was being followed by a distinguished-looking elderly gentleman. Justin turned and stared silently at his unexpected companion. "Do you know me?" the old man finally asked. Justin replied that he did not. "So why are you staring at me?" he inquired. Justin answered that he was wondering what the old man was up to in such a remote place. The old man responded: "I am concerned about some of my household. They are gone away from me; and therefore I have come to make personal search for them, if perhaps they shall make their appearance somewhere."[6] This cryptic reply makes me wonder whether the old man had been reading Luke 15 recently, and had intentionally set out to do evangelism that day.

In any case, the pair struck up a conversation and soon were engaged in a deep philosophical discourse about how to find God. Justin advocated a Platonic method whereby God was found through inner reasoning in the mind's eye. But the old man pointed Justin in a different direction: to divine revelation. "Will the mind of man see God at any time, if it is uninstructed by the Holy Spirit?" he asked.[7] The old man showed Justin that the philosophers had contradictory opinions on spiritual matters, so they could not be trusted to guide the seeker to ultimate truth. "If even the wisest teachers and philosophers do not know the truth," Justin asked, "then where should

I turn?" At this point the old man directed Justin to the scriptures. Long ago, he said, there were prophets inspired by the Holy Spirit. They wrote down messages directly from God. Whoever reads their writings in faith will find true knowledge of him. The old man urged Justin with these words: "Pray that, above all things, the gates of light may be opened to you; for these things cannot be perceived or understood by all, but only by the man to whom God and His Christ have imparted wisdom."[8] At this point the old man went on his way, and Justin never saw him again. But in his soul the young truth seeker was deeply moved by what he had heard. Justin described his conversion experience like this:

> Straightway a flame was kindled in my soul; and a love of the prophets, and of those men who are friends of Christ, possessed me; and while revolving his words in my mind, I found this [Christian] philoso-phy alone to be safe and profitable. Thus, and for this reason, I am a philosopher. Moreover, I wish that everyone, making a resolution similar to my own, would not keep themselves away from the words of the Savior.[9]

In Justin, a new kind of philosopher had been born: one who grounded his philosophy in the Lord Jesus Christ as the source of all truth. It was the beginning of an important trend in the ancient church.

Justin's Bold and Dangerous Apologetics

Justin had embraced what he thought was the most "safe and prof-itable" philosophy, but the lifestyle he chose was one of bold and sometimes dangerous confrontation. With his newfound desire to serve as a Christian philosopher, it was only a matter of time until he began to run into people with different views than his own. Justin was accustomed to travel the streets of Ephesus wearing the *pallium*. This was a square garment of coarse material, sort of like a blanket, which was folded and draped around the body. The costume was noticeably different from the more common semicircular wrap for Roman men called the *toga*. The *pallium*, a Greek fashion which signaled a simple lifestyle, identified its wearer as a philosopher. Justin was the first Christian known to adopt this mode of dress.

One day Justin was strolling along the shady colonnade of a broad avenue wearing his philosopher's robe when he was hailed by a stranger. "Good morning, Philosopher!" called the man as he joined Justin at his side. "What can I do for you?" asked Justin. The man replied that his mentor had taught him always to greet anybody wearing the *pallium*, for you never knew what piece of wisdom you might gain from that philosopher. The man introduced himself as Trypho, a Jew who had recently fled Palestine to escape the revolutionary war against Rome (instigated by a Jewish zealot named Simon Bar Kohkba, AD 132–135). Justin and Trypho began to converse about spiritual matters. Soon they were delving into biblical argumentation and theological apologetics from opposite angles. Their discussion eventually grew into a two-day debate between friendly adversaries. At the conclusion of their conversation, both parties agreed it had been a mutually profitable experience.

About twenty-five years later, Justin wrote down an account of the exchange, known to us as the *Dialogue with Trypho the Jew*. No doubt it contains some exaggerations, slips of memory, and added material. Nonetheless, most scholars believe it records the essence of a real debate between these two philosophers. In the *Dialogue* Justin offered many Christian explanations of Old Testament prophecies and defended the divinity of Christ. For his part, Trypho provided Jewish rebuttals of Christian doctrines as he argued for observance of the Mosaic law. The whole discourse was carried out with a civility that is quite rare in the history of Jewish-Christian relations. As the debate was winding down, Justin revealed his passion for soul-winning when he urged Trypho to accept Christ as his Savior: "I exhort you to give all diligence in this very great struggle for your own salvation, and to be earnest in setting a higher value on the

Christ of the Almighty God than on your own teachers."[10] Praying for Trypho and his friends, Justin said, "I can wish no better thing for you, sirs, than this: to recognize that wisdom is given to every man in this Way, so that you may be of the same opinion as me and believe that Jesus is the Christ of God."[11] With this expression of hope for his new friends' salvation, Justin set sail for a foreign destination, probably to Rome.

Although we don't know exactly when he arrived in Rome, there is no question Justin eventually made his way to the capital city of the empire. In fact it appears he lived at Rome twice in his life. There he served as a Christian teacher who instructed students in theological philosophy, and also engaged in oral and written debates with pagans, heretics, and Jews. As Eusebius put it, "Justin was especially prominent in those days. In the guise of a philosopher he preached the divine word, and contended for the faith in his writings."[12] Christian meetings took place at Justin's home along the Via Tiburtina, which today is a major highway running from the train station in Rome to the town of Tivoli.[13] This is the only Christian meeting-place Justin knew about in the city, though undoubtedly there were others. From this productive period of Justin's life three writings have come down to us today. One is the report of his exchange with Trypho that we have already mentioned. Another is his *First Apology*, which is one of the foremost examples of Christian apologetics in all of church history. We will discuss this work's themes and arguments momentarily. It was written around AD 155. A few years later, Justin added a short postscript to his major apologetic work, which has come to be called the *Second Apology*.

Justin's boldness soon brought him into confrontation with a teacher named Crescens who adhered to the philosophy of Cynicism. Justin described him as "a lover of bravado and boasting" who is "not worthy of the name of philosopher" because he "publicly bears witness against us in matters which he does not understand."[14] At one point Justin put a series of questions to Crescens, humiliating him by showing he knew absolutely nothing about Christianity and had not read the teachings of Christ. But despite his ignorance, Crescens had the skill to stir up public opinion against the Christians. One of Justin's most brilliant students, a young Assyrian named Tatian, offered this observation: "Crescens, who made his nest in the great city, surpassed all men in unnatural love, and was strongly addicted to the love of money. Yet this man, who professed to despise death, was so afraid of death, that he endeavored to inflict on Justin, and indeed on me, the punishment of death . . ."[15] Justin was well aware that Crescens was attempting to accuse him before the authorities. "I expect to be plotted against and fixed to the stake" due to Crescens' slander, he said.[16] We do not know the precise role Crescens played in Justin's arrest, but we do know that around AD 165 Justin's apologetic ministry took a deadly turn.

Justin had never been afraid to speak out against the tyrannical regime of Rome when he believed Christians' rights were being trampled. His *Second Apology* was appended to the *First* because of an outrageous instance of anti-Christian discrimination. A formerly immoral woman had become a believer and now found her husband's extreme debauchery intolerable. She wanted to divorce him, but her Christian friends advised her to stay with him in case he too might be saved. Yet the man's wanton living was so excessive that finally she had had enough. She served him with divorce papers. The man was so irked by this that he made public accusations against his ex-wife's pastoral instructor, Ptolemaeus, who had supposedly filled her head with crazy doctrines. Ptolemaeus was thrown in prison, where it just so happened that the jailer was a friend of the accuser. They conspired to trump up charges against Ptolemaeus, not based on any specific crime, but solely for adhering to the "name" of Christ (recall that Ignatius of Antioch was arrested on the same charge). On this rather tenuous legal basis, the city prefect (Rome's judicial enforcer) ordered Ptolemaeus and one of his outspoken defenders to be put to death. When Justin published his *Second Apology* to criticize this decision, perhaps Crescens used it to bring Justin to the authorities' attention as a member of an illegal sect.

It wasn't long before Justin was hauled before the prefect, along with six of his friends, to give an account of his doings. Fortunately we have a record of the proceedings, called the *Acts of Saint Justin*. The text was written several decades later than the events it describes, but scholars agree it preserves an accurate description of what transpired that day before the judge. The account is quite brief; perhaps you will want to read it for yourself.[17] The prefect Rusticus asked Justin to summarize his doctrine. Justin answered by describing his belief in one God, the maker of all things, and in his Son the Lord Jesus Christ who was predicted by the prophets. Rusticus then honed his questioning. "Are you a Christian?" he asked. Justin answered, "Yes, I am a Christian." Next Rusticus examined Justin's companions, including one woman. All of them confessed their faith in Christ. The prefect mockingly asked Justin whether he supposed he might gain some eternal reward by dying. "I do not 'suppose' it," Justin answered emphatically, "but I *know* it and am fully persuaded of it."[18] Fed up with the dialogue, Rusticus got to the point. He ordered the accused Christians to make sacrifices to the gods, which they refused to do. Justin's bold reply was, "Through prayer we can be saved on account of our Lord Jesus Christ, even when we have been punished [by you], because this shall become to us salvation and confidence at the more fearful and universal judgment-seat of our Lord and Savior."[19] Rusticus dismissed Justin and his companions to be tied to a pole and mercilessly whipped. After this agony the Christian confessors were beheaded, and some local believers came to properly bury the bodies. So it was that Justin earned the name by which he is known to history: Justin Martyr.

A Contextualized Message for a Greco-Roman Audience

Justin experienced success in his apologetic ministry because he tailored his message to his audience. Having studied all the philosophers of his era, he could speak their lingo fluently. He even wore the right kind of clothing to fit into the community he was trying to reach! Let us now examine Justin's intended audience so that we can better understand his method of evangelism.

Justin addressed his *First Apology* to the Roman emperor, but it is highly unlikely the work ever made it that far. In reality Justin was writing to Greco-Roman people with enough education to be conversant in basic philosophical issues. His audience can be described as adhering to a common worldview. Of course, there were many different philosophies and viewpoints circulating in the bubbling stew of ideas that made up the ancient Roman Empire. The conquering Romans, it turns out, were quite malleable. They borrowed elements from every society with which they came into contact. This flexibility meant that when Rome was expanding into the territories that would make up its empire, it did not really *supplant* existing cultures, but *overlaid* them, so to speak. In the Mediterranean, the dominant existing culture was Greek culture, or Hellenism. (This is why we use the term "Greco-Roman.") Two great civilizations were blended together in ancient times. The intellectuals of the Roman Empire were still working from a basically Hellenistic worldview.

Hellenistic culture had been disseminated out of Macedonia and Greece several centuries before Christ by the conquests of Alexander the Great. Alexander did much to spread a Greek lifestyle to other peoples in the Mediterranean world. But who provided the intellectual underpinnings of the Greek outlook on life? In the early Christian era, the foremost thinker was Plato. And so to understand Justin Martyr, we need to understand a bit about this ancient Greek philosopher.

Plato lived long before the Christian period (427–347 BC), but he had a profound impact on the ancient church nonetheless. He taught that there is a great gulf between our physical material world, and the world of what he called "Forms" or "Ideas." The Forms are perfect, abstract concepts—as opposed to the physical copies of those concepts that we can see all around us. For example, in the ideal world there exists the perfect Form of Beauty. It is the ulti-

mate standard of what Beauty truly is. All beautiful things are only
shadowy copies of this ideal. The Forms exist far away from us in
their eternal perfection and immutability. In contrast, our physical
world is imperfect because it is constantly changing. Now perhaps
you can see a basic problem here. The burning question of Platonic
philosophers was: how do the Forms and Matter *connect*? Plato
had said material things somehow "participate" in the Forms, but
what exactly does that mean? How does a beautiful object replicate
heavenly beauty? The great goal of later Platonism was to find the
mediating principle between "down here" and "up there." Or to put
it in theological terms: if the mysterious Maker of the universe existed in faraway solitude, as Plato taught, how was he to be found?[20]
We will now look at Justin's *First Apology* to discover the Christian
answer he gave to this Platonic dilemma.

One obvious way to connect the divine and earthly realms would
be to suggest a series of intermediate beings who could serve as go-
betweens. This is essentially the answer given by ancient pagan religion. The many gods are situated in their ranks between mere mortals
on earth and the heights of Mt. Olympus far above. Greco-Roman
religion consisted of magical rituals and prescribed customs to placate
the gods and make them give you good fortune. What did Justin have
to say about these gods? You may be surprised to learn that he did
not deny their existence in the least. He knew what many Christians
know who are in contact with animistic or idolatrous religion: that
the spiritual entities being worshiped are all too real. Justin simply
informed his pagan audience that they were actually worshiping the
wicked demons of Satan. He claimed that

> of old these evil demons, making apparitions of themselves, both
> defiled women and corrupted boys, and showed such fearful sights
> to men that those who did not use reason in judging the demons'
> actions were struck with terror. Being carried away by fear, and not
> knowing that these were actually demons, they called them gods, and
> gave them each whatever name the demon chose for himself.[21]

This assertion echoes Paul's claim in 1 Corinthians 10:20 that "what pagans sacrifice they offer to demons and not to God." Justin Martyr often mentioned the demons in his writings. He considered them to be steadfastly opposed to the Christ's ministry of enlightenment toward humankind in both the Old and New Testament eras. The demons masqueraded as gods to be worshiped in order to keep human beings in darkness and bondage. Justin even claimed their voices could be heard through evil teachers such as Simon Magus and Menander (whom we have already met as opponents of Ignatius of Antioch).[22] For Justin, a hierarchy of intermediate spirits could not be the answer to the Platonic dilemma. The demons were part of the problem, not the solution.

Many educated philosophers in antiquity found popular religion and its superstitious myths about the gods to be crude and unenlightened. They wanted a different solution to the Platonic need for mediation between the divine and human realms. By Justin's day, a concept had emerged within Platonism that borrowed a term from Stoic thought. Justin found this concept to be tremendously useful, so he made it a centerpiece of his theology. The concept is described by the Greek word *Logos*. Often this is translated in English as "word," but Logos could mean much more than that. It could refer to reason, or rationality, or the inner discourse that takes place in your mind as you think your thoughts. Over time, the word Logos had come to describe the rational Mind of God. Sometimes this Logos was portrayed as a distinct entity through which the cosmos was created and governed. It was differentiated from God himself, guiding the physical universe on his behalf. Thus, for the philosophical schools of that age, the Logos designated the mediating principle between absolute divinity and finite materiality.[23]

But what exactly was the nature of this Logos? Nobody really knew. So when Justin came on the scene as a Christian philosopher, he blazed an apologetic trail for the church by borrowing this common philosophical idea and equating it with the Lord Jesus Christ. In so doing, he used chapter one of John's Gospel as a biblical precedent:

"In the beginning was the Logos, and the Logos was with God and the Logos was God . . . and the Logos became flesh and dwelt among us." But Justin went further than John. He developed an entire theology identifying the philosophical Logos as the Incarnate Son of God. Justin could now give an apologetic answer to the great Platonic dilemma of mediation. Jesus Christ, he said, was the one and only path between the spiritual and earthly realms.

Christ the Logos

Justin's Logos Christology served him in two main ways. First, it showed that Christian teachings were compatible with accepted philosophical truths. Justin could now offer a formal theological way to conceptualize the relation of the Son to the Father, while still preserving belief in one Supreme Being (which many philosophers thought was the highest form of religion). The Logos is numerically distinct from the Father as the agent of his will, but is unified with him as well.[24] This understanding fit nicely into the Hellenistic worldview. It was also the very beginning of the church's theological reflection on the problem of the Trinity: how are monotheists supposed to articulate the truth of Christ's divinity in relation to the Father's divinity? We will discuss this issue in chapter 7.

Justin's other main use of the Logos Christology allowed him to appropriate everything good from Greek philosophy and make it belong to the church. Justin developed an idea called the "spermatic Logos," which taught that God was like a sower who had scattered "seeds" (= Greek *spermata*) of his own divine reason among people of all eras. The Logos was active not only during the time of his incarnation, but also beforehand—in the age of the Greek philosophers, for example. Whenever the ancients had come up with true insights, they did so because of the "seeds of reason" that the Logos had sown within them.[25] Justin wrote,

For each man spoke well in proportion to the share he had of the spermatic Word . . . Whatever things were rightly said among all men are the property of us Christians. For next to God, we worship and love the Word who came from the unbegotten and ineffable God. [In our day] He became man for our sakes, so that by becoming a partaker of our sufferings He might also bring us healing. But all the [pre-Christian] writers were only able to see truths dimly, through the sowing of the implanted Word that was in them.[26]

Both of Justin's uses of the Logos Christology had great apologetic value. He borrowed a well-known philosophical concept to demonstrate that Christian doctrine solved the great conundrum of the day. Furthermore, he showed that Christianity was not entirely at odds with pagan learning, but instead completed the intellectual journey that Greek philosophy had only begun.

What happens to a person who is in touch with the divine Logos? It was an axiom in ancient philosophy that true beliefs would inevitably lead to moral virtue or a life well lived. Therefore one of the main tasks Justin took on in his *First Apology* (in addition to making an intellectual defense of the faith) was to demonstrate the truth of the Christian religion by showing the kind of lives it produced. In the early church era, many pagans believed Christians were immoral reprobates. So Justin attempted to reveal what Christianity was really all about:

we who formerly delighted in fornication now embrace chastity alone; we who formerly used magical arts now dedicate ourselves to the good and unbegotten God; we who valued above all things the acquisition of wealth and possessions now bring what we have into a common stock and communicate to every one in need; we who hated and destroyed one another, and on account of their different manners would not live with men of a different tribe, now, since the coming of Christ, live familiarly with them, and pray for our enemies, and endeavor to persuade those who hate us unjustly to live in conformity to the good precepts of Christ.[27]

Justin clearly understood it was not enough to express Christian theology in philosophical jargon. He had to show that Christianity produced a lifestyle worthy of emulation by the wise man. In all these ways, Justin proclaimed a faith that would make sense to his contemporary culture, yet would remain true to its original principles.

Reflections on Justin Martyr

What are we to make of this trailblazing church father? We cannot help but discern in him certain traits common to all pioneers, such as boldness of action or courage in the face of adversity. We can also see right away Justin's remarkable skill as an apologist. He understood his age, looking for contact points to enable the gospel to make its way forward in Greco-Roman society. To a culture immersed in the worship of gods, Justin did not pretend they did not exist (for no ancient person, whether pagan or Christian, could possibly deny the existence of these spiritual powers). Instead he offered an alternate explanation of their identity according to Christian truth. To the philosopher who knew there must be a transcendent reality behind what could be seen, Justin provided a universal way to reach that Supreme Being. The Platonic Logos who governed the world as a divine mediator was shown to be none other than the Logos who became flesh and dwelt among us. The Greeks had discovered part of the truth, but now Christianity brought fuller revelation. Jesus alone, instructing our souls in divine Reason, could produce virtuous lives. For a society that valued virtue because it was so rarely found, this was a powerful argument.

Justin Martyr has often been described as "eclectic." In other words, he was wise enough to borrow what was good in Greek thought and pass over what did not seem all that valuable. This meant that for him the great philosophers were not necessarily enemies of the faith. Figures like Socrates could even be described as "Christians."[28] Justin believed some of the ancients had gained saving knowledge of God from the seeds of reason sown by the Logos prior to his incarnation. Philosophy did not have to be rejected across the board. Instead, its best teachings could be attributed to divine revelation. As we often put it today, "All truth is God's truth." Such open-minded eclecticism on the part of church fathers like Justin was absolutely necessary for Christianity to become something more than a Jewish sect with limited appeal.

At the same time, there were dangers inherent in such an approach. The Christian religion might accidentally become just another Greek philosophy—one with a touch of Jewish exoticism, while having lost its true moorings in the history of Israel and the dramatic work of God through Christ. Even Justin, for all his brilliance, did not go much beyond treating the Jewish scriptures as proof texts for the advent of the Lord. Nor did he lay out a theology of the atonement beyond making some basic Christian affirmations. We cannot fault him too much here—for how much can we really ask of the earliest trailblazers? Their task was hard enough already. Fortunately for the ancient church, two more fathers would soon come on the scene to take up the task of pushing theology further along. They were Irenaeus and Tertullian, and we will meet them in the next two chapters.

Provocative Questions

1. Justin Martyr always tried to reach people with the gospel from a position of common ground. Think about various groups in society: for example, scientists, business people, secularists, artists, politicians, or the poor. How could Christianity be presented to some of these groups in an appealing way? What might go too far, and so compromise the Christian message? Are there any "connection points" you have used to help the gospel make sense to unbelievers? How important is the testimony of a virtuous life—what we might call "lifestyle evangelism"?

2. Name some different philosophies that are widely held today. In other words, what are some common "-isms" we may run into?

Can you think of a scriptural reference that addresses one of those philosophies? What is a proper biblical attitude toward philosophy in general? See Acts 17:16–34 and Colossians 2:8.

3. Perhaps the idea of the "spermatic Logos" doesn't make much sense to you, but let's wrestle with Justin Martyr's basic contention that people like Socrates could gain saving knowledge of God through philosophy. Do you believe that (prior to the arrival of Christ) people could be saved apart from any exposure to the Old Testament or Jewish faith? If so, how would that occur? Perhaps Acts 17:30 is relevant here. Does this issue have any bearing on the status of the lost today?

4. In *Dialogue with Trypho*, Justin Martyr used the Old Testament as a collection of predictions about Christ. Is the Old Testament really about Jesus? Or is it about God's work among the Jews? Or can it be both? See Matthew 5:17–18; Luke 24:27; and John 5:46. How should you approach the Old Testament in a truly Christian way? Has the New Testament replaced the Old?

5. Justin Martyr had a lot to say about demons. So did Jesus and the New Testament writers (e.g., Luke 11:14–26; Eph. 6:10–12). What role do demons play today? Are they involved in the events of our contemporary culture? Is there a connection between demons and false human philosophies? See 1 Timothy 4:1–4. What are some demonic imitations of Christian truths we might see today?

Good Books to Dig Deeper

The best edition in which to read Justin's two apologies (accompanied by excellent background material) is:

Barnard, Leslie William. *St. Justin Martyr: The First and Second Apologies.* Ancient Christian Writers, vol. 56. Mahwah, NJ: Paulist Press, 1997.

An updated edition of the *Dialogue with Trypho* is:

Falls, Thomas B. *St. Justin Martyr: Dialogue with Trypho.* Revised by
Thomas P. Halton. Edited by Michael Slusser. Washington, DC: Catholic University of America Press, 2003.

Three fine scholarly introductions to the thought of Justin Martyr
are:

Barnard, L. W. *Justin Martyr: His Life and Thought.* Cambridge: University Press, 1967.

Goodenough, Erwin R. *The Theology of Justin Martyr.* Amsterdam: Philo
Press, 1968 (orig. pub. 1923).

Osborn, Eric F. *Justin Martyr.* Tübingen: JCB Mohr, 1973.

There is an overview of Justin Martyr designed for a popular audience in the *Shepherd's Notes* series:

Bullock, Karen O'Dell. *The Writings of Justin Martyr.* Nashville: Broad-
man & Holman, 1999.

A Taste of Justin Martyr

Dialogue with Trypho 8–9

*Justin has just given Trypho his conversion story, and now urges him
to receive Christ as his Savior. Trypho responds with his own view of
how to be saved. After this initial exchange, the pair began their two-
day discourse on divine philosophy.*

"[Trypho,] I know you're no stranger to the subject of religion.
If you care about yourself and are seeking salvation and believe in
God, then you just might come to know his Christ. Having attained
salvation, you will finally be content."

When I said this, Trypho's friends all broke into loud laughter. But Trypho himself just smiled gently.

"I approve of your other statements," he said, "and I admire your passionate desire for divine things. But you really ought to stick with the philosophy of Plato or somebody like that if you want to achieve patience, self-control, and moderation. That's better than being led astray by false teachings and becoming a follower of worthless men. For when you were pursuing your former kind of philosophy and lived a sin-free life, you had the hope of a better eternal destiny. But now that you have turned away from God and put your trust in a man, what hope of salvation is still left for you? I already think of you as a friend. So if you're willing to listen to me, here's my advice: the first thing you should do is to be circumcised. Then you should carefully observe the precepts that have been laid down concerning the Sabbath, the festivals, and the new moons of God. In short, you should fulfill everything written in the law of Moses. Only then will you perhaps find mercy from God. But if the Messiah has been born or exists somewhere right now, we don't know about it. Nor does he even know his own identity yet; and furthermore, he won't have any power until Elijah comes to anoint him and make him known to everyone. But you Christians have accepted a blasphemous rumor, and so have invented for yourselves a Messiah in whose name you are rashly going to your deaths."

I replied, "My friend, I excuse you, and may you be forgiven, for you don't know what you are saying. You have been persuaded by teachers who do not understand the scriptures, and so you blurt out whatever comes into your mind like a fortune-teller. But allow me to give you my account of Christ. I will show you that we have not been deceived, and that we will not stop confessing him even if men assail us with criticism or the cruelest tyrant tries to force us to deny Him. I will prove to you right here and now that we do not believe in baseless myths or teachings that can't be substantiated by reason. We hold to doctrines that are filled with the Spirit of God. They gush forth with power and are teeming with grace!"

First Apology 67–68

Justin has written to Emperor Antoninus Pius to defend Christianity. In this passage, he provides one of the earliest and most detailed depictions of life in the ancient church. He describes Christian behavior and worship in an attempt to show that Roman society has nothing to fear from the new religion. The Christian lifestyle is praiseworthy and virtuous. Isn't it amazing that much of what Justin described in the second century is still practiced in the church today?

[In our churches] the rich among us come to the aid of the poor, and we always stick together. For the many blessings we receive, we praise the Creator of everything through his Son Jesus Christ and through the Holy Spirit. On Sunday everyone who lives in the city or the countryside gathers together in one place, where the memoirs of the apostles or the writings of the prophets are read for as long as time allows. When the reader has finished, the leader[29] of our community gives a sermon in which he instructs us and urges us to imitate these good teachings.

Next we all stand up together and offer our prayers. When the prayers are finished, bread and wine mixed with water are brought to us, just as I described above [in the preceding chapters]. The leader offers his own prayers of thanksgiving to the best of his ability, while the people express their agreement by saying "Amen." Then the elements over which prayers of thanksgiving have been said are distributed to everyone, and all partake of them. The deacons also send portions to those who are absent that day.

Those among us who are well off, if they are willing, give an offering in whatever amount seems appropriate to them. The leader holds the collection money to be distributed as needed. He provides aid to widows and orphans, to those who are needy from sickness or some other cause, to believers who are in prison for their faith, and to Christians from other lands who may be staying with us. Basically, our leader is a caretaker for everyone in need.

We hold our shared church service on Sunday because it is the first day of the week. It was on this day that God transformed the dark and formless matter to create our world. It was also on this day that our Savior Jesus Christ rose from the dead. For he was crucified on Friday, and he appeared on Sunday to his apostles and disciples. The things that he taught them I now offer to you for your serious consideration.

Therefore [O Emperor] if my account of the Christian religion makes it seem reasonable and true, then give your respect to it. On the other hand, if you deem it to be ridiculous, then despise it as nonsense. But do not impose the death penalty on people who have committed no crimes—as if we were your enemies. For I give you this advance warning: You will certainly not escape the coming judgment of God if you persist in your injustice! But as for us, our prayer is "May God's will be done."

3

IRENAEUS OF LYONS

One Remarkable Life?

University of North Carolina professor Bart D. Ehrman is an academic expert on ancient Christianity. He has written a widely-used textbook on the historical origins of the New Testament. In it he offers an account of "one remarkable life" that will help us better understand the earliest followers of Jesus Christ. It reads this way:

> . . . I think that the most sensible place to begin our study is with the life of a famous man who lived nearly 2,000 years ago in a remote part of the Roman empire. From the beginning, his mother knew that he was no ordinary person. Prior to his birth, a heavenly figure appeared to her, announcing that her son would not be a mere mortal but would himself be divine. This prophecy was confirmed by the miraculous character of his birth, a birth accompanied by supernatural signs. The boy was already recognized as a spiritual authority in his youth; his discussions with recognized experts showed his superior knowledge of all things religious. As an adult he left home to engage in an

itinerant preaching ministry. He went from village to town with his message of good news, proclaiming that people should forego their concerns for the material things of this life, such as how they should dress and what they should eat. They should instead be concerned with their eternal souls.

He gathered around him a number of disciples who were amazed by his teaching and his flawless character. They became convinced he was no ordinary man but was the Son of God. Their faith received striking confirmation in the miraculous things that he did. He could reportedly predict the future, heal the sick, cast out demons, and raise the dead. Not everyone proved friendly, however. At the end of his life, his enemies trumped up charges against him, and he was placed on trial before the Roman authorities for crimes against the state.

Even after he departed this realm, however, he did not forsake his devoted followers. Some claimed that he had ascended bodily into heaven; others said that he had appeared to them, alive, afterwards, that they had talked with him and touched him and become convinced that he could not be bound by death. A number of his followers spread the good news about this man, recounting what they had seen him say and do. Eventually some of these accounts came to be written down in books that circulated throughout the empire.[1]

Often when I read this account aloud to my students, they sit slumped in their seats, slightly bored. They've heard it all before. But when I continue reading Ehrman's narrative, they suddenly sit up in amazement:

> . . . I suspect you have never heard the name of this miracle-working "Son of God." The man I have been referring to is the great neo-Pythagorean teacher and holy man of the first century, Apollonius of Tyana, a worshipper of the Roman gods, whose life and teachings are recorded in the writings of his later follower Philostratus, in his book *The Life of Apollonius*.[2]

All along my students had assumed I was reading about Jesus! Surely he is the only one who would fit such a description. This is an assumption we would quickly make in the twenty-first century, but it would not have been taken for granted in the first.

So what is my point? We need to recognize that in Jesus's day, there were a lot of wise sages like Apollonius who traveled around proclaiming a message of salvation. There were also numerous wonder-workers who reportedly did miracles. Therefore, Jesus would have fit a well-understood pattern in the ancient world. Or as I tell my students, "Jesus was not unique." This usually gets their attention. Maybe I've startled you, too! My point, of course, is *not* that Jesus Christ was the same as Apollonius of Tyana. The very fact that Jesus is God Incarnate and the Savior of the world makes him unique. Apollonius was a false alternative to his truth. But what I'm trying to show is that the ancients had broad exposure to savior/teachers. In the years after Jesus walked this earth, countless people explored the ramifications of his life by using their pre-existing categories to understand him. Some wanted to put him in one box, others in another. Various sects claimed to own Jesus's true legacy. He was susceptible to a variety of interpretations: magician, guru, angel, prophet. At the time, it was not at all obvious whose view would eventually win. Those we call the "orthodox" had to defend their perspective against alternate visions of what the religion of Jesus should be.

The church father Irenaeus (pronounced "eer-eh-NAY-us"), the bishop of Lyons in southern Gaul, was one of those orthodox defenders of an orthodox Jesus. The box into which he put the Lord is a box that evangelical Christians would recognize today: he was the Son of God who came in the flesh to save humankind from the sin of Adam.[3] Irenaeus lived at a strategic time, when false interpretations of Jesus were everywhere. Amidst this cacophony of voices, Irenaeus sounded the note that would eventually drown out the rest. Church historians recognize him as one of the major contributors to the emergence of a unified, catholic Christianity. One scholar writes,

> The second century was *the* century for the construction of Christian identity. One of the principal architects of that identity was Irenaeus

of Lyons. His work shaped the Scriptures, the exegesis, the theology, the institutions, and the spirituality of nascent Christianity to such an extent that his imprint is discernible almost two thousand years later.[4]

The lifetime of Irenaeus was indeed the age of a dawning catholicity, and he was one of its "principal architects." What are we to make of this?

Recall that in the introduction we talked about the word "catholic" as meaning "universal." It is a word that defines something desirable: unified, worldwide belief in the truth, instead of sectarian aberration and heretical lies. But this universal orthodoxy within the church was not achieved right out of the gate. Instead, the historical evidence shows that Jesus was almost immediately subjected to competing attempts to interpret him in various ways. Among the many attempts, the Gnostic sects were the most vocal. They advanced their own Jesuses, and thus their own Christianities.[5] Irenaeus was locked in a battle with them for the definition of authentic Christianity. But how could such a thing be determined definitively?

From our vantage point today, we might be tempted to define the "orthodox" as the group that was "biblical." But such an approach wouldn't have worked in the second century, since there was not yet an agreed-upon Bible. It took a while for the Christian church even to recognize that the Bible contained two testaments, much less to offer a precise definition of which books should be included in it. Although most of the biblical writings were already circulating among the churches, the process of delineating a proper canon still awaited finalization. As we will see, Irenaeus was one of the leading figures in establishing the canon of scripture. Until this standard was put solidly in place, the heretical factions tried vigorously to make the scriptures their own. It was not that some groups used sacred writings and others avoided them. Rather, the questions were: Which texts are authoritative? How should they be interpreted? By what authority do they speak? Whose interpretations of them are correct? These are the questions Irenaeus was attempting to answer once and for all.

The way to determine orthodoxy, according to Irenaeus, was to go back to what the apostles had proclaimed as Christ's own word. To achieve this, Irenaeus argued for three main things: (1) a catholic church whose leaders drew their authority from teaching the same doctrines as the apostles; (2) a catholic church whose Bible is comprised of two testaments, written by prophets and apostles; and (3) a catholic church whose Bible is interpreted in light of the apostolic preaching summarized in the early creeds, instead of by fanciful narratives and cosmic mythology. In this chapter we will see how Irenaeus used these three concepts—bishops, canon, and the creeds—to forge a catholic consensus that eventually defeated the many advocates of alternate Christianities. But before proceeding to discuss these matters, we should examine what we know about the life and times of Irenaeus.

A Disciple of Polycarp among the Celts

Irenaeus came to minister in the western part of the Roman Empire, but he was born in the East and retained many points of contact with his native Asia Minor. Though we don't know the exact date of his birth, scholars usually assign a date somewhere around AD 130. He grew up in Smyrna, where Bishop Polycarp (the friend of Ignatius of Antioch) presided over the church. It was Polycarp whom Irenaeus remembered as a powerful and formative presence during the early years of his life. Through Polycarp, who had been a disciple of the Apostle John, the boy Irenaeus felt that he was experiencing a living connection with the apostolic age. Writing about his childhood memories many years later, Irenaeus claimed to recall those days more vividly than the events of recent times. With obvious fond affection for his martyred mentor, he wrote:

I am able to describe the very place in which the blessed Polycarp
sat as he discoursed, and his goings out and his comings in, and the
manner of his life, and his physical appearance, and his discourses
to the people, and the accounts which he gave of his time spent with
John and others who had seen the Lord. And as he remembered their
words, and what he had heard from them concerning the Lord and
his miracles and teaching, having received it from eyewitnesses of
the 'Word of Life,' Polycarp passed on these things in harmony with
the Scriptures.[6]

Irenaeus sat in rapt attention listening to Polycarp's holy memories, "noting them down not on paper, but in my heart."[7] Can you
imagine sitting at the feet of a godly saint as he recalled the Apostle
John's recollections about his years spent with Jesus? Such was
Irenaeus's boyhood experience. It gave him a deep appreciation
for the unbroken continuity of the Christian faith since the time
of the apostles.

Eventually Irenaeus immigrated to Gaul, a western mission field
far from his home in Asia Minor. Scholars suggest that while on the
way he stayed at Rome for a time, since he later maintained close ties
with the Roman church. Could it be that during a stint in Rome he
became familiar with the work of Justin Martyr? The chronology
certainly makes this possible, for Justin was active in Rome at precisely the time Irenaeus would have been there. Irenaeus's writings
reveal that he held Justin in high regard and used him as a source
of information about heresies. Unfortunately, the exact details of
this part of Irenaeus's biography are lost to us. What we do know
is that eventually he came to the provincial city of Lyons, where he
described himself as a "resident among the Celts." Irenaeus was painfully aware of the lack of refined culture in his new surroundings.
In one of his works he even apologized for his crude writing style
because he had become accustomed to using a "barbarous dialect."[8]
However, it seems the members of his church were probably not
of Celtic stock, but were mostly Greek and Roman inhabitants of
Lyons. Let's briefly survey the history of this town.

Prior to the coming of the Romans, the land we call France had long been populated with pagan Celtic tribes. Julius Caesar conquered Gaul in 52 BC, bringing the defeated Celtic chieftain Vercingetorix to Rome in chains. The dungeon where he was held is known as the Mamertine Prison. It can be visited today as the place where, according to tradition, the Apostle Peter was later imprisoned as well. In 43 BC the Romans established a hilltop town called Lugdunum at the confluence of the Rhône and Saône rivers. It soon became the capital of Roman Gaul and served as the hub of an important road system. Though it was in a remote area, Lugdunum's residents had contact with the wider world by traveling down the Rhône to the Mediterranean, where some very old Greek seafaring colonies existed at places like Arles and Marseilles. Today, ancient Lugdunum is known as Lyons. It is France's second largest city, a major center of industry, finance, and French cuisine.

Our first historical evidence of Christianity in Gaul comes from a fierce persecution which broke out at Lyons and the nearby town of Vienne in AD 177, while Irenaeus was residing there. The ancient church historian Eusebius has preserved for us the letter that these communities sent to their sister churches (or founding churches?) back in Asia Minor. Many brave believers from Gaul went to their deaths through horrendous tortures, and they wanted their fellow Christians in other lands to know about their sufferings for the Lord. Among the martyrs was the young slave girl Blandina, whose frail, petite body made the Christians wonder whether she was strong enough to make good her confession. But Blandina put their doubts to rest by enduring the most painful agonies the Roman sadists could inflict. They tortured her in shifts from morning to evening, until at last "they acknowledged that they were conquered, and could do nothing more to her. And they were astonished at her endurance, as her entire body was mangled and broken; and they testified that one of these forms of torture was sufficient to destroy life, not to speak of so many and so great sufferings."[9] Through it all, Blandina repeated the same refrain over and over: "I am a Christian, and there is nothing vile done by us."[10]

Another famous martyr of Gaul was named Sanctus. The torturers fastened red-hot brass plates "to the most tender parts of his body," and tormented him until he was "one complete wound and bruise, drawn out of shape, and altogether unlike a human form."[11] The Romans threw him in a dungeon for a few days, and then brought him back to torture, "supposing that, with his body swollen and inflamed to such a degree that he could not bear the touch of a hand, if they should again apply the same instruments they would overcome him."[12] The letter from the churches of Lyons and Vienne claims that just the opposite happened: "contrary to all human expectation, his body arose and stood erect in the midst of the subsequent torments, and resumed its original appearance and the use of its limbs, so that, through the grace of Christ, these second sufferings became to him, not torture, but healing."[13]

Eventually Sanctus, Blandina, and many other confessors were thrown to the wild beasts in the Amphitheater of the Three Gauls (whose ruins can still be seen in Lyons today). The horrors experienced by these ancient believers can hardly be overestimated. These were the events that happened to Irenaeus's fellow believers. These were the tenuous times in which he lived.

The aged bishop of Lyons, Pothinus, also died during the persecution from suffocation in the stifling prison. When the persecution subsided, Irenaeus was named to take Pothinus's place as bishop. We don't know much about his ministry in Lyons, except that he maintained close ties with the church at Rome. When a delegation was sent there from Gaul with a copy of the letter describing the recent persecution, Irenaeus was appointed as its bearer. It has even been argued that Irenaeus wrote the account of the martyrdoms himself.[14] The letter's opening commendation reads, "We have requested our brother and comrade Irenaeus to carry this letter to you, and we ask you to hold him in esteem, as zealous for the covenant of Christ."[15] The letter goes on to say that if anyone deserves to be held in high regard, certainly Irenaeus is foremost among them. Obviously, he was greatly admired by the churches of Lyons and Vienne.

Our final glimpse of Irenaeus comes from another fragment of a letter that has survived in Eusebius's *Church History*. Once again, we discover Irenaeus's affinity with the church at Rome. In a letter to the bishop of that city named Victor, Irenaeus urged him not to act rashly in a theological dispute over the date of Easter and the practices associated with it (such as when to observe a fast). Victor had attempted to excommunicate the churches of Asia Minor because of their divergent view on these matters. As we would expect, Irenaeus sharply disagreed with this move against the beloved churches of his youth. But instead of laying into Victor, Irenaeus penned a respectful and wise letter urging him to reconsider his actions. He reminded Victor that blessed Polycarp had once come from Asia Minor to Rome (possibly while Irenaeus was there himself). At that time, the previous bishop of Rome had maintained close fellowship with the respected emissary from the East. Despite their theological differences, the churches of Rome and Asia Minor had been in full fellowship. Polycarp had even been invited to officiate at the Lord's Supper in Rome. Their doctrinal disputes were not deemed significant enough to break the unity of the whole church. So in the present case, Irenaeus insisted the churches should be in harmony with one another, and should agree to disagree about some minor questions. Irenaeus's name comes from the Greek word for "peaceful." Eusebius picked up on this meaning with his comment that "Irenaeus, who was truly well-named, became a peacemaker in this matter, exhorting and negotiating on behalf of the peace of the churches."[16] With this final act of peacemaking we lose sight of Irenaeus in the mists of history. Later tradition asserts that he died as a martyr, but no certain evidence of this fact exists.

Since we know so little of Irenaeus's life, why have we described him in this book as a spiritual forefather you should know? It is not because of his biography, but because of the writings he has left us. Irenaeus bequeathed to later generations two very significant works which make him one of the most important theologians of the early church. The first is a little book called *Proof of the Apostolic Preach-*

ing, in which Irenaeus commented on the basic creed he knew in his day and defended apostolic doctrine through scriptural exegesis. But most scholars consider Irenaeus's other surviving work to be his most significant. This great five-volume treatise is entitled *The Detection and Overthrow of What Is Falsely Called 'Knowledge.'* Today it usually goes by its shorter name, *Against Heresies.* As you might guess from the title, the treatise is an attempt to blast the Gnostics and their so-called "knowledge" out of the water. Irenaeus viewed these heretics as a deadly threat to the church. In a moment we'll examine Irenaeus's threefold response to them. But first, let's take a look at what the Gnostics actually taught.

Salvation by Knowledge

When we discussed Ignatius of Antioch in chapter 1, we learned that the Gnostics were vigorous and capable teachers who were propagating their own peculiar views of Jesus Christ. The orthodox church fathers often depicted Simon Magus from Acts 8 as the fountainhead of this heresy. While the whole Gnostic movement cannot be attributed to this one figure, it is probable that Simon represented an early version of the pseudo-Christian wisdom that other Gnostic teachers also embraced. The Apostle Paul opposed such early Gnostic-type beliefs in his epistle to the Colossians. The false teachers in Colosse had embraced human philosophies (2:8), Jewish legalism (2:16), the worship of angelic powers (2:18), and asceticism on the premise that the body is evil (2:21–23). These are some of the same features we discover in later, more developed Gnosticism. In contrast Paul says the true "treasures of wisdom and knowledge" (2:3) can be found only in Christ, who reconciled all things by the blood of His cross (1:20). The writings of the Apostle John also reveal that Gnosticizing ideas had gained a strong following in the first century. In response John says, "If anyone comes to you and does not bring this teaching [of Christ himself], do not receive him into your house or give him any greeting" (2 John 1:10). The biblical writers had very quickly identified such early Gnostic tendencies as a threat to the faith.

While an incipient Gnostic movement can be identified in the New Testament period, it is the second century which saw an explosion of formal Gnostic sects. They grew more organized, and their teachers, who were often intellectuals, grew more sophisticated. In this way many common people who had initially been drawn toward Christ were being led into error. By Irenaeus's day, the multi-hued conglomerate of Gnostic beliefs had become a potent force that threatened to swamp the orthodox church. As we have already noted, the legacy of Jesus was being hotly contested at this time. Irenaeus immediately recognized the danger. At a critical juncture in church history, he offered his book *Against Heresies* as the Christian answer.

What exactly did the Gnostics believe? Their myths seem so ridiculous to us today that we can scarcely believe anyone would ever have embraced them. But we must acknowledge that for many ancient people, Gnosticism offered an attractive alternative to orthodox Christianity. Spiritual seekers were drawn to its seeming intellectualism and mysterious insights into the cosmos. Irenaeus records the doctrines of one particular brand of Gnosticism taught by a teacher named Valentinus (or more precisely, by his disciple Ptolemy). The Valentinian Gnostics believed there was a heavenly "Fullness" which consisted of thirty angelic beings called Aeons. The Aeons always came in male-female pairs. (It is a common feature of Gnosticism that divinity consists of both genders, so that male Aeons require female consorts or counterparts.) These conjugal pairs emitted lower Aeons, and the last of these emissions was Sophia (Wisdom). But Sophia became passionate, and wickedly longed for the highest Father apart from her own consort. Though she was eventually healed from her grievous action, her evil "Thought," which had given rise to her sin, was cast out of the Fullness like an aborted fetus. This shapeless Thought took on a personified form named Mother Achamoth. She

was in a hopeless state until the "Christ" came to her and enabled
Achamoth to bring forth substances from within herself. One of the
beings she brought forth was the Demiurge. He was the ignorant
creator of the entire physical world in which we live. In many Gnostic
accounts, the Demiurge was equated with Yahweh, the Jewish God
of the Old Testament, who foolishly thought he was the one true
God. Only the enlightened Gnostics "knew" he was actually a corrupted being, far inferior to the goddess Sophia.

For the Valentinian Gnostics, there were three kinds of people,
corresponding to the division of each human being into body, soul,
and spirit. All human beings are divided into three classes: the physical, the soulish, and the spiritual. The lost "physical" people of the
world are the pagan unbelievers. The "soulish" are people like Irenaeus
who belong to the orthodox churches. Although they don't have
full *gnosis* or understanding of the truth, they can reach salvation
through good works. Of course, the highest humans are the Gnostics
themselves, who are the only true Christians. They do not have to
perform good works since their salvation is assured by their inborn
"spiritual" natures. Therefore, they can engage in certain activities
(such as attending gladiator games or seducing married women)
which are off limits to others. The rules of the common believers
do not apply to them.

In order to give secret wisdom to the spiritual Gnostics, the Demiurge (Yahweh) is said to have given birth to a son who was filled with
the spiritual seed of Mother Achamoth. This son was the "Christ"
who passed through Mary without taking a body from her. He was
just like water flowing through a tube. The Gnostics often said the
"Christ" inhabited the body of the man Jesus of Nazareth, but his
body was not made of real flesh. When we were discussing the opponents of Ignatius of Antioch, we referred to this teaching as "docetism." The docetic Christ who possessed the illusion of a body came
into the world to teach spiritual precepts that only the enlightened
Gnostics would be able to comprehend. Through the purging action
of his revealed knowledge, the Gnostics would eventually make their

way up into the Fullness as purified spirits. The ordinary Christians, however, must remain at a lesser station.

So what do we discover as the distinctive themes of Gnosticism? Allow me to name three important ones. First of all, we can easily see how it emphasized spiritual elitism. It was a system inherently designed to make distinctions between the "more spiritual" and the "less worthy." We must remember that the Gnostics by no means saw themselves as being outside the church. Rather they believed they were the most faithful expression of what Christianity was supposed to be. By claiming to have access to truths no one else had, they enticed fragile Christians from orthodox circles toward their mysterious doctrines. They also taught that they did not have to abide by the moral standards that lesser believers had to obey. Eventually the Gnostics separated themselves into competing congregations which claimed superiority over all other Christians. They alone were the spiritual elite.

Another feature of Gnosticism was its lack of historical emphasis. Since salvation came through mystical knowledge, the historical actions of Jesus Christ—which were not even performed in a real body—possessed no importance. In this way the Gnostics robbed Christianity of what is actually its centerpiece: the saving work of Christ on the cross, and his bodily resurrection from the grave. This is exactly what the apostles had emphasized so clearly. Their preaching centered on the Crucified and Risen One. Repeating a very ancient summary of the gospel, Paul wrote, "I delivered to you as of first importance what I also received: that Christ died for our sins in accordance with the Scriptures, that he was buried, that he was raised on the third day in accordance with the Scriptures" (1 Cor. 15:3–4). Irenaeus recognized that the Gnostics were not telling the same story that the apostles had told, so he made their lack of apostolicity a major part of his "refutation and overthrow."

Third, the Gnostics used a dubious method of biblical interpretation to advance their doctrines. They found secret meanings encoded in the pages of the Bible. For example, to reach the sacred number of thirty Aeons, the Valentinians added up the hours of the day when the workers were sent to the fields in the Parable of the Laborers (Matt. 20:1–7). Irenaeus believed that using cryptic symbolism and arcane codes manifestly was *not* the way the Bible should be interpreted.[17] He compared it to someone who took apart the stones in a mosaic depicting a king, reorganized them into a picture of a fox, and then called the fox the intended production! Only a fool would be carried away by such a methodology. Instead the believer should interpret scripture in light of the creed he had received at baptism, known as the Rule of Faith. This Rule served as an accurate summary of true Christianity as the apostles had always proclaimed it.

Are the religious concepts of Gnosticism still around today? Absolutely. In fact, a modern-day form of Gnosticism can be found right in my own neighborhood in Wheaton, Illinois—a place normally noted for its evangelical Christianity! Across the street from my supermarket is a stately brick building which serves as the national headquarters of The Theosophical Society in America. Although I had passed it many times, and had a general idea of what it was about, one day I decided to make a visit to do some further investigation. The folks there were very nice to me, inviting me to their upcoming festival and even offering me the chance to walk on their meditation labyrinth. Browsing through their library, I discovered books on virtually every world religion, including a section on the ancient Gnostics. While I was there I picked up several brochures about The Theosophical Society. Together they depict a movement that is stunningly akin to Gnosticism in its search for "Divine Wisdom" (which is what the word *theosophy* means). In fact, the brochure "Christianity and Theosophy" established a concrete connection between this modern movement and the "early gnostic and hermetic groups within Christianity, which later disappeared or went underground." The brochure expressed some viewpoints that Valentinus could well have endorsed.[18]

But modern Theosophy is not the only manifestation of Gnostic-type belief in America today. Another would be The Church of

Christ, Scientist.[19] And there are even a number of groups today calling themselves the "Gnostic Church" in one form or another. Just Google the term and see for yourself. One of these groups has close connections to France, where Gnostic worship of the goddess Sophia is still flourishing in the twenty-first century just as it was in the second.[20] Another group calls itself the Apostolic Gnostic Church in America—with references to Sophia, the consort of Christ, again featured prominently on its Web pages.[21] Many other occult groups would likewise fit under this general religious umbrella. And if you want to find a more popular expression of contemporary esoteric spirituality, look no further than the hit novel *The Da Vinci Code*, which is shot through with references to theosophy and Gnostic beliefs about Jesus. Do you think it is a coincidence that the lead character's name is Sophia?

Reflections on Irenaeus

Earlier in this chapter we identified three strategies Irenaeus used to counteract the false doctrines flourishing in his era. Let us now briefly examine those three concepts to see how he combated Gnosticism.

1. *A catholic church whose leaders drew their authority from teaching the very same doctrines as the apostles.* For Irenaeus, true Christianity was identical to the earliest preaching of those who had walked and talked with Christ. The bishop of Lyons lived at a time when the Christian message was transmitted through oral proclamation as well as through written texts. One of the best ways to preserve the gospel message was to follow Paul's command in 2 Timothy 2:2 that the truth should be personally entrusted to faithful witnesses who would hand it on to ensuing generations. Taking a cue from the monepiscopal church structure we have already identified in Ignatius of Antioch, Irenaeus taught that the trustworthy bishop and his council of presbyters were the ones entrusted to guard the apostolic

deposit of true faith. In contrast, the heretics boldly asserted "that they themselves are wiser, not merely than the presbyters, but even than the apostles, because they have discovered the unadulterated truth."[22] By emphasizing the apostolicity of the catholic church, Irenaeus essentially declared that he and his fellow believers (instead of the Gnostics) represented the original church of Acts in a later generation. While such claims of apostolic succession are much more difficult to make today, it was a strategy that worked quite well in the second century.

2. *A catholic church whose Bible is comprised of two testaments, written by prophets and apostles.* It may be surprising to learn that Irenaeus was the first person to use the term "New Testament" to mean what we mean today.[23] Before his time, there was no awareness within the church that the sacred books of Christianity comprised a second body of writings alongside the received Jewish scriptures. The earlier fathers certainly possessed books they revered as holy, but did not yet think in terms of a well-defined second testament. The process of determining which books were actually in the canon of scripture was just starting to occur around the time Irenaeus was pastoring his church in Lyons. In the next chapter we will look at the issue of the biblical canon in greater detail. We will learn that the orthodox believers insisted that the canonical writings of the New Testament must be closely connected with the original apostles.

3. *A catholic church whose Bible is interpreted in light of the apostolic preaching summarized in the creeds—instead of by fanciful narratives and cosmic mythology.* We have already seen how Irenaeus castigated the Gnostics for tearing apart the "mosaic" of scripture and reassembling it into something foreign. What then was the proper key for biblical interpretation? For the orthodox church, the core message of Christianity was conveniently summed up by the creed used to instruct new converts before baptism. This "Rule of Faith" provided believers with a synopsis of what the Bible was all about.[24] It certainly did not contain a bunch of myths about primal Aeons. Rather, the

Rule taught one creator God who was revealed by the Spirit through the Hebrew prophets. This Father God has been supremely revealed in the life, death, and resurrection of his Son, who was incarnate by a virgin for our salvation. The future holds a final resurrection for all, with rewards for the righteous and punishment for the wicked from the Lord Jesus Christ. So we can see that for Irenaeus, the story of salvation was a comprehensive narrative of God's redeeming work in human history. Irenaeus was one of the earliest patristic writers to see this big picture.[25] The Rule of Faith became the organizing principle of his theology, since it outlined the overarching story of Christian redemption.[26]

Since we have mentioned redemption, we should ask, "Redemption from what?" For the Gnostics, the basic human problem was ignorance. But Irenaeus believed the problem went much deeper. It was one of sin and guilt.[27] Irenaeus was the first Christian theologian to develop the Pauline understanding of the fall of humanity through Adam (Romans 5). He even borrowed a Pauline term to describe salvation: *recapitulation*, or the "summing up of all things in Christ" (see Eph. 1:10). By this term the bishop meant many things, but it all came down to this: salvation history must be centered on the historical Jesus Christ, whose obedience unto death canceled the work of Adam. Whereas the first man sinned, and so introduced sin into the world, the Second Adam lived a perfect life, and thereby reordered the cosmos the way it was supposed to be. The cross became the place where ultimate, forgiving love was poured out.[28] Sinful humans and a loving God were reconciled by the one who is both God and Man. In Irenaeus's doctrine of recapitulation, we discover a comprehensive perspective on the work of God throughout history. Instead of indulging in theosophical speculations, Irenaeus recounted the biblical story (as summed up in the Rule of Faith) which speaks of creation, prediction, incarnation, redemption, and the recapitulation of all things through Christ the Lord. This recapitulation idea will become an important patristic theme. Be looking for developments of it in chapter 7 on Athanasius, and in chapter 10 on Cyril of Alexandria.

Irenaeus's skirmishes with the Gnostics represented more than just theological squabbling over doctrinal abstractions. Two creation stories, two worldviews, two accounts of humanity's place in the cosmos, were battling for supremacy. It was a battle the orthodox catholics eventually won—though this was by no means a certain outcome when Irenaeus first put his pen to the parchment. And yet it was precisely at the time of his monumental *Against Heresies* that the tide began to turn. Through strategies that emphasized the apostolic roots of Christianity's leaders and scriptures, Irenaeus became a key architect of the unified catholicity that would eventually marginalize all other competing Jesus-religions. His anti-heretical treatise was the opening salvo; but it was the brilliant rhetorician Tertullian who dealt the death blow. After these two writers finished their apologetic efforts, an established catholicity was firmly in place. Never again would Gnosticism pose the threat of becoming the authentic version of genuine Christianity. In the next chapter we will meet Tertullian, one of Irenaeus's collaborators in defense of the true faith.

Provocative Questions

1. Irenaeus gave wise counsel to Victor concerning theological disagreements. He said that the churches of Rome and Asia Minor should agree to disagree on some practices, while still holding on to the essential Christian doctrines. Which do you tend to favor: theological truth, or unity in the body? Can we have both today? See Ephesians 4:1–6 and 2 Timothy 4:1–5.

2. Speaking of essential doctrines, let's recall how the Rule of Faith served the early church as a synopsis of the apostolic preaching. As such, it was a succinct expression of core

Christian beliefs. What do you think are the non-negotiable doctrines of the faith? If you were preparing a short creed for some new converts preparing to be baptized, what would you write?

3. While there may not be people in your church forming their own separate cults like the Gnostics, perhaps you have encountered spiritual elitism or exclusive cliques in your congregation. What are some ways that the "elite" exclude other people? Do they do it through pretensions of superior knowledge? Do certain popular leaders sometimes serve as the focal points of such cliques? How should you approach this situation? Are you contributing to factions in any way? The Corinthian church faced the problem of divisions and spiritual elitism—what does scripture have to say in response? See 1 Corinthians 1:10–13; 3:1–6; 4:6–7; 8:1–3; 13:4–7.

4. What are some groups today that claim to be "Christian," but do not hold to the true, biblical faith? Have you ever had personal contact with members of a pseudo-Christian cult? Is your church engaged in refuting aberrant beliefs? How important is it for orthodox Christians today to "detect and overthrow" heresies like Irenaeus did? In what ways does your pastor guard you from false doctrine? See 1 Timothy 6:3–5, 20–21. (Does v. 20 ring a bell?)

5. Irenaeus is known for his cosmic understanding of the work of Christ. It is more than just personal and individualistic—the Lord's victory has touched every part of creation. Irenaeus's term "recapitulation" meant that the universe which was disordered because of Adam's sin is triumphantly put right by the Second Adam's perfect obedience (see Rom. 5:12–19; Col. 1:15–23). Of course, we do not yet live in a perfected world. Nevertheless, what are some concrete ways that Christ's reign as Head of the church should affect our world?

Good Books to Dig Deeper

Irenaeus's *Against Heresies* is in complete English translation only in the *Ante-Nicene Fathers* series, Volume 1. For more recent translations of selected portions, see:

Grant, Robert M. *Irenaeus of Lyons*. New York: Routledge, 1997.

Unger, Dominic J. *St. Irenaeus of Lyons Against the Heresies: Book I*. New York: Newman, 1992.

For an overview of Irenaeus's theology, see:

Donovan, Mary Ann. *One Right Reading? A Guide to Irenaeus*. Collegeville, Minn.: Liturgical Press, 1997.

Lawson, John. *The Biblical Theology of Saint Irenaeus*. London: Epworth Press, 1948.

Minns, Dennis. *Irenaeus*. Washington, DC: Georgetown University Press, 1994.

Osborn, Eric. *Irenaeus of Lyons*. Cambridge: Cambridge University Press, 2001.

A Taste of Irenaeus

Against Heresies 1.10.1–2

In this text Irenaeus describes the Rule of Faith which is shared by the whole church. Notice how he draws his ideas from scripture. The Rule is a synopsis of biblical belief, a summary of mere Christianity. We can easily see how it served as an outline for an orthodox understanding of God's saving work in the world. For Irenaeus, the fundamentals of the faith were held in common by all Christians in all lands. This is the essence of the catholicity he strived so hard to establish.

The church which is scattered over the whole world all the way to the ends of the earth received from the apostles and their followers this faith: We believe in one God the Father Almighty, "who made heaven and earth and the sea and all that is in them" (Exod. 20:11); and in one Christ Jesus, the Son of God who became incarnate for our salvation; and in the Holy Spirit, who through the prophets predicted the plans of God.

These divine plans included the first advent; the birth from a Virgin; the passion; the resurrection from the dead; the bodily ascension of our beloved Lord Jesus Christ into heaven; and his second coming from heaven in the glory of the Father to "recapitulate all things" (Eph. 1:10) and to resurrect the bodies of the whole human race, so that to Christ Jesus our Lord and God and Savior and King "every knee shall bow, in heaven and on earth and under the earth, and every tongue shall confess Him" (Phil. 2:10–11). This was the good pleasure of the invisible Father.

Christ will raise the dead in order to execute righteous judgment upon everyone. Into eternal fire he will send the "spiritual forces of wickedness" (Eph. 6:12), and the angels who sinned and became apostate, and every person who is profane, unjust, sinful, and blasphemous. But there are others: the righteous and holy, and all who have kept his commandments and remain in his love (John 15:10). The apostles persevered from the very beginning of his ministry (John 15:27), while others began at the point of their own repentance. To all of these he will give incorruptible life by his grace, and will clothe them with eternal glory.

Now as I was just saying: the Church which is spread out through the whole world has received this preaching and this faith. And so we Christians diligently guard it as if we were living together in a single house. Or to put it another way: clearly we all believe these things so much, it's like we have a single heart and soul (Acts 4:32). We so consistently preach, teach, and hand down these truths, it's as if we have but one mouth.

For although the languages of the world are dissimilar, the meaning of our tradition is one and the same. The churches founded in Germany do not believe or hand down anything different; neither do the churches established in Spain, or among the Celts, or in the Far East, or in Egypt, or in Libya, or in the middle of the world. Just as the sun which was created by God is one and the same throughout the whole world, so the light which is the preaching of Christian truth shines everywhere, and illumines everyone who wants to come into knowledge of the truth.

No pastor of any congregation, even if he is extremely eloquent, will say anything that varies from the truth. For we all recognize that "no one is above the Master" (Matt. 10:24). Likewise, the pastor who is lacking in eloquence will not diminish the tradition. For since the faith is one and the same, he who can discourse at length about it does not really add to it, and he who is less theologically capable does not diminish it in any way.

4

TERTULLIAN

Have you ever stopped to think how difficult it must have been to be a cowboy in the days of the Wild West? Our American mythology paints a picture of the cowboy riding lazily through stunning Western scenery, with a hearty meal of fresh beef around a campfire in the evening, and a good night's sleep under a star-studded sky. But historical accounts tell a different story. Here are some selections from cowboy George Duffield's diary describing a cattle drive from Texas to Iowa in 1866:

> (May) 8th. All 3 heards are up and ready to travel off together for the first time travelled 6 miles rain pouring down in torrents and here we are on the banks of a creek with 10 or 12 ft water and raising crossed at 4 Oclock and crossed into Bosque Bottom found it 20 ft deep Ran my Horse into a ditch and got my Knee badly sprained—15 Miles . . .
>
> 13th. Big Thunder Storm last night Stampede lost 100 Beeves hunted all day found 50 all tired. Every thing discouraging.

14th. Concluded to cross Brazos swam our cattle and Horses and built Raft and Rafted our provisions and blankets &c over Swam River with rope and then hauled wagon over lost Most of our Kitchen furniture such as camp Kittles Coffee Pots Cups Plates Canteens &c &c.

15. Back at River bringing up wagon Hunting Oxen and other lost property. Rain poured down for one Hour. It does nothing but rain got all our traps together that was not lost and thought we were ready for off dark rainy night cattle all left us and in morning not one Beef to be seen.

16th Hunt Beeves is the word—all Hands discouraged and are determined to go 200 Beeves out and nothing to eat.

20th. Rain poured down for two hours Ground in a flood Creeks up—Hands leaving Gloomey times as ever I saw . . .

23rd. Travelled 10 Miles over a beautiful Prairie country such as I expected to see before I came here . . . Hard rain that night and cattle behaved very bad—ran all night—was on my Horse the whole night and it raining hard.

31st. Swimming Cattle is the order We worked all day in the River and at dusk got the last Beefe over—and am now out of Texas—This day will long be remembered by men—There was one of our party Drowned to day (Mr Carr) and several narrow escapes and I among [them].

June 1st. Stampede last night among 6 droves and a general mix up and loss of Beeves. Hunt cattle again Men all tired and want to leave . . . Horses *all* give out and Men refused to do anything . . .

5th. Oh! what a night—Thunder and Lightning and rain—we followed our Beeves *all* night as they wandered about—put them on the road at day break . . .

12th. Hard Rain and Wind Big stampede and here we are among the Indians with 150 head of Cattle gone hunted all day and the Rain pouring down with but poor success Dark days these are to me Nothing but Bread and Coffee Hands all Growling and Swearing—every thing wet and cold . . . Last night 5000 Beeves stampeded at this place and a general mix up was the result.

19th. Good day 15 Indians come to Herd and tried to take some Beeves. Would not let them. Had a big muss One drew his Knife and

I my revolver. Made them leave but fear they have gone for others they are the Seminoles.[1]

The litany of misery continues like this for months, with such added trials as cattle-thieving rustlers, sickness, blisters, being attacked by an ornery steer, heat, flies, legal troubles, cold nights, and a "severe pane in my neck." This hardy cowboy wasn't able to head home until October 3—six and a half months after he first set out! As we read such an account, we can't help but admire his courage and toughness. When the other cowhands were packing their bags and quitting the drive, George Duffield stayed in the saddle.

What does George Duffield of the Brazos country have to do with Tertullian of ancient Carthage? I want to suggest that in many ways the two men were cut from the same cloth. Both possessed a kind of dogged determination in the face of adversity; both refused to shrink from a challenge; both were audacious in what they dared to attempt. Tertullian lived at a time when his "herd" was not safely corralled, and so was exposed to danger from all sides. Instead of backing down, Tertullian rode into the fray with a rebel yell and both guns blazing. He did not take on the heretics with the kind of plodding and disjointed argumentation that we sometimes find in Irenaeus's writings. Rather, with a biting wit unmatched among the church fathers, Tertullian fired white-hot pamphlets at the heretics like bullets from his six-gun. Certainly he was a larger-than-life personality among the ancient Christians. He possessed the cowboy's zest for danger and boldness in the face of opposition. And yet if we are honest we must admit he also possessed the cowboy's cantankerous personality. But when the chips were down, you definitely wanted him on your side.

Tertullian never had to corral a herd of unruly cattle, but he did build a "fence" of a different kind: a safe enclosure into which the Christians of his day could be herded for protection against the heretics lurking without. He constructed this corral not by the sweat of his brow or the edge of an axe, but by the pen he so deftly wielded as an accomplished writer. Tertullian was a master of the Latin language—the first Christian author to use this noble tongue instead of Greek. Although his abbreviated style often made it difficult to ascertain his exact meaning, nobody could miss his main points. Even today he is famous for his pithy expressions, such as the critique of philosophy in his question, "What does Athens have to do with Jerusalem?" or the celebration of martyrdom in his slogan, "The blood of Christians is seed."[2] Tertullian protected the Christians of his day by enclosing them in a fence made of words. Unfortunately, he kept making the enclosure smaller and smaller until eventually only a few were left inside.

We can see Tertullian's fence-building at its best in his work called *Prescription Against Heretics*.[3] In this treatise he marked out a safe space for the orthodox believers to live, and in so doing excluded the heretics from their midst. Tertullian was irritated (as he often was) by the Gnostics and others who constantly quoted Jesus's words "Seek and you shall find" as justification for their unlimited theological deliberation. The heretics never actually arrived at a position, but constantly offered speculative theories, dragging the more simple believers into their controversies. Tertullian responded emphatically, "My first principle is this: Christ laid down one definite system of truth, which the world must believe without qualification, and which we must seek precisely in order to believe it when we find it."[4] Once Christ's authoritative teachings have been found, philosophical "seeking" should end, replaced by firm belief. The teachings of Jesus served as the "boundary" for true Christians. Believers should not go searching for wisdom outside of his revealed truth.

In the material world, of course, fences are visible to the eye and clear for all to see. When it comes to something abstract like doctrines or ideas, how are we to know where the boundary line is drawn? In other words, how do we know what Christ really taught? For Tertullian the essentials of the church's faith had been clearly demarcated in the baptismal creed. Like Irenaeus before him, Tertullian believed the most convenient synopsis of Christian truth was found in the

Rule of Faith. Within its defined contours, theological seeking was perfectly acceptable. "Let us now seek in our own territory," he writes, "from our own friends and on our own business, and let us seek only what can come into question without disloyalty to the Rule of Faith ... Provided the essence of the Rule is not disturbed, you may seek and discuss as much as you like."[5] Or as he puts it a few lines later with his typical wit, "To know nothing against the Rule is to know everything."[6] The Rule of Faith emphasized the Creator God who sent his Son to be born of a virgin, to die and rise again, to ascend to heaven, and to return for final judgment. By laying out the basic framework of salvation history, the Rule erected a visible fence that separated those inside the corral from the predators outside with their destructive cosmic myths.

Did Tertullian's appreciation for the Rule of Faith mean he preferred it over the scriptures? Such an idea would have been absurd to him. The Rule is nothing but an accurate summary of what the apostles taught as the word of Christ. Tertullian did not think the Rule was inspired like the Bible; yet he did think both contained the same basic ideas. They were not in conflict with one another, for the Rule was simply a distillation of scripture's more complete message. But Tertullian was practical enough to realize that the scriptures could be subjected to many different interpretations—some true, others false; some right, others wrong. How could one know the difference? For Tertullian (as for all of the church fathers) the criterion for Christian truth was agreement with the teachings of Jesus Christ himself. But since the Lord was no longer present on earth, who could be identified as the authentic inheritors of his message? Obviously it was the apostles—those to whom Christ had revealed himself directly. And so, assuming the Rule was a summary of the apostles' teaching, it was the key by which scripture's true meaning could be unlocked. In contrast, the interpretations of the heretics, which did not conform to the Rule, were shown to be erroneous because they lacked congruence with apostolic doctrine.

Tertullian vigorously challenged the heretics on their lack of apostolicity. They could make no claims to possess the truth, he said, for their pedigree did not go back to the founding of the church. They were "latecomers." As such, they had no right of access to the Word of God. Tertullian was very protective of the scriptures. He wanted to insure that the Bible would be interpreted not by endless heretical speculations, but by the received summary of Christian truth. He even attempted to prevent the heretics from debating about the Bible's meaning at all. It was simply not their book. Since they are not apostolic, they have no right to offer any interpretations of it. This is what Tertullian meant when he called his treatise a "prescription" against the heretics. The *praescriptio* was a Roman legal concept that excluded certain parties from bringing a suit in court. We still use this principle today. For example, I cannot sue someone about a property dispute that my friend may be having. If I am not the legal owner of the property, I have no right to come before the bench to litigate about it. I am "proscribed" from further legal action by nonownership. In the same way, Tertullian argued that the heretics had no right of ownership to the Bible. It belonged to the orthodox catholics, who were the only rightful heirs of the apostles. So the heretics should keep their hands off what is not their property.

Are you catching a sense of Tertullian's sheer audacity here? Don't miss it. As we now turn to a brief account of Tertullian's life setting, I hope you have already come to appreciate this cowboy of a church father. In keeping with our Western imagery, we might say he's like the lone sheriff who was bold enough to run the gang of bandits out of town. Of course, I do not want to portray Tertullian in an idealistic way. He is a conflicted character, and there is much about him to dislike. We'll mention some of his faults and errors in this chapter. At the same time, I don't want you to miss the stubbornness, the flair, the true grit—even the cockiness—of this ancient church father. He had an aura about him that George Duffield would have appreciated.

"Give Me the Master"

The force of Tertullian's personality reverberated well beyond his lifetime. Decades later, the respected bishop of Carthage named Cyprian would ask his secretary to bring him Tertullian's writings every day with the request, "Give me the master."[7] Obviously, later generations found much to value in Tertullian's thought. But for someone who was such a towering figure in North African Christianity, we know very little about his life. The traditional picture is as follows: Tertullian was born around the year AD 160, the son of a Roman centurion. As an adult he practiced law at Rome until he converted to Christianity from paganism. He became a presbyter in the church at Carthage (near modern-day Tunis in Tunisia), serving there until he broke away from the catholics as he became increasingly attracted to a sect of Spirit-filled prophets called the Montanists. He died at an old age, estranged from the catholic community. But modern scholarship has blurred this already vague picture of the man. Now it is widely accepted that Tertullian was not a soldier's son, was not a presbyter, was not formally trained in law, and may not have died as an old man.[8] Furthermore, the precise nature of his association with the Montanists is debated today. (We will discuss Montanism in chapter 5.) So our final picture of Tertullian really is quite fuzzy. When we examine his writings we can see he was highly educated in both Greek and Latin. He knew philosophy, literature, rhetoric, and legal theory. His writings span the years AD 197 to 212, and include a treatise on marriage called *To My Wife*, from which we can assume he was a married man.[9] Beyond this meager information, not much more can be said.

Nor do we know exactly how Christianity came to Tertullian's home city of Carthage. Perhaps the faith arrived from Rome, since he said it was from there that the African believers made their connection to an apostolic church.[10] Others have theorized that the Christian community grew out of Jewish-Christian congregations.[11] In any case, history reveals that the church's character in North Af-

rica was very much like Tertullian's own personality: morally rigorous, radically devoted, and steadfastly opposed to the pagan world.
These traits are the perfect formula for producing martyrs, which
the North African church had in abundance. Indeed our earliest
evidence of North African Christianity is a text commonly called
The Acts of the Scillitan Martyrs. On July 17 in the year AD 180,
twelve Christians from the town of Scilli were brought before the
proconsul and ordered to swear religious devotion to the emperor.
From their names we can deduce that they were common people
of the land, not nobles. However, they were not all illiterate: their
leader Speratus had brought the epistles of Paul (his Bible, in other
words) to the trial.[12] When the confessors were urged to renounce
Christianity, all twelve utterly refused to do so and were sentenced
to execution. Their passion story concludes, "And so they all together
were crowned with martyrdom; and they reign with the Father and
the Son and the Holy Ghost, for ever and ever. Amen."[13] But while
North Africa was definitely a land of radical Christian commitment, it didn't only produce rustic martyrs. Two centuries later the
region would be home to the most influential church father of them
all: Augustine, who taught at Carthage for a time and later became
a bishop in the nearby city of Hippo. Interestingly, he sometimes
preached in a church dedicated to the Scillitan martyrs. Yet despite
such a profound legacy of North African martyrs and theologians,
today there is virtually no Christian presence there. The region is
completely dominated by Islam.

But back in the third century, long before fundamentalist Islam
had come on the scene, fundamentalist Christianity was alive and
well in Tertullian's writings. It is perhaps the church's finest tribute
to him that so many of his works have been preserved to our times.
Today we possess thirty-one of them in the original Latin, most of
which are very substantial theological discourses. Compare that to
the great bishop Irenaeus: only two of his writings now survive, and
neither is in his original Greek (except for a few fragments). Among
the Latin church fathers, only Augustine is on par with Tertullian

as having earned such high regard among later scribes. Tertullian's longest work is a five-volume anti-heretical treatise which is notable not only for its bulk, but because it blossomed into a sustained effort at verse-by-verse scriptural exegesis. As such it is considered one of the first Christian biblical commentaries. The work is known as *Against Marcion*, which immediately causes us to ask: Who was this fellow Marcion? And what made Tertullian direct the full force of his debater's rhetoric against him in five long volumes? It is time to get acquainted with the man whom Tertullian obviously viewed as an archenemy of the church.

Confrontation with the "Shipmaster of Pontus"

Marcion was a rich businessman with an interest in church affairs. As is often true in such cases, his money gave him the opportunity to propagate his own peculiar theology. He was from Sinope, a port city in the region of Pontus along the Black Sea. From that base he made his fortune in international shipping. But even as a young man, his theology was beginning to go astray. Marcion's father, who was probably a bishop, was forced to excommunicate his son for heresy.[14] So what was a young, rich, charismatic, excommunicant to do? Go to Rome, of course, and see what doors his money might open there. Marcion did just that. Around the year AD 140 he arrived in Rome and made a huge donation to the church. But when the leaders found out what he was actually teaching, to their credit they returned the sum in full and excommunicated Marcion again. Yet this powerful man did not disappear off the scene. He became the overseer of a widespread network of Marcionite churches—which the orthodox church leaders understood to be the work of Satan. Justin Martyr, who was living in Rome at the time, wrote, "Many have believed this man [Marcion], as if he alone knew the truth; and they laugh at us, though they have no proof of what they say, but are carried away irrationally as lambs by a wolf, and become the prey of atheistic doctrines and of devils."[15] Likewise we learn that Polycarp once ran into Marcion at Rome but completely ignored him. Apparently Marcion was feeling a little insecure about his reputation that day, for he demanded of the bishop, "Acknowledge me!" "I do acknowledge you," replied Polycarp. "You are the firstborn of Satan!"[16] This was probably not the reply Marcion was looking for.

What made the church fathers so angry at Marcion? Why would Tertullian take five volumes to demolish this heretic? The nature of his doctrine was so egregious that the orthodox writers—from Justin Martyr to Irenaeus to Tertullian and beyond—all felt compelled to refute him. In a nutshell, Marcion taught that there are two Gods. Playing off Marcion's former occupation, Tertullian wrote, "The heretic of Pontus introduces two Gods, like the twin Clashing Rocks of his own shipwreck: One whom it is impossible to deny, our Creator; and one whom he will never be able to prove, a god of his own."[17] The God that Marcion saw in the Old Testament was cruel, arbitrary, petty, warlike, and stupid. He was more than simply a God of strict justice: he was literally a very mean God.[18] This deity even said horrible things such as "I create evil" (Isa. 45:7). In contrast, Jesus came to announce a new or "alien" God. The Father God was loving, kind, and forgiving. According to Marcion, the Jews worshiped the old Creator who had fashioned our contemptible world. But all along there has always been another God. Formerly unknown to humankind, he eventually sent Jesus to tell us that our sins are automatically forgiven without any punishment. Jesus's purpose was to announce universal salvation for everyone. To do this he did not really need a human body; so Marcion (like the Gnostics) was a docetist who denied a real incarnation. Against such nonsense Tertullian fired this sarcastic bullet: "You may, I assure you, more easily find a man born without a heart and brains, like Marcion himself, than without a body, like Marcion's Christ!"[19] For the orthodox church fathers, Marcionite theology simply was not Christian doctrine.

Let us not overlook the element of anti-Semitism at work here. Marcion rejected the God of the Jews, and therefore believed the religion of Christianity bore no connection to the salvation history of Israel. The greatest modern commentator on Marcion, Adolf von Harnack, wrote that "his entire attitude toward the Old Testament and Judaism can best be understood as one of resentment . . . his Christianity is built upon a resentment toward Judaism and its religion."[20] In a classic work of patristic studies, von Harnack portrayed Marcion as an early Martin Luther. How so? Like Marcion, Luther certainly was known for making a sharp distinction between the law and the gospel—and also, unfortunately, for his pronounced anti-Semitic bias. But scholars today do not view Marcion as the heroic proto-Protestant, proclaiming a gospel of grace and freedom, that von Harnack envisioned him to be.[21] Perhaps it is not surprising to recall that von Harnack was writing as a liberal Protestant in Germany at the beginning of the twentieth century. That was hardly a time and place known for its affection toward Jews. Yet Marcion shows us that anti-Semitism could rear its ugly head in ancient times as well as modern.

Marcion's dislike for the God of the Jews had profound implications for his understanding of the Bible. He completely rejected the Old Testament as being relevant for Christians. With respect to the New Testament, Marcion accepted only the Gospel of Luke and the letters of Paul.[22] Why these works alone? Marcion saw himself as the true inheritor of Paul. Only the great Apostle to the Gentiles got the message right and remained uninfected by Jewish ideas. From Marcion's radical point of view, the law/grace distinction in Paul's writings became a distinction between two different deities, each with his own set of scriptures. Marcion thought that the letters of Paul and the "Gentile" Gospel of Luke contained many statements that were antithetical to the God seen in the Old Testament. Of course, anything that smacked of high regard for Judaism in Luke and Paul was edited away as a supposed corruption of their actual teaching. By settling on an edited form of the Pauline epistles and the Gospel of Luke, Marcion was one of the first figures to delineate which writings he viewed as "biblical." For this reason he was an influential figure in the history of the canon of scripture.[23] As I promised in chapter 3, I will now say a few words about that subject.

The Canon of Scripture

The word "canon" comes from the Greek word *kanon*, which referred to a straight reed used as a measuring rod. Books that are canonical "measure up" to the ultimate standard, thus becoming a measure of truth themselves. The process of canonization for the Old and New Testaments followed different courses. The early Christians had embraced the Jewish scriptures from the very beginning. While they were not always clear about the exact boundaries of some disputed writings, the core books of the law and the prophets invariably possessed authoritative status in the church. However, the ancient Christians did not at first refer to these works as the "Old Testament." They were simply called "Scripture," and quotations were often introduced with the formula "It is written . . ." The earliest believers did not have any awareness of a second "Testament" to complement the first.[24] For them the scriptures were the sacred writings that Jesus himself had read and interpreted. It took some time for the church to realize that another distinct Testament had been delivered to the human race. In this process of recognition, we can discern four stages:

1. *First Century: Writing of the Biblical Texts.* Most evangelical scholars would agree that all twenty-seven books which comprise the New Testament were completed by the end of the first century. It is important to note that from a theological perspective, the inspired books *are* scripture from the very moment of their writing. So when we discuss the issue of the canon, we are talking about the biblical books being *recognized* for what they are. This process took several centuries. The ancient church did not create God's Word, but simply identified it as such over time.

2. *Second Century: Authoritative Core Texts, With Some Dispute.* During the second century the core of the New Testament came to

have widespread authority throughout the church. This is not to say the biblical writings had possessed no authority before, for they certainly did. But what we find in the early to mid-second century is that Christianity became more of a book-based religion than it had been previously. Back in the apostolic days, the eyewitnesses of Jesus were still alive, so Christianity was spread through verbal proclamation rather than through texts. At that time it was still primarily an oral religion. The situation obviously changed in the second century, and thus the faith became more literary. There was a greater sense that the Christian religion possessed its own central books. During this period the four Gospels and the letters of Paul crystallized as core works. Other important writings such as Acts, 1 John, and 1 Peter were widely viewed as authoritative as well. However, there were some New Testament books that the early believers were unsure about (such as the tiny letters of 2 and 3 John). And there were other uninspired writings, such as an epistle thought to have been written by Barnabas, which some Christians believed might belong in the canon. So the shape of the canon at this time was an authoritative core, with fuzzy edges.

3. *Third Century*: *Awareness of a Two-Testament Bible*. As we said in chapter 3, Irenaeus was the first to use the term "New Testament" in connection with a body of writings. A little later Tertullian was even more clear in his usage of this term. In fact, he is the church father to whom we assign the honor of giving us the literal term "New Testament" (from the Latin *novum testamentum*). If Irenaeus was somewhat vague about what he meant, two decades later Tertullian certainly operated with a conception of the "New Testament" as a distinct scriptural corpus.[25] We see, then, that at the dawn of the third century a new awareness arose among the Christian faithful: that their Bible was comprised of both an Old and a New Testament. The church continued to function with this awareness for more than a century, until Emperor Constantine's imperial acceptance of Christianity finally enabled church leaders to make some official pronouncements about the extent of the biblical canon.

4. *Fourth Century: List-Making, Exclusion, and Final Closure of the Canon.* When the church found itself no longer persecuted by the Roman authorities, and instead being favored by the emperor, it gained new opportunities to define its sacred canon. Emperor Constantine told his trusted adviser Eusebius to have fifty official copies of the scriptures made for use in prominent congregations.[26] Eusebius took great interest in the matter of the canon, listing out those books he believed to be definitely canonical, possibly canonical, and certainly not canonical.[27] His canon list was one of many written up during the fourth century.[28] The first canon list in all of church history to clearly and unequivocally accept the twenty-seven books of the New Testament was composed by Bishop Athanasius of Alexandria in the year AD 367. Thirty years later, a council at Carthage ratified this same list (except for Revelation, which was added a few years after that). So we must view the canonization of the New Testament as a centuries-long process. It was begun informally as soon as people like Peter started calling Paul's epistles "scripture" (2 Pet. 3:16). But it wasn't really completed until around the year AD 400. From this point on, the church has possessed a closed New Testament canon.

Reflections on Tertullian

Tertullian played a vital role in the canonization process. He was not the only important figure; indeed there was no one person who defined the biblical canon for the church. Yet he was writing at that crucial time when heretics were being vigorously refuted, and the unified catholic church was being formed to stand against them. When we discussed Irenaeus in chapter 3, we discovered three main strategies in this effort: apostolic bishops, apostolic creeds, and an apostolic Bible. Tertullian followed the same threefold strategy as his predecessor Irenaeus. He grounded the church in the deposit of faith received from those who had walked and talked with the Lord

Jesus. And so we discover that to determine which books were in the Bible, *apostolicity* was the number one criterion that had to be met.[29] Tertullian wrote,

> I lay it down as my first position, that the evangelical Testament has apostles for its authors, to whom the Lord Himself assigned this job of publishing the gospel . . . Of the apostles, John and Matthew [who were Jesus's disciples] first instilled faith into us; and the apostolic men Luke and Mark renewed it afterwards. These men all started with the same principles of the faith: the one and only Creator God, and His Christ who was born of the Virgin and came to fulfill the law and the prophets. Never mind if some variation occurs in the order of their narratives, provided that there is agreement in the essential matter of the faith—in which there is [total] disagreement with Marcion.[30]

Tertullian's statement here represented the policy of the entire catholic church with regard to canonization: the books which were to be read as authoritative must bear an intimate connection with the apostles. This was the church's way of guaranteeing that heretical ideas would be excluded.

We should note, however, that for Tertullian the issue was bigger than simply accepting the apostolic "New" Testament alongside the prophetic "Old." The *real* issue was the unity of God and Christ which is expressed in the harmony of their dual revelation. Tertullian's most important contribution to church history was his portrayal of God's work as a single narrative of divine redemption. Following the principles he discerned in writers like Irenaeus, Tertullian's treatise *Against Marcion* laid out his case for a unified salvation history with a theological depth no Christian author had yet achieved. The words of Jesus came often to his mind: "I have not come to abolish the law but to fulfill it" (Matt. 5:17). For Tertullian, the relationship between the law and the gospel was one of preparation and fulfillment. Certainly there was a separation between the two, but it was:

a separation achieved through reshaping, through amplification, through progress, just like fruit is distinct from its seed, although fruit comes out of seed. So also the gospel is separated from the law, because it advances from out of the law—something other than the law, but not alien to it, different, though not opposed.[31]

Tertullian believed there was a single and indivisible salvation history in which the seed planted in the Old Testament bore fruit in the coming of Christ. While there was obviously an advancement, there was no fundamental rupture between the two covenants—just as there can be no rupture between the Creator and his Christ. It was this vital truth that made Marcion's lies so dangerous.

Tertullian's doctrine of the unity of God and Christ laid an important foundation for future theological debates within the church. (The Holy Spirit was of course acknowledged too, but most of the discussion at that time revolved around the Father and the Son.) Marcion had attempted to introduce ditheism, but Tertullian clung tenaciously to the Judeo-Christian monotheism he had received from the beginning. Yet he did so in a way that made room for diversity in the Godhead as well. In fact, Tertullian was the first known writer to use the term "trinity" to express the relationship of three-in-one that characterizes the Christian God. To explore this concept, he employed several images to depict the divine balance of unity and diversity. For example, picking up on the idea of the Logos which we have already seen in Justin Martyr, Tertullian pictured Christ as the inner rational discourse within God's mind.[32] The Logos has always existed as distinct from God, and yet is united with him just as our own thoughts innately belong to us. When we humans think about something, it's as if we have a separate mental conversation partner in our heads, even though we are single individuals. So too, God is both unified and complex: he is one God, yet he eternally discourses with his own inner Word or Reason. Other images Tertullian favored were a tree and its root, the sun and its ray, and a spring and its stream.[33] All of these metaphors attempted to highlight the unity of the Godhead, while at the same time acknowledging its inherent diversity of persons. The heavenly Father sent forth from himself a Son who is clearly separate, yet who is always inseparable from him. These paradoxical principles will set the stage for the subsequent early church debates about the Trinity and Christology.

What can we conclude about Tertullian? There are ten spiritual forefathers described in this book, and eight of them are called saints today because of their holy lives. Tertullian is one of the two exceptions. (The other is Origen.) This fact should tell you something about his personality. Certainly he was a deeply flawed character. He could be harsh and moralistic, especially later in his life. In fact, he once wrote an entire treatise telling women what kind of clothes and makeup they should wear! There was also a legal or contractual aspect to his understanding of salvation which opened itself to the idea of earning merit with God through penitential actions. But as we consider these errors, perhaps we can return to the image we painted at the outset. The old cowboys were often hard-talking men—yet they performed their arduous work with a brand of courage most of us do not possess today. In the same way, while Tertullian could be ornery at times, we still have to admire the chutzpah of his bold assault on all the heretics. In the late second century the church was under assault from a plethora of heretical groups. But by the time Tertullian was finished writing in AD 212, the situation had changed dramatically. Marcionism had been roundly defeated and was in decline. Gnosticism, while by no means gone, never again significantly threatened the orthodox church in the great cities of the Roman Empire. Of course there were many reasons for the triumph of the catholic Christians during this era. But of the many reasons, none could be greater than the massive literary firepower brought to bear against both pagans and heretics by the fiery, enigmatic, and always entertaining Tertullian of Carthage.

Provocative Questions

1. Tertullian was a man with great gifts, but great personality flaws as well. Have you ever known anyone like that? Do you see such flaws in your own life? How does it affect your ability to serve God? Does God use deeply flawed people to do great things? Give some examples. What is the difference between boldness and harshness?

2. The heretics were always "seeking" new theological ideas, whereas Tertullian wanted to hold on to an already established faith. What are some new theologies hitting the church today? How should we respond to them as we balance new and old ideas? Read Matthew 7:7–12. What kind of "seeking" did Jesus have in mind?

3. Marcion wanted to divorce Christianity from the Old Testament God of the Jews. While Marcionism is no longer around, anti-Semitism still is. In what ways do Christians display anti-Semitic attitudes today? Is your Christian faith rooted in Israel's history of salvation? Is the God of the Old Testament truly your God? What is Romans 11:1–32 trying to say about this issue?

4. Evangelicals believe scripture is always the inspired Word of God (2 Tim. 3:16 and 2 Pet. 1:20–21). Nevertheless, history reveals that it took time for the church to recognize which books were inspired and canonical. Why do you think God allowed the church to take so long to establish its canon? How can it be possible for such an important issue as the canon to be determined by fallible people over an extended period? What are the implications of this point for understanding how God works through the church?

5. Tertullian believed biblical interpretations had to line up with the Rule of Faith's summary of the Bible's message. Do we have any sources today that help us interpret scripture? Can we ever be completely free from traditional understandings of God's Word? What about our own denominational or theological traditions—should they function as interpretive guides for us?

Good Books to Dig Deeper

The *Prescription Against Heretics*, along with some other selections from Tertullian, can be read in:

Greenslade, S. L. *Early Latin Theology*. Library of Christian Classics, Volume 5. Philadelphia: Westminster, 1956.

The best translation of *Against Marcion* is by Ernest Evans (who has also translated several other treatises by Tertullian).

Evans, Ernest. *Tertullian's Adversus Marcionem*. Oxford: Clarendon Press, 1972.

A good introduction to Tertullian, with some selected translations, is:

Dunn, Geoffrey D. *Tertullian*. New York: Routledge, 2004.

The most authoritative English-language study of Tertullian is:

Barnes, Timothy David. *Tertullian: A Historical and Literary Study*. Oxford: Clarendon Press, 1971, 2nd ed. 1984.

A wealth of background information and English translations of Tertullian's writings can be found on Roger Pearse's excellent Web site, The Tertullian Project, at www.tertullian.org.

A Taste of Tertullian

Prescription Against Heretics 36–37

Tertullian makes an argument here for the apostolic pedigree of the catholic churches. We are reminded that he stood no great historical

*distance from the world in which the apostles lived. He could appeal
directly to the original Christian congregations for confirmation of the
truth.*

*For Tertullian's church in Carthage, Rome was the nearest apostolic
community. So he cites its Rule of Faith as the standard of orthodoxy.
Notice the Rule's emphasis on the unity of the Creator and his Christ.
Only the catholics who adhered to this Rule could rightly come to the
Christian scriptures. All impostors were excluded. Tertullian offers a
legal argument to dispossess the heretics as false heirs who have no claim
to the inherited estate of the apostles.*

Come now, all you who wish to make better use of your curiosity in
the business of your own salvation! Run through the list of apostolic
churches. In them you can still find the very thrones of the apostles
presiding over their regions. The authentic letters of the apostles are
still recited there today, sounding forth their voices and bringing the
face of each apostle to our minds.

If you are close to Greece, you have Corinth. If you are not far from
Macedonia, you have Philippi and Thessalonica. If you can travel to
Asia, you have Ephesus. If Italy is nearby, you have Rome—which
is the nearest authority for us too [here in Africa]. How blessed is
the church of Rome! For that is where the apostles poured out not
only their complete teaching, but even their very blood. There Peter
suffered a passion like his Lord's own [crucifixion], and Paul was
crowned with a death [of decapitation] like John the Baptist, and
the Apostle John was immersed in boiling oil but was not harmed,
and was banished to an island.

Let us see what Rome has learned, what doctrine she has taught,
what bond of friendship she has had with the African churches. The
church knows one Lord God, the Creator of the universe; and Jesus
Christ, born of the Virgin Mary, the Son of God the Creator; and the
resurrection of the flesh. The church harmoniously joins[34] the law and
the prophets with the writings of the evangelists and apostles. From
this source she drinks in the true faith—a faith which the church
signifies with the water [of baptism], clothes with the Holy Spirit,

feeds with the Lord's Supper, and encourages with martyrdom. The church accepts no one who stands opposed to this teaching.

This is the teaching . . . from which heresies "went out." But they were not "of it" when they took a stand against it (1 John 2:19). A rough wild olive sometimes sprouts even from the kernel of a mild, rich, and useful olive. The empty and useless wild fig grows up even from the seed of the most delightful and sweetest of figs. In the same way, the heresies come from our plant, but they are not really the same kind as us. They may sprout from the cultivated seed of truth, but because of their lies they belong among the overgrown weeds!

It is confirmed, then, that the Truth must be judged as belonging to we who "walk according to this Rule" (Gal. 6:16). The church has handed down the Rule from the apostles, and the apostles from Christ, and Christ from God. Therefore the principle I have already laid down is firmly established, by which it is ruled that the heretics are not allowed to make any appeal to scripture. Even without using scripture, I have proved that they have nothing to do with the Bible.

If they are heretics, they cannot be true Christians. They adopt the names of the heretics because they have not received from Christ what they instead pursued of their own free choice.[35] Since they are not Christians, they have no right of access to the Christian scriptures. We are completely justified in saying to them, "Who are you? From when and where did you come? What do you have to do with me, you stranger? By what right do you cut down my trees, Marcion? What allows you, Valentinus, to divert my streams? By what authority, Apelles, do you move my boundary markers? This is *my* land. What is this? Why are all the rest of you heretics freely sowing and grazing on my property? I repeat: this is my land! I have owned it for a long time, well before you came along. I have valid deed papers from the original owners of the estate. I am the true heir of the apostles. Just as they decreed in their will, and ordered it to be held in trust, and swore under oath, so do I now rightfully hold their property. But as for you heretics: the apostles unquestionably have disinherited you forever, and have disowned you as strangers and enemies!"

5

PERPETUA

The following account appeared on the Reuters news service. Be warned: it is shocking.

April 6, 2004 LONDON—A woman in Mexico gave birth to a healthy baby boy after performing a Caesarean section on herself with a kitchen knife, doctors said Tuesday. The unidentified 40-year-old woman, who lived in a rural area without electricity, running water or sanitation and was an eight-hour drive from the nearest hospital, performed the operation when she could not deliver the baby naturally. She had lost a previous baby due to labor complications.

"She took three small glasses of hard liquor and, using a kitchen knife, sliced her abdomen in three attempts . . . and delivered a male infant that breathed immediately and cried," said Dr R. F. Valle, of the Dr. Manuel Velasco Suarez Hospital in San Pablo, Mexico. Valle recounted the event in a report in the International Journal of Gynecology and Obstetrics.

Before losing consciousness, the woman told one of her children to call a local nurse for help. After the nurse stitched the wound with a sewing needle and cotton thread, the mother and baby were transferred and treated by Valle and his colleagues at the nearest hospital.

"This case represents an unusual and extraordinary decision by a woman in labor who, unable to deliver herself spontaneously, and with no medical help or resources, decided to perform a Caesarean section upon herself," Valle said.

Virtually every American who reads this account—accustomed as we are to the highest standards of medical care—will be amazed at the fortitude displayed by this desperate Mexican woman. It is something we can scarcely comprehend. No doubt the mothers among us can understand it on a deeper level than I can, for they know how compelling is the urge to defend the life that has been growing inside them for months. This poor woman had previously lost a baby to labor complications. Alone and afraid, she was now facing another such loss. In a last-ditch attempt to bring her child into the world, she was willing to slash open her own body to deliver the infant just before losing consciousness. Such is the raw power of the maternal instinct.

When we consider this kind of intense devotion of mother to child, the story of Vibia Perpetua of Carthage becomes all the more remarkable. Perpetua was a young woman of aristocratic lineage, born into the noble family of the Vibii. She was a newlywed with an infant son at the breast when, at age twenty-one,[1] she was imprisoned in a Roman dungeon for being a Christian. There she proved that not even the love of a mother for her son can take priority over her love for Christ. Renouncing her family and even her baby, Perpetua went to her death as an heroic martyr. Her narrative of sacrifice and passion in the year AD 203 has inspired countless generations of believers. Perhaps she has a message for you too.

Perpetua the Woman

We do not know Perpetua's full life story. Like Ignatius of Antioch, she appears out of nowhere, a shooting star blazing across the sky, headed for martyrdom. Perpetua's life has been vividly imagined by my friend Amy Rachel Peterson in her novel *Perpetua* (Relevant Books, 2004). Peterson offers a plausible account of the events that led up to Perpetua's dramatic confession of faith. For those wishing to journey with Perpetua from paganism to Christ and ultimately to martyrdom, the book is a great read. Nevertheless, a novelist's imagination is all we can offer to reconstruct Perpetua's biography. Beyond a few basic details, her life prior to her arrest eludes the firm grasp of the historian. She was born in the late second century to a high-ranking official in Roman North Africa. Her family included two brothers still living, and one who had died of facial cancer at age seven. One of the living brothers was, like Perpetua, a *catechumen*—a person who had committed to the Christian faith but had not yet been baptized. In fact, it is possible all her family members were believers except her father, who remained steadfastly opposed to his daughter's faith.[2] What about Perpetua's husband? His absence from her story is something of a mystery. Perhaps he had already died, or was out of town at the time, or was ashamed of his wife's Christianity and wanted nothing to do with her. A more interesting suggestion is that he was Saturus, one of the characters described in her passion narrative, who seems to have had a special relationship with her as they walked the road of suffering together.[3] In any case, Perpetua's story doesn't focus on her personal biography. The church fathers only saw fit to tell us about her final weeks as she prepared to give her life for Jesus in a Carthaginian arena.[4]

What do we know about Carthage? When we discussed Perpetua's contemporary Tertullian, we learned it was a prominent city in the ancient world. In fact, it was second only to Rome in the western empire. According to legend, it had been founded around 800 BC by a Phoenician queen named Dido. As the Republic of Rome began to grow in power, Carthage became its chief rival, resulting in the Punic Wars of the third and second centuries before the Christian era. Among the many heroic escapades of those wars was the daring invasion of Italy by the Carthaginian general Hannibal, who even brought war elephants across the Alps to fight the Roman legions. Eventually Rome triumphed and Carthage was razed to the ground, where it lay abandoned for a century. Then Caesar Augustus resurrected it to serve as the capital of the newly-created province of Africa. By Perpetua's day, Roman Carthage was a thriving, cosmopolitan city with a hilltop forum full of temples, a large amphitheater, a circus for chariot racing, two theaters, and many bath houses. Its houses and countryside villas were adorned with fountains and mosaics that spoke of the city's affluence. The fertile area quickly became the breadbasket of Rome. Large ships laden with African wheat often made the three-day sail from Carthage's circular harbor to the imperial capital. Thus we can imagine Perpetua would have been raised in a culture of wealth and sophistication. Devotion to the pagan gods and the Roman way of life were ingrained in her from birth. This fact makes the Christian devotion she displayed in the final weeks of her life even more profound.

Perpetua's story is a woman's story. One of the most remarkable things about the surviving text, *The Passion of Saints Perpetua and Felicity*, is that it contains Perpetua's own firsthand account of her imprisonment.[5] This is quite uncommon among patristic texts, which were usually written by men. But here in Perpetua's own words we discover a heartrending story that offers a rare window into the world of women in the early church. As we peer through that window we immediately discern the deep affection shared between the Christian woman Perpetua and her pagan father Vibius. Yet we also see a stark contrast between her inner tranquility and his anguished grief as he lost his only daughter to the shame and agony of public execution. Perpetua is revealed to be a quintessential Roman daughter—except that she had formed an uncompromising allegiance to Christ which was so powerful it could supplant even the father-daughter bond. Because of this story's vividness and poignancy, it is worth telling in detail.

Perpetua had been placed under house arrest for her Christian faith along with two household slaves, Revocatus and Felicity, and two other companions named Saturninus and Secundulus. Perpetua knew her father's paternal love would make him very upset at this turn of events. He fervently implored her to discard her foolish religion and be freed. She must deny that she was a Christian. In response, Perpetua picked up a small pitcher. "Father," she asked, "do you see this water pot? Can it be called anything else than what it is?" No it cannot, he admitted. "So too," replied Perpetua, "I cannot be called anything other than what I am: a Christian." At the word "Christian," the enraged Vibius flew at Perpetua as if he would tear her eyes out. But eventually he retreated, taking with him the anti-Christian arguments that Perpetua knew to be the devil's work. Although she loved her father very much, she was comforted by his absence, for he represented a strong temptation to apostasy. During this respite, Perpetua was baptized.

Eventually Perpetua and her friends were thrown in jail. As a girl of refined upbringing, she was terrified at its horrors. Now Perpetua's father grew more desperate. He begged her to deny her faith. When he arrived at the prison, she immediately noticed he was physically consumed with worry for her. "My daughter," he cried, "have pity on me!" Just now, as I was typing these forlorn words, my own five-year-old daughter came into my study and gave me an affectionate hug and kiss. No doubt Perpetua's father had experienced something similar many times in his Roman villa. The emotions he must have been feeling with his daughter in mortal danger can be understood by all who deeply love their little girls. His urgent pleas, resounding in the dark dungeon, are captivating:

> "Have pity, my daughter, on my grey hairs! Have pity on your father, if I am worthy to be called a father by you. If with these hands I have brought you up into the flower of your age, if I have preferred you to all your brothers, do not deliver me up to the scorn of men. Have regard to your brothers, have regard to your mother and your aunt, have regard to your son, who will not be able to live after you. Lay aside your courage, and do not bring us all to destruction; for none of us will speak in freedom if you should suffer anything." These things

my father said in his affection, kissing my hand, and throwing himself
at my feet; and with tears he called me not 'Daughter' but 'Lady.'
And I grieved over the grey hairs of my father, that he alone would
not rejoice over my passion. And I comforted him saying, "On that
scaffold [where I will be tried or executed] whatever God wills shall
happen. For know that we are not placed in our own power, but in
that of God." And he departed from me in sorrow.[6]

The reversal of roles here is startling when we consider the normal
relationship between Roman men and their daughters. In ancient
times the daughter was the property of the father, who held absolute power of life and death over his children. When a female child
was born she was laid at the feet of her father as the supreme head
of the family. At that moment he decided whether to rear her as
a daughter, or send her outside to die of exposure.[7] Elite Roman
girls who were accepted as daughters were given a feminine form
of the father's family name, often being distinguished only by their
birth order. Today it would be as if I had several daughters named
"Litfina Elder," "Litfina Second," "Litfina Third," and so on. Among
the most prominent virtues expected of a highborn daughter were
total devotion and unquestioning respect toward her father and his
clan. In return the father was to protect the daughter's interests by
arranging a good marriage and providing a dowry or an inheritance.
Roman fathers, despite their absolute authority in the home, often
were very affectionate toward their daughters—more so than was
acceptable for sons. The great orator Cicero stands out among the
many examples of paternal warmth in Roman literary sources because
of his extraordinary fondness for his daughter Tullia. When she died
giving birth to her second child, Cicero never fully recovered from
his profound grief. He once asked, "What is a more worthy object
[than a daughter] on which to lavish all our care and tenderness?"[8]

Seen in this historical context, Perpetua's rejection of her father's
pleas represented far more than girlish rebellion. As Vibius lay weep-
ing at her feet—just as she had been laid at his feet as a newborn—

Perpetua inverted everything her society stood for. Roman culture did not value independence, feistiness, and a free spirit in women. Her responsibilities were to fear the gods and her father like a good girl, and to marry and bear children. Strict social codes inextricably bound a daughter to the family of her birth. Indeed, many Roman marriages did not legally transfer the bride to the home of her husband. She remained in the hand of the father even while living in her new husband's home. So when Perpetua steadfastly resisted her father even though he tore out his beard, and threw himself on the ground before her, and cursed his old age, and uttered "such words as might move all creation," we are witnessing a scene of extraordinary Christian renunciation by this noble daughter.

Perpetua's father caused such a commotion at her trial that the governor ordered him to be beaten with rods. Perpetua was anguished over this: "My father's misfortune grieved me as if I myself had been beaten. I so grieved for his wretched old age!"[9] Nevertheless, she did not change her mind. She consistently viewed her father as an obstacle to making a bold confession. Perhaps we might recall the words of Jesus in this regard: "If anyone comes to me and does not hate his own father and mother and wife and children and brothers and sisters, yes, and even his own life, he cannot be my disciple. Whoever does not bear his own cross and come after me cannot be my disciple" (Luke 14:26–27). Similarly, the church father Jerome applied Psalm 45:10–11 to a woman's relationship to Christ: "Hear, O daughter, and consider, and incline your ear: forget your people and your father's house, and the king will desire your beauty. Since he is your lord, bow to him."[10] The ancient Christians took the Lordship of Christ very seriously. No other loyalties could supersede their devotion to him.

We have seen how Perpetua's absolute commitment to Jesus was expressed in her role as a daughter. Yet there was another role in which she practiced Christian self-denial: as a mother. When she was thrown into the filthy darkness of the prison, with its stifling heat and cruel soldiers, she carried the additional burden of being separated from her baby. "I was extremely distressed by my anxiety for my infant," she wrote.[11] Then some Christian deacons bribed the guards to allow Perpetua to be moved to a better part of the prison. Finally she could nurse her son, who had grown faint with hunger. Arrangements were made for Perpetua to keep her baby in the jail. "I grew strong and was relieved from distress and anxiety about my infant," she wrote, "and the dungeon became to me as a palace, so that I preferred being there to being anywhere else."[12]

But those who opposed Perpetua saw an opportunity. Perhaps her maternal love could be used to break her resolve? When she appeared before the local governor for trial, her father pulled her aside and held out her only son, imploring, "Have pity on your baby!"[13] Likewise the governor said to her, "Spare the infancy of your boy, and offer sacrifice for the well-being of the emperors." But in the presence of her father and the watching crowd, Perpetua resolutely answered, "I will not do so." "Are you a Christian?" the governor asked. "Yes," replied Perpetua, "I am a Christian." The death sentence was passed, and she was removed with the other confessors to await the day they would be condemned to the beasts. This was the last time Perpetua ever saw her little boy, for now her father refused to give him back to her. But Perpetua praised God that the child miraculously no longer desired the breast. She even added a detail only a nursing mother would think to record: she did not suffer the mastitis that typically accompanies sudden cessation of breastfeeding. In this tender detail we see glory ascribed to God for one of the little miracles that so often grace a woman's life.

There was another Christian mother in prison with Perpetua. The slave girl Felicity, whom many have identified as Perpetua's own handmaiden, was pregnant when she was arrested. Now in her eighth month, Felicity grew worried because she knew the governor would not execute an expectant mother. She feared that her companions would go to their martyrdom without her, leaving her to be executed at a later time with the common criminals. For their part, her fellow Christians were concerned they would be forced to leave behind such a worthy comrade. The language of intimacy here between slaves and masters reveals how the Christian faith overcame the social barriers that normally characterized interpersonal relations in the Roman world. In the unity shared by these imprisoned believers, we witness the fruit of scripture's promise that "There is neither Jew nor Greek, there is neither slave nor free, there is neither male nor female, for you are all one in Christ Jesus" (Gal. 3:28; cf. 1 Cor. 12:13).

Felicity was blessed. The jailed Christians prayed—not as we would have, to be freed from prison—but that Felicity might suffer with them. "Joining together their united cry they poured forth their prayer to the Lord three days before the exhibition. Immediately after their prayer, her pains came upon her."[14] Felicity was laboring heavily because in the eighth month her body was not yet ready for delivery. As she cried out in pain, the guards mocked her: "You who are in such suffering now, what will you do when you are thrown to the beasts? Little did you think of them when you refused to sacrifice to the emperor!"[15] To this taunt came Felicity's confident reply from the darkness: "Now it is I that suffer what I suffer; but then there will be another in me, who will suffer for me because I also am about to suffer for Him." Felicity gave birth to a daughter, who was raised by a Christian sister as her own child. And so Felicity was able to receive the crown of martyrdom with her companions. The narrator says that she "rejoiced that she had safely given birth so that she might fight with the wild beasts—going from one kind of blood to another, from the midwife to the gladiator, to wash after childbirth in a second baptism."[16]

In *The Passion of Saints Perpetua and Felicity* we are indeed fortunate to gain a firsthand perspective on the experiences of women in the early church. Perpetua is revealed to be a godly Christian woman— one who affirmed the high calling of being a daughter and mother, yet who put her loyalty to Jesus Christ before even those worthy vocations. Because of her close walk with the Lord, she became a spiritual leader of her band of confessors. The towering respect she earned among her jailed companions was based on the depth of her spiritual life. Her piety lent her a reverence and authority not normally accorded to women in Roman society. In the next section we will learn something else about Perpetua's deep spirituality: that she was in touch with the Holy Spirit in an especially dramatic way.

Perpetua the Prophetess

The Passion of Saints Perpetua and Felicity is acknowledged by most scholars today to reflect a theological outlook called Montanism.[17] What was Montanism? It was an ancient church movement advocating direct revelation from God to Spirit-filled prophets. We should distinguish between Montanism's origins in Asia Minor (where its revelations competed against scripture) and its later appearance in the North African context of Tertullian and Perpetua (where it was a more biblical and orthodox movement). The movement began inauspiciously when a prophet named Montanus claimed to receive visions in the Asian region of Phrygia—an area already known for extreme devotion to the goddess Cybele, whose followers went into trances and mutilated their bodies.[18] Montanus had similar ecstatic experiences during which he claimed to utter oracles received from God.[19] Using the term for the Holy Spirit in the Gospel of John, Montanus said he was possessed by the "Paraclete" while in an unconscious state.[20] He was soon joined by two female companions who left their husbands to take up an itinerant prophetic ministry with him. They declared themselves the very mouthpieces of God, like passive harps whose strings were plucked by the divine Harpist. The Montanists adhered to a strict legalistic lifestyle, expected the return of Christ very soon to set up an earthly millennium, gave prominent roles to women leaders, and experienced revelation through dreams, visions, and unintelligible speech. Their own name for their movement was not Montanism, but the New Prophecy.

The church leadership in Asia Minor soon discerned in this New Prophecy a worrisome threat to the Christian faith. Any claim to receive personal revelations from God would undermine the authoritative and correct reading of the Bible.[21] In fact, the Asian Montanists had their own special books containing prophecies that carried the same weight as the established apostolic writings. In other words, the New Prophecy offered a private, mystical alternative to scripture. For this reason (among several others) the bishops of the eastern cities began to combat the movement in their region. Some bishops even attempted to exorcize Montanist prophets of demons. In later generations, Montanism would come to be viewed as a dangerous heresy of the early church. This was due in no small part to its extrabiblical, and seemingly demonic, revelations.

But when the New Prophecy migrated west to North Africa, it took a notably different form. It was not seen as a diabolical heresy that competed against scripture. Rather, it was accepted within the church as a biblical ministry of the Holy Spirit as described in 1 Corinthians 14 (where Paul regulates speaking in tongues). We do not know when Montanism arrived in Carthage, but we might guess it was somewhere around the year AD 200. Tertullian would not have allowed a known heresy to gain an inroad in his city. Likewise, Perpetua would not have been so enthusiastically embraced as a martyr if her spiritual tendencies were already a significant problem. Since both Tertullian and Perpetua were positively inclined toward the New Prophecy, apparently it was not yet viewed as a heresy or a breakaway movement from the catholic churches.

Furthermore, North African Montanism was orthodox on the essential doctrines of Christianity. Tertullian emphasized he was not changing the basic Rule of Faith, but was only adding a stricter rule of discipline.[22] He always tested Montanist visions by scripture as the final authority.[23] This is what made the New Prophecy in Carthage different from its Asian origins. In Africa it was not a heresy *per se*, but was a subcommunity within the overall church that advocated higher standards of Christian commitment and the ongoing revelation of the Holy Spirit.[24] In this sense, we might view it as analogous to the modern-day charismatic movement, which exists (uneasily at times) within larger evangelicalism.

What overtones of the New Prophecy do we find in Perpetua's story? We learn immediately that she was in close communion with God. She wrote,

> Then my brother said to me: "Dear sister, you are greatly privileged; surely you might ask for a vision to discover whether you are to be condemned or freed." Faithfully I promised that I would, for I knew that I could speak with the Lord, whose great blessings I had come to experience. And so I said: "I shall tell you tomorrow."[25]

Perpetua asked God and received a vision. She saw an immense bronze ladder reaching into the sky. On its sides were fastened sharp daggers and hooks that would mangle the flesh of someone who did not climb carefully. Guarding the bottom of the ladder was a fierce dragon. Saturus, identified by some as Perpetua's husband, went up first. (He was not among those originally arrested but had turned himself in and joined his friends in prison.) In the vision he reached the top of the ladder and looked back at Perpetua, beckoning to her. "Perpetua, I am waiting for you," he said. "But take care; do not let the dragon bite you." "He will not harm me," she replied, "in the name of Jesus Christ." She boldly stepped on the dragon's head (an allusion to Gen. 3:15) and climbed the ladder. At the top Perpetua found herself in a luxurious garden where a shepherd was milking sheep amidst thousands of people clad in white. The shepherd said, "I am glad you have come, my child." He gave her a mouthful of milk as everyone cried, "Amen!" Then she awoke with the taste of sweetness still in her mouth. Convinced that she would certainly be martyred, Perpetua decided to "no longer have any hope in this life."

Perpetua received another vision the night before she was to be thrown to the wild animals. She dreamed of confronting a vicious Egyptian gladiator before an immense crowd. She was stripped and rubbed with oil in the manner of a gladiator, and even became a man in order to fight her foe. Alongside the two combatants there was a mighty onlooker: a giant man clad in a purple tunic with sandals of silver and gold. He was a sort of referee or trainer who promised to award the final prize to the victor. Perpetua engaged in a furious battle with the Egyptian. She was lifted off the ground as she kicked and struggled with all her strength. Finally she threw down her opponent and stepped on his head in victory. Perpetua's companions began to sing psalms. She approached the referee and was given a victor's branch bearing golden apples. The trainer kissed her and said, "Daughter, peace be with you."[26] Then she awoke. In her diary she wrote, "I realized that it was not with wild animals that I would fight, but with the Devil—but I knew I would win the victory."

In these visions we see how Perpetua's prophetic abilities supplied strength in her moment of deepest need. Far from being in a frenzied state of spirit-possession, she instead received the kind of visions we find biblical characters receiving as well. Her dreams had the same realism and authenticity that we find, for example, in Peter's vision of the sheet in Acts 10, or in Jacob's vision of the ladder in Genesis 28. In her day, Perpetua was honored by her fellow Christians as a mighty prophetess like Miriam, Deborah, or Anna.[27] The church at Carthage believed the New Prophecy was the realization of Joel 2:28 and Acts 2:17–18: "In the last days it shall be, God declares, that I will pour out my Spirit on all flesh, and your sons and your daughters shall prophesy . . . even on my male servants and female servants in those days I will pour out my Spirit, and they shall prophesy."[28] In other words, some Christians of the third century understood the events they were witnessing to be the fulfillment of a biblical promise. What is your opinion of Perpetua the prophetess?

As Perpetua wrapped up her first-person account of her hardships and heavenly comforts in prison, she concluded with these simple words: "So much for what I did up until the eve of the contest. About what happened at the contest itself, let him write of it who will."[29] We can imagine that in the flickering light of an oil lamp she put down her pen and papyrus with an air of finality and resignation. All was now in God's hands. She knew that with the first light of dawn, she would go to face her ordeal in the arena. Let us turn now to the climactic story of Perpetua's final hours.

Perpetua the Martyr

As we approach Perpetua's story, we might reasonably ask, "Why were Christians persecuted in the early church?" There is no single answer. Sometimes prejudice and mob violence instigated the persecutions. Other times local governors took the lead. At first, the persecutions tended to be sporadic and local. Later on, persecution would be empire-wide as the result of imperial edicts. One of the main sticking points in all the decades of Christian persecution was the practice of emperor worship. Roman subjects considered it a religious duty to offer a sprinkling of incense or a cupful of wine to the "genius" of the emperor, hailing him with the words, "Caesar is Lord!" Many Christians today might say to themselves, "So what is the harm in that? Just fake a little devotion and save your life." This was exactly the temptation offered to the great martyr Polycarp. "What harm is there in saying 'Caesar is Lord?'" he was asked by the prosecutor. "Swear by the genius of Caesar! Revile Christ!" Polycarp's noble reply was, "Eighty and six years have I served Him, and He never did me any injury: how then can I blaspheme my King and my Savior?"[30] As one pagan observer noted, you could never make a true Christian deny Christ even under the threat of death.[31] Why were the early Christians so adamant about this?

When martyrs like Polycarp or Perpetua refused to swear to the emperor, they were not being needlessly stubborn. The emperor's *genius* to which sacrifices were made referred to his guardian spirit, or the divine power that gave him his vitality.[32] The Greek word for this spiritual power was *daimon*. So for the early Christians, the issue was clear-cut: either you could curse Christ and worship the demonic spirit that empowered the pagan emperor, or you could remain faithful to your Savior. Caesar was not the true Lord. Only

Jesus Christ deserved that title in worship. Wasn't the scripture quite clear on this matter? Paul wrote that "no one speaking in the Spirit of God ever says 'Jesus is accursed!' and no one can say 'Jesus is Lord' except in the Holy Spirit" (1 Cor. 12:3).[33] Jesus himself taught that "everyone who acknowledges me before men, I also will acknowledge before my Father who is in heaven, but whoever denies me before men, I also will deny before my Father who is in heaven" (Matt. 10:32–33). Rejection of emperor worship was considered a duty of utmost importance in the ancient church. To capitulate would be to reject the Lordship of Jesus Christ, to worship demons, and to reap the dire consequences of denying the Savior.

Perpetua and her companions knew this full well. On the day of their confession, they handled themselves with a holy boldness befitting those who are confident of their eternal destiny. They marched from the prison to the amphitheater trembling with joy, not fear. The face of Perpetua, "the wife of Christ," shone with a tranquility that made the onlookers avert their gaze. The Roman authorities wanted to dress the martyrs in the robes of pagan religion, but Perpetua rebuked the judge for such injustice. We have come here freely, she said, with the understanding that you would not make us do this shameful thing. In the face of her criticism the judge relented. The Christians were not forced to don the demonic garments.

As the martyrs entered the arena, Perpetua began to sing psalms. She was "already treading under foot the head of the Egyptian."[34] The enraged crowd demanded the martyrs be whipped before a line of gladiators; and so the bloodied Christians rejoiced that they had obtained a share of the Lord's sufferings (Phil. 3:10; Col. 1:24). Saturninus and Revocatus were attacked by a leopard, then bound in the stocks to be accosted by a bear. Saturus was tied to a wild boar, but the animal gored the handler to death while only dragging Saturus around a bit.

As for the women, the Devil had inspired the gladiators to match them with a female animal: a very fierce heifer. Perpetua and Felicity were stripped and led out to the sandy floor of the arena before the hungry crowd. The narrator records that the Romans were ashamed when they saw the women's naked bodies, for they could see Perpetua was in the flower of her youth and Felicity's breasts were still dripping with milk from her recent childbirth. The onlookers demanded the martyrs be clothed in tunics to ease their guilty consciences. Then they were returned to the arena. Straightaway the heifer charged Perpetua and knocked her over. When her tunic was ripped she demurely pulled it down to cover herself, "mindful of her modesty more than her suffering."[35] She also looked for her hairpin to bind her hair, lest its disheveled appearance make it seem she was mourning instead of rejoicing. Felicity had been crushed to the ground by the cow, but Perpetua helped her up. They were led out of the arena to await more torment later.

Waiting in the gateway, Perpetua's battered body could barely stand. Yet she was so caught up in the Spirit that she asked when she was going to be offered to the heifer. She did not realize she had just been mauled. Only by looking at her gashes and bruises could she accept that the attack had already occurred. The early martyrs believed that in their moment of greatest suffering, Jesus would bear the pain with them. Perpetua, in this heightened state of spiritual communion, exhorted her comrades to stand firm and to love one another to the end. Meanwhile Saturus was using the brief respite to strengthen a brand-new believer. In prison he had been sharing his faith with a guard named Pudens who was drawn to the martyrs' spiritual power. Eventually Pudens had put his faith in Christ, and now Saturus hoped to confirm that faith.

The ravenous crowd called for the martyrs once again. When Saturus was led out, a leopard tore him open in a shower of blood. The onlookers yelled "Well washed!"—the customary greeting for a person coming from a bath. Certainly Saturus bore witness that day to the washing of his soul by Christ. Wanting to perform one final act of encouragement, he took Pudens's ring and dipped it in his blood as a memento of his martyrdom. As he lay dying he said to Pudens, "Farewell, and be mindful of my faith. Do not let these things disturb you, but confirm you."[36] Then the martyrs willingly mounted a platform in view of everyone, where the executioner murdered each one with a sword. Perpetua was the last to die. With great dignity she even guided the trembling hand of the young gladiator to her throat. In this way the daughter of Christ went to her eternal reward.

As we remember these heroic martyrs, let's not overlook the new believer Pudens standing in the shadows, clutching his bloodstained ring. Even as some Christians were dying in the arena, others were being born again. The word *martyr* means "witness," and that is exactly what Perpetua and her companions did that day. They bore witness to their faith in Christ—a faith that could not be compromised by family ties or the threat of immense suffering. In their deaths, Tertullian's oft-quoted words came true: "The more we are mown down by you [pagans], the more in number we grow; the blood of Christians is seed . . . Christians are teachers not just by their words, but by their deeds."[37]

Reflections on Perpetua

Perpetua was a figure of biblical proportions. Her passion narrative helps us see what the early church honored in a woman. Today it is common in scholarly circles to explore Perpetua and other early Christian women from the perspective of power.[38] Did women have the authority to lead in worship? Could they preach to men? How did the male-dominated hierarchy suppress women's rights and marginalize them in the institutional church? Feminist scholarship uniformly insists upon a story of male oppression. But in doing so, it invests the idea of "power" with aspects foreign to Perpetua herself. The early Christians weren't focused on power as dominance over others, but on the power of godliness. It was Perpetua's deep spirituality that brought her esteem in the eyes of the church. She was lauded for her intimacy with the Lord and her steadfast commitment to him—even when a mother's love for her baby or a daughter's love for her father tugged at her heart.

Around two hundred years after these events, the great bishop Augustine of Hippo preached three sermons to commemorate the sacrifice of Vibia Perpetua and her handmaiden Felicity. Perhaps we will let his words tell us how the early church treasured its holy daughters. "What could be more glorious," he asked, "than these women, whom men can more easily admire than imitate? But this [glory] redounds supremely to the praise of him in whom they believed, and in whose name they ran the race together."[39]

Or, if we long for a tribute even more simple than this, we can recall the words engraved on a stone from the ancient Carthaginian church where the martyrs' remains were kept. The engraving reads, "Perpetua, sweetest daughter."[40] These three words poignantly remind us of the cherished woman who left behind the family of Vibius to join the family of God.

Provocative Questions

1. Family and parenthood are highly valued among evangelicals today. It often goes unquestioned that our family members should be our highest priority. Do you think this is true from a Christian perspective? Are we too preoccupied with family relations? What did Jesus mean in his hard sayings of Matthew 10:37 and Luke 14:26? What would the renunciation of children or parents for the sake of Jesus look like today?

2. Consider the inclusion of women among the heroes of faith in Hebrews 11:11, 31 (and see vv. 35–38 for a description that fits Perpetua's situation). What have you learned from Perpetua that has affected your understanding of the admirable qualities of a woman's character?

3. Perpetua received the kind of spiritual blessings described today as "charismatic gifts" or a "word of knowledge." What is your view on this? Have prophecies and divine visions ceased,

or are they still being given? See 1 Corinthians 13:8, but also 14:1 and 2 Corinthians 12:1–4. How is the Holy Spirit's power manifested in the church today? Do we make enough room for his remarkable and unexpected work in our midst? Do we overemphasize dramatic and direct revelation as proof of his presence? How does scripture serve to reveal God's truth by the Spirit?

4. The early Christians believed sacrificing to the Roman emperor's "genius" was an act of devotion toward demons. Today we're not urged to worship demonic powers directly. But can you think of any ways we give our deepest affections to people, things, or ideals other than God? Do we worship the Devil in not-so-obvious ways?

5. Martyrs bear witness to Christ by making the ultimate sacrifice. Is there anything you would be unwilling to sacrifice for the name of Jesus? Is he "Lord" over every part of your life? Is your bold and fearless testimony for him ever compromised by reluctance to let go of something you hold dear? If Perpetua could leave behind all she loved, shouldn't we likewise be willing to give up the things we love? For example, shouldn't we relinquish our reputation or human esteem in order to bear witness to Christ? What is meant by Matthew 10:33; Mark 8:38; Luke 9:26; and 2 Timothy 2:12?

Good Books to Dig Deeper

The account of Perpetua's martyrdom may be read in the *Ante-Nicene Fathers*, volume 3. The text is also widely available on the Internet. The best modern translation is found in:

Musurillo, Herbert. *The Acts of the Christian Martyrs*. Oxford: Clarendon Press, 1972.

Two good overviews of Perpetua's life and historical setting are:

Salisbury, Joyce E. *Perpetua's Passion: The Death and Memory of a Young Roman Woman*. New York: Routledge, 1997.

Walsh, Joseph J. *What Would You Die For? Perpetua's Passion*. Baltimore: Apprentice House, 2005. (Designed for college students, the commentary and translations are written in a breezy and appealing style.)

A riveting fictional account of Perpetua's life has been written up as an historical novel:

Peterson, Amy Rachel. *Perpetua: A Novel*. Lake Mary, FL: Relevant Books, 2004.

Augustine's sermons 280, 281, and 282 on Perpetua and Felicity can be read in:

Hill, Edmund. *Sermons 273–305A On the Saints*. The Works of Saint Augustine: A Translation for the 21st Century. Vol. 3, Pt. 8. Hyde Park, NY: New City Press, 1994.

A Taste of Perpetua

The Passion of Saints Perpetua and Felicity 20–21

Here is the account of Perpetua's final end. Along with the other martyrs, she and Felicity were brought to the amphitheater at Carthage to face the wild animals in front of the savage crowd. Notice how the narrator highlights Perpetua's godliness and spiritual strength.

The Devil had prepared a very fierce heifer for the young women. Though this was unusual, it had been devised so that the sex of the martyrs might be rivaled by that of the animal they faced. Perpetua and Felicity were stripped naked and draped in nets [to hamper their movement]. Then they were led [into the arena]. But the crowd was horrified when they noticed that one was a delicate young woman, and the other had only recently come from childbirth with her breasts still dripping. So the women were recalled and dressed in loose robes [then sent back into the arena].

The heifer first tossed Perpetua in the air so that she landed on her back. Sitting up she noticed her robe was ripped away from her side. So she pulled it back in place to veil her private parts—for Perpetua was more mindful of her modesty than her agony. Then she searched for her hairpin to bind up her disheveled hair. She knew it wasn't right for a martyr to suffer with her hair in disarray, lest she appear to be mourning in her moment of triumph.[41]

When she stood up she noticed Felicity had been crushed [by the heifer]. Perpetua went over and took Felicity by the hand to help her up. The two of them stood side by side. For the time being, the hard-hearted cruelty of the crowd was appeased, so the women were called back through the Gate of Life.[42] There Perpetua was held up by a Christian catechumen named Rusticus who stayed close by her side. She was so enraptured and caught up in the Spirit that she seemed to awake from a kind of sleep and began to look around. To everyone's amazement she asked, "When are we going to be thrown to that heifer or whatever it is?" And when she was told it had already happened she wouldn't believe it until she noticed the gashes on her body and the rips in her dress. Then she called together her brother and Rusticus, exhorting them with the words, "Stand firm in the faith and love one another! Don't let our suffering become a stumbling block to you."[43]

Here the narrative switches scenes to describe the exchange between Saturus and Pudens. Saturus was ripped open by a leopard, and collapsed from loss of blood. His final act was to give a bloodstained ring to Pudens. Then Perpetua and her companions were led to their execution.

Saturus's unconscious body was tossed with the rest of the martyrs in the place where victims normally have their throats cut. But the mob demanded they be brought out in the open. So when the sword pierced the martyrs' bodies, the onlookers joined in the deed with their eyes and became accomplices to murder. Without being asked, the martyrs stood up and went willingly to the place where the crowd wanted them. Kissing each other, they consummated their martyrdom with the ceremonial kiss of peace.[44] The martyrs all took the sword silently and without moving—especially Saturus. Just as he had been the first to ascend [the ladder in Perpetua's dream], so he was the first to give up his spirit. Once again, he was waiting for Perpetua.

But Perpetua still had to taste some pain. The executioner, who was a beginner, accidentally pierced Perpetua between her collarbones. She screamed in agony. Then she herself guided his errant hand to her throat. It was as though so great a woman, who was feared by the demonic spirit within the executioner, could only be killed if she herself willed it.

O most brave and blessed martyrs! Truly you have been called and chosen for the glory of our Lord Jesus Christ! All who magnify, honor and adore him should definitely read these accounts. They are just as much for the church's edification as the older examples of faith. These new examples of miraculous power bear witness to the one and only Holy Spirit who is at work even now, and to God the Father Almighty, and to his Son Jesus Christ our Lord—to whom be glory and infinite power for ever and ever! Amen.

6

ORIGEN

On a cold night in a faraway land two girls sat alone in the forest grieving their deepest loss. They had spent all their tears in wrenching sobs as the dark hours passed. Now a thin light began to edge the eastern horizon. The girls were quiet, their souls numb. Suddenly the stillness was broken by a loud crack!

"What's that?" said Lucy, clutching Susan's arm.

"I—I feel afraid to turn round," said Susan; "something awful is happening."

"They're doing something worse to *him*," said Lucy. "Come on!" And she turned, pulling Susan round with her.

The rising of the sun had made everything look so different—all the colours and shadows were changed—that for a moment they didn't see the important thing. Then they did. The Stone Table was broken into two pieces by a great crack that ran down it from end to end; and there was no Aslan.

"Oh, oh, oh!" cried the two girls rushing back to the Table.

"Oh, it's *too* bad," sobbed Lucy; "they might have left the body alone."

"Who's done it?" cried Susan. "What does it mean? Is it more magic?"

"Yes!" said a great voice behind their backs. "It is more magic." They looked round. There, shining in the sunrise, larger than they had seen him before, shaking his mane (for it had apparently grown again) stood Aslan himself.

"Oh, Aslan!" cried both the children, staring up at him, almost as much frightened as they were glad.

"Aren't you dead then, dear Aslan?" said Lucy.

"Not now," said Aslan.[1]

You've probably recognized this scene as the climax of C. S. Lewis's *The Lion, the Witch and the Wardrobe.* The great lion Aslan, who had been slain on the Stone Table in the magical land of Narnia, now appeared in resurrection glory to his two friends. No reader can miss the point here; indeed the author did not intend to hide it. Aslan teaches us about Jesus Christ, the Lion of Judah who died and rose again.[2]

Why does Lewis's tale always affect its readers so profoundly? Why has it served as such a powerful vehicle of timeless truth since it was published in 1950? Perhaps it is because Lewis understood the transformative potential of narrative. When stories are told well, they elevate the reader to a higher plane of understanding. The plotline of the narrative becomes a pathway to hidden meaning. Of course, young children can read *The Chronicles of Narnia* and enjoy them as simple stories. But those who are more mature, who have greater wisdom, can read them on another level. Lewis wanted his stories to function this way. For him the purpose of allegory was to lead the reader to deeper insight. He wrote, "It may encourage people to suppose that allegory is a disguise, a way of saying obscurely what could have been said more clearly. But in fact all good allegory exists not to hide but to reveal . . . For when allegory is at its best, it approaches myth, which must be grasped with the imagination, not with the intellect."[3] Lewis believed "the function of allegory is not to hide but to reveal, and it is properly used only for that which cannot be said, or so well said, in literal speech. The inner life, and specially the life of love, religion, and spiritual adventure, has therefore always been the field of true allegory."[4] Allegory transports the mature reader to a foreign land.

C. S. Lewis understood that our present world is barely separated from the wondrous spiritual realm beyond. The barrier between them is as thin as the back panel of a wooden wardrobe. Lewis was at home in both worlds. He was a noted scholar and literary critic at Oxford University, yet was a man of deep Christian spirituality. His religious life was not the dry stuff of academia, the intellectual "head knowledge" that remains aloof from the heart. He was no cold rationalist proving God's existence through reason alone. To the contrary, his devotional life was so deep and contemplative he can rightly be called a mystic. "For him, Christian faith was not merely a set of religious beliefs or institutional customs or moral traditions. It was rather the recognition of a profound cosmic drama, an ongoing struggle between good and evil."[5] Through narrative, Lewis transcended the mundane world to explore the epic themes of God's universal story.

In many ways, C. S. Lewis resembles the subject of our present chapter: Origen of Alexandria, the greatest scholar of the early church.[6] Like Lewis, Origen understood that the spiritual world lies just beyond the visible one. He believed the wonderful realm of the spirit could be explored by applying the allegorical method—not to a child's fairy tale, but to the very words of scripture itself. Origen longed for mystical union with God through Jesus Christ.[7] He interpreted the Bible allegorically to find Christ on every page. He also practiced self-discipline to purge all distractions to his study of the Word. In this chapter, we will get to know a church father who searched for the things of God with all his heart and soul and mind and strength. Origen shows us that a brilliant intellect and a passionate heart for the Lord do not have to be mutually exclusive.

An Alexandrian Intellectual

Origen was born around the same time as Perpetua, in the year AD 186. He was seventeen when the same persecution under which Perpetua was martyred came to his hometown of Alexandria in Egypt. Though his life was not snuffed out in its prime like hers, Origen did suffer great loss: his father Leonides was beheaded for believing in Christ. With all the zeal of a teenager, Origen wanted to rush to the prison to join his father in death. But as the church historian Eusebius reports, Origen's mother, unable to bear the loss of her son as well as her husband, hid all his clothes so he could not go outside. In this way she prevented Origen's martyrdom as a young man (though later as an old man he would die from wounds received in torture for his Christian faith).

The death of Leonides dealt a heavy blow to Origen's family. Leonides had loved his children very much. Often he came into Origen's room at night and was so moved with tender love that he kissed his sleeping boy's bosom "as if the Divine Spirit were enshrined within it, considering himself blessed in his excellent offspring."[8] But all was not fun and games at Leonides's house. He homeschooled Origen with unusual rigor, giving him a fine education that prioritized scripture and also grounded him in the Greek liberal arts. Leonides drilled Origen in the Bible and made him recite daily. Yet this was not an unpleasant task for the young prodigy, who often astonished his father with the deep questions he asked. In his heart Leonides "rejoiced greatly and thanked God, the author of all good, that he had deemed him worthy to be the father of such a child."[9] When Leonides was executed and his property confiscated, Origen drew upon the solid education his father had given him to become a private tutor. As the oldest of seven sons, it fell to Origen to support his now impoverished family through teaching.

Teaching was a respected occupation at Alexandria, a city known throughout the world for its intellectualism. Indeed the preeminent library of antiquity was located there. It was the ancient equivalent of Oxford or Harvard University. Alexandria had been founded in 332 BC by the Greek conqueror Alexander the Great, who personally laid out the lines of the city that would bear his name. He chose a strip of land in the Nile delta between the Mediterranean shoreline and a freshwater lake. Two great harbors for sea traffic were built, while canals gave access to the Nile River and the Red Sea. Comfortable breezes blew from offshore to provide relief during the hot Egyptian summers. The fertile delta soil produced an abundance of crops that guaranteed the region's prosperity. Merchant ships came from everywhere to trade, guided into port by a 400-foot-tall lighthouse that was one of the seven wonders of the ancient world. By Origen's day the city was second in importance only to Rome—but it was certainly Rome's superior in terms of scholarship. This was because Alexander the Great had ordered a magnificent library to be built in his city. His successors established a temple to the gods of intellectual inspiration known as the Muses. Soon Alexandria's "Museum" became a kind of university for scholars, with a great library at its heart. In the third century before the Christian era, the library housed around 500,000 books and scrolls (including many items ransacked from passing ships or permanently "borrowed" from other great cities).[10] Alexandria's library made it a magnet for intellectuals from every corner of the world.

The intellectual heritage of Alexandria exerted a profound influence on Origen. The overarching worldview permeating the city came from the ancient Greek philosopher Plato. Though he was long dead by Origen's day, Plato's philosophy lived on in his writings and his school of thought. Among the many Platonist philosophers of Alexandria, we should note in particular the Jewish sage named Philo, a contemporary of Jesus. We can hardly overestimate the impact Philo had on the early church. He was the first to try to reconcile Greek philosophy with the revelation of the Bible through an allegorical method of interpretation. Thus he provided a model that later Christian intellectuals like Justin Martyr and Origen would emulate. In a moment we will take a deeper look at Origen's interpretive method and his Platonic approach to theology.[11]

We don't know exactly when Christianity arrived in Alexandria, but from the beginning, the faith there appears to have been highly intellectual. We see this even in New Testament times. In Acts 18:24–28, Apollos appears as an Alexandrian convert to the faith. He is described as eloquent, well-versed in the scriptures, and a powerful apologist—obviously a very learned man. Yet we have no evidence that he planted a church in his hometown. In fact, it is quite possible the first "Christian" communities at Alexandria were not orthodox at all, but were second-century Gnostic sects led by figures such as Valentinus (whom we met in chapter 3).[12] It is only in the late second century that we begin to see orthodox churches functioning in the city. These Christians had to be very academic to combat the Gnostics' preoccupation with "knowledge." For example, one of Origen's forerunners, Clement of Alexandria, was an orthodox teacher in the city starting around AD 180. Clement's apologetic writings were very cerebral and mystical. Although Origen never mentioned Clement by name, their similarities testify to the common shape of Christian theology at Alexandria. This theology, with Philo as its precedent, was characterized by the allegorization of scripture and the harmonization of biblical ideas with Greek philosophy.

All this to say, when Origen became a teacher in the wake of his father's martyrdom he inherited a longstanding tradition of high intellectualism. He soon found himself teaching not only arts and letters as a private tutor, but also serving his local church as an instructor in basic theology for new converts. The young Origen went on to achieve unheard-of stature for a Christian theologian. He began to earn respect even from the secular philosophers of Alexandria. His brilliance soon became legendary, and pagan intellectuals from around the Mediterranean came to dispute with him. Unfortunately, such acclaim brought Origen into conflict with his bishop, Demetrius. Eventually it led to Origen's departure from Alexandria on bad terms. But before we continue that story, we should spend some time trying to understand the contours of this great thinker's mind. To do this we must begin at the place where Origen himself always began: the Holy Scriptures.

The Body and Soul of Scripture

Origen receives a lot of criticism today because of his allegorical interpretive method. Many evangelical Christians suppose he wanted to undermine the true meaning of the Bible. Nothing could be further from the truth. Origen was a man who loved the scriptures immensely, just as he had been taught by his beloved father Leonides. Origen used allegory precisely because of his deep and abiding respect for the Word of God. While it is not a method we moderns would use, we should not for a minute think it was anti-biblical. I dare say Origen knew the scriptures far better than most American believers in the pews today. He memorized vast portions of the sacred text and constantly immersed himself in God's Word. One of his greatest works was a line-by-line comparison of Bible translations in six columns of Greek and Hebrew with scholarly notations. He was so prolific that he needed a team of stenographers, copyists, and calligraphers to take down all the sermons, biblical commentaries, and theological treatises that poured from his mind.[13] Of course, we must admit Origen produced some remarkable interpretations we wouldn't want to follow ourselves. But no one should accuse this church father of not loving the inspired Word of God.

To understand Origen's approach to scripture, we must recall the Platonic outlook that permeated his culture. When we studied Justin Martyr in chapter 2, we learned that Plato made a distinction between the higher realm of pure truth and the material world we see around us. The goal of Platonism was to move from "down here" to "up there." For Christians—as Justin Martyr had already shown—Jesus Christ served as the great road linking the two realms. Since Jesus has provided the means for the soul to look upon God, Christians ought to embark on that journey by contemplating divine ideas. Origen's basic assumption was that the spiritual realm has been opened up for exploration (though he readily acknowledged not every Christian is equally prepared for the trip). Those who are spiritually mature have no business remaining "down here" when the riches of deeper insight have been made accessible by Christ.

Perhaps this sounds like a lot of mystical or philosophical nonsense to you. But don't write off Origen just yet. Try to understand where he was coming from. Often we are so conditioned by our modern mind-set that it's hard to appreciate a man like him. We are set in our ways. But it is always a good idea to evaluate modern viewpoints in light of church history. This is especially true when it comes to biblical interpretation. We may be surprised at what we discover in the comparison! For example, our tendency is to approach the scriptures as something external to us, like scientists seeking to discover meaning in a concrete object. In contrast, Origen thought of interpretation as an inner quest: the soul's yearning to find its way back to God. This distinction makes all the difference in how we do exegesis. I do not mean to imply that we are impersonal and rational, while the ancients were warm and emotional. It is more complicated than this. Let me see if I can explain what I mean.

The difference between Origen's exegesis and our own has to do with the stance of the human interpreter in relation to the Bible. More specifically, it has to do with the place for *movement* in biblical interpretation. Whether we are aware of it or not, we stand still when we read the Bible. We know we live in the twenty-first century, and we also know the Bible was written long ago. So we perceive ourselves as standing *here*, while we are looking *over there*. We try to discover the original historical setting of the passage we are studying, as we examine communication that occurred way back then. Once we have understood the biblical writer's intent, we try to bring his message forward, applying it to our own situation. Only then do we move as we apply the Bible's message to our lives. I am not saying this is a coldhearted or detached process. Most of us read the Bible as a warm spiritual exercise. Yet we do it from a very fixed position. Our feet are planted here, while biblical events happened over there. It's up to us to use our interpretive tools to bridge the historical divide. We can only do that by *looking at* the past from our present location.

But for Origen, movement has to take place *during interpretation*. The interpreter's movement is not just an "application" that comes at the end of critical study. Interpretation itself is a journey in which the interpreter travels deeper into God's mystery. In Origen's understanding, it is impossible to interpret the Bible unless we move—and this is inevitably a movement upward. We must ascend to a higher level. We must enter a foreign land. I'm not talking about traveling from modern times to Bible times. Though Origen was aware of the need to build that particular bridge, he believed studying the original context of a verse was only a small part of good interpretation. What mattered most was finding the treasure that lay beyond the bare bones of the obvious. Interpretation calls for vigorous exercise in which the interpreter moves into scripture's field of words and images. He is not a scientist investigating an external object, but a frontier woodsman who is actually traipsing around inside the forest. As he parts the branches to see what's next, unexpected surprises await him.

Because of his two-realm perspective, Origen understood the text of scripture to be multifaceted. There had to be different layers of meaning in these holy and sacred words. As C. S. Lewis knew when he wrote his *Chronicles of Narnia*, written texts have the power to reveal truths we wouldn't perceive otherwise. In the same way, Origen didn't want to miss any spiritual truths that might be latent within the Bible. One of his guiding principles was drawn from 2 Corinthians 3:6: "The letter kills, but the Spirit gives life." He understood this verse to say that the letters of scripture, taken by themselves, are dead. They are just ink on paper. It is only when God reveals their spiritual meaning that they bring life. Origen took it as unquestionably true that physical things often contain spiritual realities hidden within. For example, we humans have physical bodies. At the same time, we are created in the image of God. We are made for higher things than mere animals because, unlike them, we have souls in addition to our bodies. And this brings us to a fundamental point of Origen's interpretive mind-set: he believed the Bible likewise has a "soul" within its outer "body." In other words, there is much more to scripture than meets the eye.

Origen's most famous book was called *First Principles*.[14] The title indicates his purpose: to lay out the fundamentals of the Christian faith. Book 4 provides his basic rules for interpreting scripture. The first thing Origen wished to establish was that the Bible is the inspired Word of God. But then he points out an undeniable problem: divine inspiration does not prevent some people from interpreting scripture poorly. Where did they go wrong? Origen tells us:

> Now the cause of the false opinions, impious statements and ignorant assertions about God appears to be nothing else than not understanding the Scripture according to its spiritual meaning, but interpreting it according to the mere letter. And therefore, to those of us who believe the sacred books are not the compositions of men but were composed by the inspiration of the Holy Spirit, we must point out the method of interpreting them which appears to be correct to us, [namely, to recognize] that there are certain mystical economies made known by the holy Scriptures.[15]

Origen was saying that most people fail to recognize the deeper truths enshrined within the pages of the Bible. Too often, interpreters stay at a superficial level, instead of perceiving the "mystical economies"—the spiritual insights to which the outer words of scripture often point. The interpreter is urged to move beyond the Bible's "body" to discover its inner "soul."

Origen famously identified three (or sometimes four) "senses" of scripture. Usually he began with the text's literal sense.[16] By literal sense he meant the historical meaning of a Bible verse based on its original context and the principles of grammar. This is where our modern exegesis tends to focus—and so the literal sense is our only basis for making contemporary interpretations and personal applications. But

Origen would not settle for this. While he acknowledged the edifying value of the literal sense, he insisted that more capable interpreters must constantly be on the move. They must journey into scripture's very soul: its allegorical or spiritual sense. The spiritual sense of scripture could take several forms. First and foremost, it offered a Christ-centered interpretation (even in obscure texts that did not obviously seem to be speaking about him). Other aspects of Origen's spiritual sense included moral applications to the soul's relationship with God, or cosmic explanations about the final destiny of our world.

According to Origen, God had intentionally invested the Bible with multiple layers of meaning. Think about what this means. The great beauty of Origen's system—which is lacking in our modern interpretive methods—is that any verse can become a rich source of christological truth. Even the most baffling prescriptions from the law of Moses, or the most mundane details of an historical narrative, have the potential to be unlocked by the key of allegory. Ask yourself: when you read the Book of Leviticus with all its Jewish legal technicalities, how on earth do you make it relevant if you can only rely on the literal sense? It's pretty difficult to apply the Mosaic regulations about sacrifices and ritual purity to our lives today. In contrast, Origen's sermons on Leviticus make room for Jesus Christ at every turn.[17] Origen viewed all of scripture as wondrously fertile and packed with allegorical possibilities. He believed this was the Bible's own method of interpretation, for the Apostle Paul had said in Galatians 4:24 that an Old Testament reference "may be interpreted allegorically."[18] By means of divine allegory, every word on every page of scripture could be made to speak with overflowing richness about Jesus Christ, the Christian life, and the Christian's eternal hope.

The Limits on Allegory

Origen's use of allegory opened abundant interpretive possibilities. But perhaps you have already sensed a basic problem here. Many observers have pointed out that the greatest strength of Origen's system is also its Achilles' heel: its unlimited freedom.[19] How can we restrain the flights of fancy an interpreter might take? How do we keep him from reading into the text a meaning of his own invention? How do we guarantee that the interpretation is God's message to us, not man's creative but flawed imagination? Origen was well aware of this problem, though it did not concern him greatly. I would like to suggest he had three safeguards in place to deal with the problem of the interpreter's subjectivity.

First, Origen fully embraced the catholic church's Rule of Faith as a theological guide. Although he believed he had great freedom in how to handle a biblical text, Origen didn't grant himself license to come up with any interpretation whatsoever. An interpreter's conclusions had to be congruent with what the Christian church believed and taught. In his preface to *First Principles*, Origen provided a summary of apostolic doctrine that more or less corresponded to what we've already seen in Irenaeus and Tertullian.[20] Like his predecessors, Origen established the axiom that every interpreter must use the truths of the Rule of Faith as the "elementary and foundational principles" in constructing a systematic theology.[21] Thus, the received teaching of the catholic community served as a boundary to exclude the allegorical fantasies of the Gnostics and other heretics. There was a limit to what allegory could be made to say—and it was the orthodox Rule of Faith that set the limits.

Origen's second safeguard against allegorical fancy was grounded in the very nature of the Bible itself. He understood it to be, at its heart, a message about the Logos who became incarnate as Jesus Christ. But it was more than that. Not only was it *about* him, it was also *from* him.[22] Just as the Word became flesh and dwelt among us for a time, so he continues to speak as God's Word to humanity through the Bible. One of the greatest modern scholars to study Origen's exegesis, Henri de Lubac, had this to say about the Christ-centered focus of sacred allegory:

In short, the spirit of the letter is Christ . . . Therefore, Jesus Christ brings about the unity of Scripture, because he is the endpoint and fullness of Scripture. Everything in it is related to him. In the end he is its sole object. Consequently, he is, so to speak, its whole exegesis . . . Scripture leads us to him, and when we reach this end, we no longer have to look for anything beyond it . . . Inasmuch as he is the exegesis of Scripture, Jesus Christ is also the exegete. He is truly Scripture's Logos, in an active as well as a passive sense: "Christ, who alone unlocks an understanding of the Scriptures." It is he alone who explains it to us, and in explaining it to us, he gives us an explanation of himself.[23]

Origen believed his Christocentric interpretive method had Jesus's own support. He often quoted the Savior's words in John 5:39, "You search the Scriptures because you think that in them you have eternal life; and it is they that bear witness about me."[24] Since the Bible was understood to be entirely about Christ, Origen never was too worried that he might "miss the point" because of his allegory. As long as he proclaimed the Lord as revealed elsewhere in scripture, he could be confident he had discovered the correct interpretation. Besides, the Logos's own work of revelation always guided the interpreter to exegetical outcomes that were "worthy of God."[25] Origen believed that when he journeyed into the spiritual sense of the text, Jesus would be there to reveal himself accurately in the sacred words of scripture.

The third safeguard against frivolous allegory was the upright character of the exegete. Origen believed gaining insight into the deepest meaning of scripture required moral excellence. What did Jesus have to say about this? "Blessed are the pure in heart, for they shall see God" (Matt. 5:8). Follow Origen's logic here. Jesus seems to be saying that the vision of God requires purification from sin. But seeing God is not something reserved only for the future. Christ the Logos can begin to reveal God to us even now. To what kind of person would we expect the Logos to offer his divine illumination? Obviously he would give greater discernment to those whose spiritual lives are receptive to gifts from above. He reveals himself to those who seek hard after him. Interpreters marked by such godly maturity and wisdom would not be likely to make drastic mistakes in their exegesis.

Today we often suppose anybody can get an interpretation "right." In other words, even an unbeliever or a person who denies the value of God's Word could figure out what a particular verse is trying to say. But Origen did not think so—at least not when it comes to the fullest meaning of the text. Interpretation in the ancient church was a spiritual quest, so everything depended on your heart for the Lord. Godliness was required for true comprehension, not just a good mind. The lifestyle of the interpreter genuinely mattered. Origen valued what we call the "spiritual disciplines" as the way to gain scripture's wisdom. He did not discipline himself in order to earn grace through works salvation. Rather, he knew he couldn't grow in biblical understanding unless he possessed a degree of sanctification worthy of God's holy Word. Let us now return to Origen's biography as we learn more about his rigorous pursuit of moral excellence.

The Man of Steel

When we left Origen's story he was a young man serving as a tutor to support his family. At the same time, he was ministering as a catechist (a teacher of new converts) in his local church. Though he was an outstanding intellectual, Origen was no wimpy academician in an ivory tower. He was a bold man of action who became famous in Alexandria for his courageous witness. Despite the danger from the Roman authorities during a time of Christian persecution, Origen continued to instruct new believers in the essentials of the faith even when other teachers had fled the city. In fact, several of his students went on to be martyred. At great personal risk Origen visited them in prison to encourage them; for he was more than just their teacher—he was their mentor and discipler.[26] Eusebius writes,

> not only was he with them while in bonds until their final condemnation, but when the holy martyrs were led to death he was very bold

and went with them into danger. As he acted bravely, and with great boldness saluted the martyrs with a kiss, oftentimes the heathen multitude around them became infuriated and were at the point of rushing upon him . . . So great was the enmity of the unbelievers toward him, on account of the many people that were instructed by him in the sacred faith, that they placed bands of soldiers around the house where he lived. Day by day the persecution burned against him, so that the whole city could no longer contain him.[27]

Here we see a man who considered himself dead to the things of this world and alive only to Jesus Christ. In a little book of encouragement called *An Exhortation to Martyrdom*, Origen put it this way:

I think that God is loved with the whole soul by those who through their great longing for fellowship with him draw their soul away and separate it not only from their earthly body but also from every corporeal thing . . . If such a view seems hard to anyone, then he has not [truly] thirsted for God, the Mighty One, the living God.[28]

Origen's zeal for martyrdom marked him as a Christian who understood the cost of discipleship. He wanted to purge his soul of any earthly affection that competed with the love of God.

While Origen's reputation as a fearless advocate of the Christian faith continued to grow, he also became known for his life of austerity and physical renunciation. For example, when he discovered his work as a liberal arts teacher interfered with his blossoming apologetic ministry, he gave up the steady income of his secular job to focus solely on Bible study and Christian scholarship. He sold his library of non-Christian books and lived off the meager amount the sale provided. His nights were marked by extreme limitation of sleep so he could spend extra hours in the Word. He never slept on a bed, preferring the bodily discipline of sleeping on the floor. He fasted constantly, went barefoot, and abstained from alcohol and sex. So rigorous was his lifestyle that he was physically weakened by the mortification of his flesh. It was in this context that Origen did something foolish: taking Jesus's words in Matthew 19:12 literally, he castrated himself to become a "eunuch for the kingdom of heaven." Later he regretted the act and wrote that it should not be done. At the very least, it reveals the strength of his desire to overcome the flesh. Though some might look at Origen's lifestyle with skepticism, we should recognize that the holiness he displayed drew the admiration of Christian and non-Christian alike in Alexandria. In the ancient world, his self-denial served as a powerful form of "lifestyle evangelism." We'll explore the subject of asceticism further in chapter 8.

Eventually Origen's prominence in Alexandria brought him into conflict with the bishop Demetrius. Perhaps jealousy was involved. It appears Demetrius felt threatened by this extremely devoted and obviously brilliant young man. On the other hand, there could have been a certain arrogance on Origen's part. No doubt he sometimes went out on a theological limb, and was not willing to be disciplined by his church. As Origen matured and became the leading Christian intellectual in the city, the conflict with Demetrius came to a head. Origen finally decided to move to Caesarea in Palestine, where the bishop was more favorably disposed toward him. He went on to have a long and productive career there. One of the great benefits of this new location was the availability of Jewish rabbis with whom Origen could have scholarly discussions about the manuscripts and meaning of the Hebrew scriptures. He also profited from his proximity to the lands of the Bible. He could actually visit the lands he was studying as he produced the numerous commentaries and sermons that marked this phase of his life.

Unfortunately, those peaceful decades of productive ministry would not conclude with the gentle death of a respected scholar—though Origen probably wouldn't have had it any other way. During the hot persecution of Emperor Decius which began ravaging the church in the year AD 250, Origen was thrown in prison as a prominent Christian leader. Eusebius says that "the demon of evil marshaled all his forces and fought against Origen with his utmost craft and power, assaulting him beyond all others against whom he contended at that time."[29] Origen adamantly held on to his faith during the horrific tortures in the Roman dungeon. He endured burning by fiery implements and the extreme stretching of his limbs in the stocks. Though he was not killed in prison, the trauma of torture (on top of all the bodily hardships he had long endured) finally claimed Origen's life. Later generations coined a nickname for Origen. They called him *Adamantius*, which means "made of steel." But there is another meaning for this Latin term, which is perhaps even more fitting. *Adamantius* can refer to a diamond. It is an image that captures not only the great hardness, but also the great beauty and value, of a man like Origen of Alexandria.

Reflections on Origen

The Man of Steel has not been impervious to later attacks. While there were many who cherished Origen's legacy, others found him problematic. Origen did teach some doctrines that are now viewed as unorthodox. For example, he said there is a hierarchy within the Trinity, so that the Son is subordinate to the Father, and the Holy Spirit is a created being. To be fair we must remember that the theological position of the Christian church on these points had not yet been firmly established. Only in the time of Athanasius (as we will see in the next chapter) did the equality of the three persons of the Trinity become official doctrine. But when Origen taught that our resurrection bodies will not be physical, or that eventually the purifying fires of hell will reform all creatures (even the Devil!) back to a state of obedience to God, he was arguing for views that the catholic church had never embraced.[30] For this reason a backlash developed against Origen among certain church fathers.[31] Then at a council in AD 553, some of his views were formally condemned. Because of Origen's controversial legacy, he is one of two figures in this book (along with Tertullian) whom the decision makers of church history have not seen fit to name as a "saint."

Origen has been accused by modern commentators of downplaying "history" in favor of spiritual truths.[32] There is something to be said for this argument. Though he did not deny the importance of God's saving work through physical means, in practice Origen put less emphasis on salvation history than he did on abstractions. If we recall what we said in the introduction about Christianity being a record of the *res gestae*, the "events that have occurred," we can see that such an abstract approach is misguided. With his philosophical bent, Origen sometimes failed to adequately capture the real-world aspect of the Christian faith. Yet what he did perceive about Christianity's spiritual dynamic was so profound that—despite his errors—he certainly deserves a place among the greatest of Christian thinkers. The eminent church historian Henry Chadwick got it right when he compared Origen to the little girl in the Longfellow poem who had a curl in the middle of her forehead: "When she was good, she was very good indeed, but when she was bad, she was *horrid*."[33] So too, Origen has been known to inhabit the extremes of the theological spectrum.

Where does that leave Origen? It has often been observed that there are many Origens. It all depends on the Origen you want to find. Perhaps it was inevitable that so brilliant a man would leave us such a conflicted inheritance. In cases like this it's best to give the author himself the last word. Origen told us how he wanted to be remembered when he wrote, "As for myself, my wish is to be truly a man of the church, to be called by the name of Christ and not of any heretic, to have this name which is blessed all over the earth; I desire to be, and to be called, a Christian, in my works as in my thoughts."[34] With that no follower of Christ can disagree.

Provocative Questions

1. Have you ever read a great book that conveyed truth in a way you hadn't thought of before? Describe a time you learned

something profound about God or the world through a written narrative.

2. What do you think of allegory? Can it be applied to scripture? Why or why not? What dangers are present? Which is more necessary to interpret the Bible—your mind or your heart? Assuming we can't employ Origen's type of allegory today, what would it look like to find authentic "spiritual meaning" in a biblical text? Describe a proper method of interpreting the Bible. How do you find God's timeless truth in this ancient book?

3. If you hunger for the soul of scripture, here is some in-depth study you can do. Read Galatians 4:21–31. Then compare it to Isaiah 54:1, and also Genesis 16; 18:9–15; and 21:9–21. How would you characterize the interpretive moves Paul is making in Galatians? How does he take truth from the Old Testament and apply it to Christianity? Now ask the same questions of 1 Corinthians 10:4–6 in comparison with Exodus 17:1–7 and Numbers 20:1–11. What does Paul mean in 1 Corinthians 10:6 when he says, "these things took place as examples for us"?

4. Origen lived a rigorous lifestyle of self-denial. In what contexts do we practice self-denial today? In other words, what are our normal motivations for denying our bodily urges? Read 1 Corinthians 9:24–27. What would it look like to "buffet our body" like Paul did? In what ways have American Christians become self-indulgent or morally lax? How could we practice a higher degree of asceticism than we currently do? At the same time, how can we avoid legalism and spiritual elitism?

5. Origen was a great scholar of the Bible and theology. Are academicians and scholars respected at your church? Is theology emphasized, or rarely mentioned? Do you tend to be suspicious of scholars? Or are you too trusting? Can excessive learning take a person away from the simple gospel? Is simple theology best? Do we honor God if we remain at the simple level?

Good Books to Dig Deeper

The standard English edition of *First Principles* is:

Butterworth, G. W. *Origen: On First Principles.* London: SPCK, 1936. Reprint, Harper Torchbooks, with an introduction by Henri de Lubac, 1966.

One of Origen's most important philosophical works, *Against Celsus*, is translated in:

Chadwick, Henry. *Origen: Contra Celsum.* Cambridge: Cambridge University Press, 1953.

Some selections from Origen's writings with good introductory material can be found in:

Greer, Rowan. *Origen: An Exhortation to Martyrdom, Prayer and Selected Works.* New York: Paulist Press, 1979.

Oulton, John Ernest Leonard and Henry Chadwick. *Alexandrian Christianity: Selected Translations of Clement and Origen.* Library of Christian Classics. Philadelphia: Westminster Press, 1954.

Trigg, Joseph W. *Origen.* The Early Church Fathers. New York: Routledge, 1998.

Three excellent overviews of Origen's life and thought are:

Crouzel, Henri. *Origen: The Life and Thought of the First Great Theologian.* Translated by A. S. Worrall. San Francisco: Harper & Row, 1989.

McGuckin, John Anthony. *The Westminster Handbook to Origen.* Louisville, KY: Westminster John Knox Press, 2004. (This book is topically arranged like an encyclopedia.)

Trigg, Joseph W. *Origen: The Bible and Philosophy in the Third-century Church.* Atlanta: John Knox Press, 1983.

A Taste of Origen

Commentary on the Song of Songs 1.2.1–4, 7–8

Origen's Commentary on the Song of Songs *is a classic exposition of this little book, much emulated in later centuries. He says in his preface that it is a love song celebrating Solomon's marriage to his bride. But it is more than that. Origen explores the spiritual meaning hidden in the outer form of the drama. It describes the soul's love for Christ the Bridegroom.*

Here Origen is commenting on Song of Songs 1:2, "Let him kiss me with the kisses of his mouth. For your breasts are better than wine, and the fragrance of your perfumes is better than all spices." (Modern Bible translations read "your _love_ is better than wine," but the Hebrew text is ambiguous, and Origen's Greek version said "breasts.") He first interprets the text literally: it portrays the romantic longings of a betrothed princess for her fiancé. Then he moves to an allegorical interpretation in which the Bride desires teachings from the very bosom of Jesus. Notice how Origen pays close attention to biblical words, and uses scripture to interpret scripture.

Let's begin with the historical drama portrayed here. You should understand that the bride has poured out her prayer to God the Father with her hands lifted up. She has prayed that the bridegroom might come to her right away and lavish on her the kisses of his own mouth. But even as she is supplicating the Father by saying "Let him kiss me with the kisses of his mouth," she is getting ready to add further words to her prayer. She says that as she began to speak those words, the bridegroom suddenly became present to her and stood beside her while she prayed. His breasts were revealed to her, and he remained there with her. He was anointed with a sumptuous perfume by which a bridegroom properly exudes a pleasant aroma.

The bride perceived that the one whose presence she had prayed for had come. While she was still speaking, he offered her that for which she had been praying. He bestowed on her those little kisses she so

urgently desired. This filled her with joy! She was deeply moved by
the elegance of his breasts and his pleasing fragrance. So she altered
the words of her intended prayer to adapt to the presence of her
bridegroom. Whereas before she had said, "Let him kiss me with the
kisses of his mouth," now that the bridegroom had come she spoke
to him directly, adding, "Your breasts are better than wine, and the
fragrance of your perfumes is better than all spices."

For the moment, that's enough of the literal meaning, which as I
said earlier is composed in the form of a romantic drama. Now let
us inquire into what the more profound meaning might hold.

In the divine scriptures we find the concept of *the heart* called
by many different terms, according to the particular circumstances
under discussion in each case. Sometimes it is simply called "the
heart," as in "Blessed are the pure in heart" (Matt. 5:8) or "With the
heart we believe unto righteousness" (Rom. 10:10).

But if the setting is that of a meal, and the purpose is to describe
the appearance and order of those reclining at the table, it is referred
to as the "bosom" or the "chest." For example, John refers in his
gospel to "a certain disciple whom Jesus loved" who "reclined on
his bosom" or "his chest" (John 13:23–25). This disciple is in fact
the one to whom Simon Peter gestured and said, "Ask him who he
is speaking about." And then it says, "Leaning back on Jesus's chest,
he said, 'Lord, who is it?'" Now this is certainly what the text means:
John is said to have reposed on the seat of Jesus's heart, that is, on
the inner meaning of his teachings. There he sought and investigated
"the treasures of wisdom and knowledge that are hidden in Christ
Jesus" (Col. 2:3). And so I don't think it's inappropriate to refer to
the place of his holy teachings as "the bosom of Christ."

. . . In this present passage [from the Song of Songs] which describes the behavior and conversation of lovers, I think it is entirely
fitting that the same inner seat of the heart should be described as
"breasts." Therefore the breasts of the Bridegroom are good, because
in them "are hidden the treasures of wisdom and knowledge." The
Bride, moreover, compares these breasts to wine. In fact she says the

breasts are better than wine. Now the "wine" is intended to refer to the ordinances and teachings which the Bride had become accustomed to partake of through the law and the prophets, before the advent of the Bridegroom.

But now when she considers the teaching that flows from the breasts of the Bridegroom, she is amazed and struck with awe. She can see it is far superior to the wine that was served to her by the holy fathers and prophets—the "spiritual" wine, so to speak, that used to gladden her heart before the advent of the Bridegroom. Indeed, [the Old Testament saints] used to plant vineyards like this and cultivate them. Noah did so first (Gen. 9:20), and later Isaiah also planted one "on a fertile hill" (Isa. 5:1). However, the Bride can now see that far greater precepts and knowledge are to be found with the Bridegroom. From him flows a more perfect teaching than what was found among the ancients. That is why she says, "Your breasts are better than wine." [Christ's teaching] is certainly much more wonderful than the teaching with which the ancients used to delight her!

7

ATHANASIUS

In 1865 American writer Mary Mapes Dodge published a fictional story about a brother and sister in Holland trying to win a pair of silver skates. The boy, eight-year-old Hans Brinker, has passed into folklore because of the heroic act he is said to have performed. One evening he was walking along a canal near Haarlem thinking about the dikes that kept the sea from inundating the low-lying countryside. Then he heard the sound every Dutch child fears: the trickling of water that signaled a hole in the dike!

> The boy understood the danger at a glance. That little hole, if the water were allowed to trickle through, would soon be a large one, and a terrible inundation would be the result.
>
> Quick as a flash, he saw his duty. Throwing away his flowers, the boy clambered up the heights until he reached the hole. His chubby little finger was thrust in, almost before he knew it. The flowing was stopped! Ah! he thought, with a chuckle of boyish delight, the angry waters must stay back now! Haarlem shall not be drowned while I am here!

This was all very well at first, but the night was falling rapidly. Chill vapors filled the air. Our little hero began to tremble with cold and dread. He shouted loudly; he screamed, "Come here! come here!" but no one came. The cold grew more intense, a numbness, commencing in the tired little finger, crept over his hand and arm, and soon his whole body was filled with pain. He shouted again, "Will no one come? Mother! Mother!" . . . He tried to whistle. Perhaps some straggling boy might heed the signal, but his teeth chattered so, it was impossible. Then he called on God for help. And the answer came, through a holy resolution: "I will stay here till morning." . . .

The midnight moon looked down upon that small, solitary form, sitting upon a stone, halfway up the dike. His head was bent but he was not asleep, for every now and then one restless hand rubbed feebly the outstretched arm that seemed fastened to the dike—and often the pale, tearful face turned quickly at some real or fancied sounds.

How can we know the sufferings of that long and fearful watch— what falterings of purpose, what childish terrors came over the boy as he thought of the warm little bed at home, of his parents, his brothers and sisters, then looked into the cold, dreary night! If he drew away that tiny finger, the angry waters, grown angrier still, would rush forth, and never stop until they had swept over the town. No, he would hold it there till daylight—if he lived! He was not very sure of living. What did this strange buzzing mean? And then the knives that seemed pricking and piercing him from head to foot? He was not certain now that he could draw his finger away, even if he wished to.

At daybreak a clergyman, returning from the bedside of a sick parishioner, thought he heard groans as he walked along on the top of the dike. Bending, he saw, far down on the side, a child apparently writhing with pain.

"In the name of wonder, boy," he exclaimed, "what are you doing there?"

"I am keeping the water from running out," was the simple answer of the little hero. "Tell them to come quick."

It is needless to add that they did come quickly . . .[1]

The image of the little Dutch boy defying the angry waters has come
to represent anyone who takes a stand against dangerous forces that
threaten to overwhelm. According to legend, if this small yet stal-
wart guardian had not remained at the dike, the whole area would
have been swamped by a deadly flood. Yet he stayed there through
the cold night with his finger holding back the entire weight of the
ocean until the danger passed. His tenacity saved the day.

The early church father Athanasius of Alexandria has often been
viewed as the same kind of hero as the little Dutch boy. The ancient
Christians portrayed him as a solitary resistance fighter standing firm
while the waters of heresy raged about him. Today the expression is
often used, *Athanasius contra mundum*, or "Athanasius against the
world."[2] At times it certainly seems as if this were true. Exiled on five
occasions by three different emperors, Athanasius spent seventeen
out of his forty-six years as a bishop in exile.[3] Yet even in the face of
imperial opposition, he clung tenaciously to his belief in the equality
of the Father, Son, and Holy Spirit. It's probably not an exaggeration
to say that if it were not for his efforts, a heretical view of the Trinity
known as Arianism would have won the day. Indeed, one observer of
those times wrote that the Roman Empire awoke one day and "was
astonished to find itself Arian."[4] For several decades Athanasius was
a lonely defender of the orthodox doctrine of the Trinity against the
Arian view. Only at the end of his life did his efforts begin to pay off
as Arianism was finally rejected. In this chapter we will meet a man
who was not afraid to stand "against the world" on the doctrine of
the Trinity.

But before we turn to the Arian controversy, we must take note of
the dramatically different situation that faced the early church in Athanasius's day. In the previous chapters we've seen Christianity being
persecuted by the Roman authorities. In spite of this, it was growing
and making many converts. However, it was nowhere near being an
overwhelming cultural force. In contrast, Christian theology in the
fourth century was the subject of widespread discussion throughout the empire. The faith had become ubiquitous. How did such a

drastic change come about? At the beginning of the fourth century, the church crossed a threshold that altered everything. Christianity went from being the object of imperial persecution to the religion of the emperors themselves. The Roman Empire quickly became a Christian Empire. This spectacular conversion began under a man we met in the introduction: Constantine the Great. As a backdrop to Athanasius, let's take a moment to look at the new era of Christian history that was ushered in by Emperor Constantine.

Conquered by the Cross

The year AD 303 was not a good one for the Christian church. In that year the reigning emperor, Diocletian, began to issue a series of edicts against the faith. First, church buildings were leveled and Bibles burned. Then church leaders were thrown in prison or compelled to make sacrifice to the gods under threat of torture. Finally the persecution was extended to all Christians. Things began to spiral out of control. It was as if a mad rage had taken hold of the Roman Empire, particularly in the eastern provinces. Untold numbers of Christians were tortured in the most hideous ways.[5] Eusebius records that entire towns were massacred for confessing Christianity.[6] This dark hour of church history has come to be called the Great Persecution.

In AD 311 the mistreatment of the Christians abated somewhat. Yet there was no guarantee it would not start up again. In fact, persecution did continue sporadically in the East. Meanwhile a young prince named Constantine was mobilizing his army in an effort to claim the imperial throne. (Diocletian had abdicated several years earlier, leaving a gaping power vacuum in the Roman Empire.) The main rival who emerged to oppose Constantine was Maxentius. Constantine moved toward Rome to meet his enemy head on. At this critical moment, he claimed to see a miraculous sign in the heavens. Above the noonday sun there appeared a cross of light inscribed with the words, "Conquer by this." Constantine then had a dream telling him to fashion a Christian banner decorated with gold and jewels. Emboldened by this apparent aid from the Christian God, Constantine marched against Maxentius with his soldiers fighting under the banner of Christ. The two armies met outside Rome at the famous Battle of the Milvian Bridge in AD 312. Though Constantine's forces were badly outnumbered, he pulled off a stunning military victory. Maxentius's army was completely defeated, and he was drowned in the Tiber River. Constantine now took sole possession of the Roman Empire's western half.

Constantine attributed his great victory to the God of Christianity. Though historians often debate whether his conversion was heartfelt or opportunistic, what can't be debated is that Constantine became a lifelong supporter of the Christian faith. Immediately he arranged a meeting at Milan with an ally from the East, Licinius. Together they issued a famous document called the Edict of Milan. It proclaimed that "the Christians and all others should have liberty to follow that mode of religion which to each of them appeared best . . . All who choose [Christianity] are to be permitted, freely and absolutely, to remain in it, and not to be disturbed or molested in any way."[7] The Edict of Milan symbolizes the dramatic transition from the era of Christian persecution to the era of imperial support for the faith. Licinius, however, did not remain true to his promise. He continued to persecute Christians when he found it expedient. Eventually Constantine realized his former ally would have to be confronted in battle. In AD 324 Constantine defeated him, becoming sole ruler of the Roman Empire in both the western and eastern halves. And now, for the first time in history, a Roman emperor sought to unify his empire around the religion of Christianity instead of paganism.

Eusebius, the ancient Christian historian to whom we owe much of our knowledge of the early church, lived through these events. Their significance was not lost on him. He tried to give a theological interpretation to what he was witnessing. Eusebius had been born around AD 260, probably at Caesarea in Palestine. There he studied under a teacher he greatly admired named Pamphilus. For a time they worked as a scholarly team and published books together. Eusebius even adopted the name of Pamphilus as if he were his son. But during the Great Persecution, Eusebius's beloved teacher and father figure was martyred. To chronicle the important events of those days, Eusebius embarked on a journey around Palestine and Egypt collecting eyewitness accounts of the torture and heroism of the early Christians. Therefore we must understand this church historian in the context of his very real experience within Christian persecution. His firsthand observations, as well as his own personal loss, help explain the prominent attention he devoted to the persecuted church in his historical studies.

This context also helps us understand Eusebius's perspective on the rise of Emperor Constantine. He viewed the emperor as a divinely appointed savior who delivered the church from its fiery trials. Constantine's conversion was the fulfillment of a predestined plan in which Christianity assumed its rightful place as the religion of the empire.[8] Though Rome had previously been a mortal enemy of the Christian faith, now the emperor was professing personal devotion to Christ! This could only be the hand of God. Eusebius believed it was the church's destiny to reign triumphantly over its pagan culture. He therefore articulated a theological vision for what has been called "Imperial Christianity." It is a Christianity no longer experiencing deadly opposition from its culture. Rather, Christianity has won the day.

In ancient times there was no "separation of church and state." The only question was which religion would be the state religion. According to Eusebius, Constantine's embrace of the true God was the key decision that allowed the church to defeat paganism and bring the empire under Christian influence. In a flattering biography called the *Life of Constantine*, and also in a great oration delivered on the thirtieth anniversary of the emperor's ascension to power, Eusebius depicted Constantine as Christ's own representative on earth. The emperor ruled the world on behalf of God by always looking to Christ as his perfect pattern. Preaching from the brand-new Church of the Holy Sepulcher in Jerusalem, with Constantine himself in attendance, Eusebius said that "our emperor whom God loves brings those whom he rules on earth to the only-begotten Word and Savior, making them fit subjects for his kingdom."[9] The emperor is making Christian disciples—what a difference from the experience of the ancient martyrs!

As we said in the introduction, we need not think of this era as the "fall of the church." No doubt, new challenges faced the Christians now that their faith was favored by the emperor. Money and power were available in ways they had not been before. Yet this does not necessarily mean the church fell away from the truth. Instead, Christianity did what it has always done: it learned to express itself in a new cultural setting even as it sought to bring the culture under the Lordship of Jesus Christ. We can see the process of Christianization reflected in the biblical values that were brought to the law.[10] For example, Emperor Constantine issued legislation limiting child trafficking, the abduction of girls, and divorce. Likewise he decreed that a slave should not be branded on the face to mark ownership because "man is made in the image of God." He even made Sunday a day of rest.

We can also see the Christianization of culture in the way that theology penetrated to all levels of society in the fourth century. Theological arguments were everywhere. One eyewitness put it like this: "All the affairs of the city are full of this stuff! The alleys, the markets, the wide avenues, and the neighborhood streets! The clothing merchants, the bankers, and those who sell us food! If you ask someone for a penny, he philosophizes to you about the Begotten and the Unbegotten. If you should inquire about the estimated price for a loaf of bread, he answers, 'The Father is greater, and the Son is subordinate.' And if you ask, 'Is the bath suitable?' the attendant declares that the Son is derived out of non-being."[11] In other words, everyone from the emperor to the common man was debating Christian doctrine. This can be a very healthy thing. But what happens if the theological consensus starts to settle upon an incorrect view? In that case it would be very difficult to overturn, for there are political ramifications connected to various doctrinal positions. This is precisely what happened in the time of Athanasius. The views of Arius began to receive imperial favor and were accepted by many bishops across the empire. Athanasius seemed to stand alone against a world that had gone completely Arian. His challenge was far more difficult in this new age of Imperial Christianity. Now he faced not only his theological opponents, but the all-powerful Roman emperors whose politics were tied to theology. With this radically altered context in mind, let us return to the story of the one man who had the courage to stick his finger in the dike to hold back the waters of Arianism.

A Trickle Becomes a Torrent

Athanasius was born around AD 299 in the prominent Egyptian city of Alexandria. He was short and dark-skinned, with a fiery and stubborn personality. Apparently he did not receive a theological education in the great school where Origen had taught; yet this did not prevent him from being noticed by the city's bishop, Alexander. According to several ancient accounts, Alexander happened to glance up one day before breakfast to see some boys playing on the beach. The boys were pretending to be at church, going through the motions of the liturgy and performing mock ceremonies. At first, their game made Alexander smile. But then he noticed the boys were attempting to baptize their playmates! He called the boys together and demanded to know what words they had uttered. Come to find out, Athanasius (the ringleader) had performed all the proper rituals and had spoken the precise words of the baptismal liturgy without error. After consulting some of his assistant pastors, Alexander decided a valid baptism had been performed! He also realized the promise of this precocious boy. So he took Athanasius under his wing and made sure he got a very good Bible education. In fact, it was said that Athanasius "meditated on every book of the Old and New Testament with a depth that no one else had ever applied even to one of them."[12] Under Alexander's guidance, Athanasius emerged as a rising young star.

One day in the year AD 318, a problem within the church at Alexandria came to Bishop Alexander's attention. Arius, a popular pastor who presided over an influential parish in the city, was teaching some strange ideas about Jesus Christ.[13] But Alexander did not jump to conclusions. He respected Arius, a likable man known for his ability in logic. So Alexander gathered together the church leaders under his jurisdiction to investigate the matter. The key issue was this: How should the Son of God be differentiated from God the Father? Is he the same being as God? Is he a manifestation of God? Does he emanate out of God? Is he created by God? The relationship of the Son to the Father was the topic under discussion. Confusion reigned.

At last Alexander articulated his own position. He said there is a fundamental *unity* between the Father and the Son which must not be breached. Therefore both of them must be eternal. This is where Arius jumped in. He challenged his bishop's view, even calling him a heretic. Arius offered a new doctrine that had never been officially taught in the church: the Son of God is a created being, not eternal at all. He is separate from, and inferior to, the Father. Now the accusations were flying left and right. Many Alexandrian church leaders agreed with Arius, while others (such as the bishop's young secretary Athanasius) agreed with Alexander. Like a spark falling on dry tinder, the controversy spread like wildfire. The Arians even made up theological drinking songs to teach their views to the common people. What began as a doctrinal debate had blossomed into a full-fledged church split.

Bishop Alexander had no choice but to excommunicate Arius, who fled to Palestine and Syria. Fortunately for him, he continued to find ample support for his views in those regions. Soon the whole

Christian church was in an uproar over whether the Son was eternal like the Father, or was a created being. And all this was happening precisely when Constantine was trying to unify his empire around the cohesive religion of Christianity! As you might imagine, the emperor was not pleased with the development of a theological schism in the church. So he decided to call a major council to set the matter straight. But before describing what happened next, I'd like to take a moment to look at the theological background of the Arian controversy. Such an important doctrine as the Trinity deserves some in-depth explanation. Hang with me as we look at some complex theology.

The Theological Road to Nicaea

As our basic context, let's recall the Logos theology that we have already encountered in Justin Martyr, Tertullian, and Origen. When we discussed those figures, we learned that the concept of God's Logos (or Word) was helpful to the church fathers in describing the divine existence of Jesus Christ before his Incarnation, while at the same time maintaining his distinction from his heavenly Father. The Logos is God's eternal conversation partner. This conceptualization allowed him to be *united with* God the Father, yet *distinct from* him as well. Among the church fathers, Tertullian was particularly clear in explaining the Trinity along these lines. (Perhaps you recall he was the first writer to use the term "trinity" to describe God.) Tertullian defined the Trinity as three unique persons with one shared substance. These are precisely the terms that would be considered orthodox by later Christians. Tertullian's only real problem was that he did not use the term "Son" to describe the eternal existence of the Second Person. Rather, it was the Logos whom Tertullian called eternal. The Logos later became a "Son" for the purpose of carrying out God's will in creation and salvation. From the perspective of later developments in the doctrine of the Trinity, this aspect of Tertullian's thought might seem a little off because he did not make the Father/ Son relationship eternal. For the most part, however, Tertullian accurately anticipated the orthodox doctrine of the Trinity. He clearly believed the essential doctrine that the Logos has always existed. He simply did not refer to him as a "Son" for all eternity. Fortunately, his "error" was corrected by Origen of Alexandria as we will see in a moment. In turning to Origen, however, we must first take into account the way in which he was an influence on both sides of the argument between Arius and Alexander.[14]

Two distinct trends in Origen's thought are relevant to the ancient Trinitarian debates. On the one hand, some of Origen's writings indicate the Son is subordinate to the Father. This view is not without biblical support, at least with respect to his humble obedience. Jesus himself said, "The Father is greater than I" (John 14:28), but Origen actually thought of the Son as secondary in a hierarchy of three. Along these lines, Arius could claim to be following Origen. However, he took the idea of subordination much further than Origen ever did. He said the Son was fundamentally a lesser being than the Father. What kind of being must he then be? Arius alleged he was a *created* being. In a slogan for which he became famous, Arius claimed, "There was, when he was not." In other words, there was a time when the Son of God did not exist at all—not even as the Logos. Logically, this must mean he is an inferior being who is not essentially God. Arius believed God does not come from somewhere else. He just *is*. But the Bible says in verses like John 3:16 that Jesus Christ was "begotten." So Arius took that to mean the Son must have been generated by the Father at an identifiable moment—and before that moment, *he did not exist*! In arguing that Jesus Christ, the Logos of God, was not eternal but a created being, Arius stepped outside of what the ancient Christians had come to believe about their Savior.

On the other hand, Origen taught the doctrine known as "the eternal generation of the Son." This aspect of his thought was an exceptionally helpful refinement of Christian reflection on the relationship between God the Father and God the Son. By "eternal generation" Origen meant that God the Father always continually "begets" his Son in an eternal and ongoing act of divine generation. There was no time when the Father did not have his Son. Their relationship is always one of Begetter and Begotten, or of Father and Son. This is where Origen can be understood to "correct" Tertullian. Though Tertullian and others had thought the particular role of sonship was not eternal, they had always believed in the eternality of the Logos (i.e., Christ). But now Origen demonstrated that the Logos was always the "Son" as well.

In all this theologizing, don't miss the main point: the previous church fathers had uniformly insisted that the Logos, who became incarnate as Jesus Christ, was not a creature made at some moment in time. Instead, he was a being uniquely begotten of God before the creation of the world and all creatures—an eternal being.[15] So Bishop Alexander was following long-established Christian teaching when he made this claim.

The Nicene Creed

The theological argument between Bishop Alexander and Arius threatened Constantine's plan to use Christianity as a unifying force in his empire. So he decided to call a council for the bishops to settle the matter once and for all. It was to be held in the town of Nicaea (modern Iznik, Turkey), where Constantine owned a nice summer palace on the shore of a placid lake. He sent messengers across the empire inviting the bishops to attend the council at imperial expense. Two or three hundred bishops were able to come—most from the eastern regions, though a few westerners came as well, including two representatives from the bishop of Rome. Of course Bishop Alexander was there, and so was the young Athanasius.

Let's not overlook what a dramatic turn of events this council represents. Many of the bishops had been maimed in the Great

Persecution. One of them could not use his hands because red-hot irons had destroyed the nerves. Others had had their eyes dug out or their arms cut off. "In short, the Council looked like an assembled army of martyrs," remarked one ancient historian.[16] And now here they were—dining at a lavish banquet with the emperor himself! Eusebius gushed, "Not one of the bishops was missing at the imperial banquet, which was splendid beyond description . . . Some were the emperor's own companions at his table, while others reclined on couches arranged on either side. One might have thought that a picture of Christ's kingdom was here shown forth—a dream rather than reality!"[17]

On a June morning in AD 325, the bishops gathered expectantly in the imperial palace's great hall. A hush fell over the room as the emperor entered. He wore a dazzling purple robe and a golden crown encrusted with diamonds. Recognizing he was not an ordained clergyman, Constantine politely asked to attend the council. When the bishops agreed, Constantine delivered an opening speech urging them to find a path to unity. Then the theological wrangling began. Different factions presented their creeds in an attempt to find the right wording to express such complex doctrine. But the bishops under the guidance of Alexander and Athanasius refused to allow anything that might suggest Christ was a created being. Soon their "Nicene" party began to prevail.

At last a creed was formulated with which almost all the bishops could agree. In its most important sentence it claimed that Christ was "of the substance of the Father, God of God, Light of Light, true God of true God, begotten not made, consubstantial with the Father." Here the creed introduced a nonbiblical word which has nevertheless become the hallmark of Nicene Trinitarianism. It is still taught today by evangelicals as orthodox doctrine. The Greek word for "consubstantial" was *homoousios*, "of the same substance." This was a term the Arians could not get around. If the Father and the Son shared the same substance, then certainly the Son could not be a created being. To make sure the Arians were excluded unequivocally, the Nicene Creed added a conclusion which said, "The catholic and apostolic church condemns those who say 'There was when he was not,' or 'Before he was begotten he was not.'" This was a devastating blow to the Arians. Virtually everyone sided with Bishop Alexander and his protégé Athanasius. A couple of bishops refused to sign the creed, but they were promptly deposed. Arius was banished by the emperor himself. Even St. Nicholas (apparently not feeling so jolly that day) supposedly punched Arius in the nose! Though this story is no doubt as legendary as the later Christmas myths that developed around the saint, the overall picture we get is one of complete triumph for the Nicene party. Judging from the events at the Council of Nicaea, it would seem the Arians had been roundly defeated. But history still had some surprises in store.

Athanasius *Contra Mundum*

Bishop Alexander died three years after Nicaea. The natural choice to be the next bishop of Alexandria was Athanasius (though some claimed he was too young for the position since he was not quite thirty). Meanwhile, Emperor Constantine realized the theological debate had not disappeared. Though he had supported the decision of Nicaea, many of his actions after the council favored the Arians in an attempt to make everybody happy. He endorsed a middle-of-the-road position as exemplified by Eusebius (who tended to be, shall we say, more diplomatic than dogmatic on such matters). Soon Constantine ordered Bishop Athanasius to readmit Arius to the church. But Athanasius refused to do so because he believed Arius did not really accept the vital principle of Nicaea: *homoousios*, the identical substance of the Father and the Son.

Still trying to resolve the thorny debate, Constantine convened another council at a city called Tyre. Athanasius came reluctantly, but soon realized the council leaders had stacked the deck against him. So he slipped out of Tyre on a raft at night to evade his enemies, and headed up to Constantinople (the new imperial capital) to appeal directly to the emperor. But Constantine had gone to Jerusalem to attend the dedication of the Church of the Holy Sepulcher. There the bishops who had been at Tyre managed to win a declaration that the Arian position was congruent with the emperor's view. So they quickly reinstated Arius as a pastor. When Constantine arrived back in Constantinople, Athanasius finally got his audience with the emperor. But Athanasius's enemies had followed him from the council at Tyre to charge him with a new crime: not only was he guilty of opposing Arius, who had just been judged orthodox; he was even accused of hindering the precious Alexandrian grain shipments from reaching the capital city! Constantine demanded to know whether such high treason had any basis in fact. Athanasius vehemently denied the charges. Growing angry, he warned the emperor that God would be his judge in these matters. Because of the hot words thrown around that day, Athanasius was exiled to Trier on the German frontier. It would not be the last time the bishop would see exile.

When Constantine died in AD 337, the empire was divided among three of his sons. Eventually the middle son, Constantius, emerged as the most powerful of them. He would go on to have the longest reign. Unfortunately for Athanasius, Constantius favored the doctrines of Arius. By now Arianism had grown much bigger than its namesake could ever have imagined. Arius's theological views continued to spread throughout the East, though Arius himself had recently died. (He dropped dead in the bathroom from an explosive intestinal disorder—a death Athanasius considered to be a reflection of God's opinion of the man!)[18] Seeing that Arianism was thriving, the new co-emperor Constantius made it his imperial policy to propagate Arian Christianity throughout his jurisdiction. During the ensuing decades, Arianism grew even stronger. In fact, a neo-Arian party emerged which went so far as to say that the Son is "dissimilar" from the Father. This was a radically subordinationist view of Jesus Christ, against which Athanasius expended a great deal of effort.

Eventually Athanasius was allowed to return to his home church in Egypt. Nevertheless, Emperor Constantius made his life very difficult. The emperor once wrote a letter to the citizens of Alexandria in which he called Athanasius an "impostor and cheat" from the "lowest dens of infamy" who deserved to be killed "ten times over."[19] In another particularly dramatic incident, Athanasius's church was stormed during a midnight service by a mob of soldiers sent at Constantius's order. Somehow the bishop was able to slip through their midst, which he viewed as miraculous.[20] Yet he still endured several periods of exile over the years. These examples illustrate the lonely fight Athanasius waged against the great heresy of his day.

As we consider the difficulties Athanasius faced, we should acknowledge that he was not completely without friends. Athanasius had several strategic allies in his anti-Arian campaign. For one, the bishops of Rome through these decades supported the Nicene view against the Arian bishops. Athanasius often was able to find refuge in the Latin West under the protection of the Roman church. In addition, we would be remiss if we did not mention the three eastern church fathers who emerged in the AD 360s to defend Nicene Trinitarianism. They were from the region of Cappadocia, and so are called the Three Cappadocians: Gregory of Nazianzus, Basil of Caesarea, and his younger brother Gregory of Nyssa. The great Cappadocians were Athanasius's theological allies in the battle against Arianism. But Athanasius probably found his most loyal bastion of support among the monks who lived in the Egyptian desert. In particular, an elderly and pious monk named Anthony, whose biography Athanasius wrote and widely disseminated, was held in high esteem throughout the Christian world. Athanasius portrayed Anthony as a staunch opponent of the Arian heresy.[21] As time went on, efforts like these started to have an effect. Through vigorous networking with like-minded allies, and also through a massive outpouring of anti-Arian writings, Athanasius began to see his polemical efforts pay off. The torrent of Arianism at last slowed to a trickle.

In the last seven years of his ministry, Athanasius lived in Alexandria unmolested. The people of Egypt adored him, considering him a great hero of the faith. Arianism was finally on the decline, at least within the borders of the Roman Empire. When Athanasius died on May 2 in the year AD 373, he was celebrated by his people as having steadfastly defended the true doctrine of God and Christ. Unfortunately, he did not live to see Nicene Trinitarianism formally triumph. That occurred under Emperor Theodosius, the first emperor to be a staunch supporter of orthodox Christianity against the Arians. In AD 381, Theodosius convened the second universal council of the church: the great Council of Constantinople. Here the "Nicene Creed" assumed its final form—the form that is still used by Christians today. And at its heart remained the word *homoousios*, that essential theological term which declared the Father and Son to share the same substance. Both of them are fully God; both of them are eternal. If someday you should recite the Nicene Creed in church, perhaps you can think of the tenacious little bishop of Alexandria with a great big smile on his face.

Reflections on Athanasius

Why all this fuss? It's a reasonable question. Why was Athanasius so tenacious? What was the big deal here? Isn't this just quibbling about words? Certainly the Roman emperors thought so. They wanted peace and quiet in their realm, at any price. But Athanasius saw things differently. As we finish our journey with Athanasius, let's take a look at what was at stake for him theologically.

Athanasius possessed a profound understanding of the incarnation of Jesus Christ. The whole question of the Son's divinity was not some intellectual premise that could fit into a logical syllogism, as it was for many of the Arians. Rather, it mattered deeply to Athanasius because it was a question of Christian salvation.[22] For Athanasius, salvation meant much more than individually "getting saved" so as to escape hell or get to heaven. His theology centered on the relationship between the created world and the Uncreated God. The Bible assures us of God's loving disposition toward his creation, especially humankind. However, we must remember that God is immeasurably beyond us. We are separated from him by our status as created beings. Just as we were created out of nothing, so too, apart from God's grace, we will naturally fall back into nothingness. This situation has created a divine dilemma for God: he has made us in his image, yet as sinners we are perishing. What is to be done about this? The answer is the incarnation. In Christ, the one who is fully God in every respect became fully man as well. This perfect joining of divinity and humanity made it possible for all people to be joined with God. In a delightful treatise that every modern believer should read, called *On the Incarnation*, Athanasius lays out the patristic doctrine of salvation in very clear terms. He shows that the Word of God became flesh and dwelt among us, not only to reveal the Father, but to die on the cross in place of sinners who were fading into oblivion. In the resurrection, he triumphed over death. Only through Christ can humans transcend their finite creaturehood. In him, we share by grace in what God possesses by nature: eternal life. That is why Athanasius famously said, "He was made man so that we might be made God."[23] The Incarnate Christ had to be fully man and fully God in order to lift human beings back into God's life. Therefore, the full divinity of Christ was absolutely essential to human salvation—and Arius had to be refuted!

Athanasius's book *On the Incarnation* is widely available today in a little volume with an introduction by C. S. Lewis. Perhaps Professor Lewis's words will serve to summarize Athanasius's for relevance today. Lewis writes, "There is a strange idea abroad that in every subject the ancient books should be read only by the professionals, and that the amateur should content himself with the modern books . . . This mistaken preference for the modern books and this shyness of the old ones is nowhere more rampant than in theology."[24] Lewis urges all Christians to be like Athanasius: to steadfastly preserve the faith, and not be "drawn away into sub-Christian modes of thought" because of our "curious modern assumption that all changes of belief, however brought about, are necessarily exempt from blame."[25] Lewis goes on to say that Athanasius's enduring value comes from his willingness to

> [stand] for the Trinitarian doctrine, "whole and undefiled," when it looked as if all the civilised world was slipping back from Christianity into the religion of Arius—into one of those "sensible" synthetic religions which are so strongly recommended to-day and which, then as now, included among their devotees many highly cultivated clergymen. It is his glory that he did not move with the times; it is his reward that he now remains when those times, as all times do, have moved away.[26]

In our age of undiscerning Christianity, when churches too often have bought into American popular culture, nothing is needed more than believers like Athanasius who are willing to live boldly *contra mundum*.

Provocative Questions

1. Where is the "hole in the dike" today? What cultural forces threaten the church in the twenty-first century? In other words, as you observe the Christian scene, what teachings do you find most dangerous to the body of believers? What specific things could you do to "put your finger in the hole"?
2. Athanasius staked his life on the doctrine of the Trinity. Is this a doctrine worth defending today? Or is it something about which Christians can disagree? To ask it another way: Does scripture clearly teach it, or is it a matter of personal interpretation? See Genesis 1:26; Deuteronomy 6:4; Isaiah 48:16; Matthew 28:19; Luke 3:21–22; John 1:1–3; 20:28; and 2 Corinthians 13:14. Is the Trinity something you would speak about when witnessing?

3. What if Christ were not viewed as fully divine? Imagine he is a great moral teacher, a man of wisdom, a courageous social reformer—yet not God. What implications would this have in theology? What practical impact would this have on the Christian faith? Have you ever heard anyone say that Jesus was only a man? What would you say in response?

4. When Constantine came to power, church and state became linked together. Think about the good things this brought: persecution ceased; Christian values were added to the law; church leaders had influence with government officials; money was available to be spent on Christian purposes; the person of Jesus was widely discussed among the citizenry. In our own times, what benefits could come from evangelical Christians having political influence and money? Give specific examples. In what ways (if any) is political power a good thing for the church?

5. Now let's think about some negatives of close church-state relations. In what ways could evangelical Christians be corrupted by having political influence today? Again, give some examples. Having thought about the issues of questions 4 and 5, do you believe Constantine represents a triumph or a fall for the church? (Don't just take my position on this—what do you really think?) Drawing upon the lessons of history, how would you recommend evangelicals relate to government today?

Good Books to Dig Deeper

Many of Athanasius's writings can be found in the *Nicene and Post-Nicene Fathers*, Second Series, volume 4. A more readable edition of *On the Incarnation* is:

Athanasius: On the Incarnation: The Treatise De Incarnatione Verbi Dei. Introduction by C. S. Lewis. Crestwood, NY: St. Vladimir's Seminary Press, 1998 (orig. 1944).

The best scholarly survey of Athanasius's life in historical context (though it is not very sympathetic to Athanasius) is:

Barnes, Timothy D. *Athanasius and Constantius: Theology and Politics in the Constantinian Empire*. Cambridge, MA: Harvard University Press, 1993.

An overview of Athanasius's life and thought, with selections from his writings, is:

Anatolios, Khaled. *Athanasius*. New York: Routledge, 2004.

Two in-depth academic treatments of Athanasius's theology are:

Anatolios, Khaled. *Athanasius: The Coherence of His Thought*. New York: Routledge, 1998.

Pettersen, Alvyn. *Athanasius*. Ridgefield, CT: Morehouse Publishing, 1995.

The most comprehensive overview of the Arian controversy is:

Hanson, R. P. C. *The Search for the Christian Doctrine of God: The Arian Controversy 318–381*. Edinburgh: T&T Clark, 1988.

A Taste of Athanasius

On the Incarnation of the Word, various selections

This is Athanasius's most popular work. He wrote it early in his life, before the Arian controversy had reached crisis proportions. Yet the theology we discover here is the theology that would make Nicene Trinitarianism so worthy of unyielding defense. The dauntless bishop of Alexandria argued that the full deity of Christ is necessary for human salvation.

The treatise is addressed to a Christian, reminding us all of the saving truths in which we have believed. It also explains and defends the gospel to those who might raise skeptical questions. Athanasius articulates the essence of the Good News: humans are sinners separated from God; but Christ, who is both God and Man, is worthy to die in place of sinners and to offer eternal life through his resurrection. No one in the ancient church was more clear on this point than Athanasius. He is truly our spiritual ancestor.

Death was conquering us more and more. Corruption remained upon all humanity. Therefore the human race was falling into ruin. Man, who was rational and made in the image of God, was disappearing. The very handiwork of God was being destroyed. There was a law that we could not escape, because God had laid it down due to the original Transgression. From that time on, death legally prevailed against us. What was happening here was truly improper and unworthy!

So, with his rational creatures going to ruin, and such great works on the way to destruction, what was the good God to do? Was he supposed to let corruption master them? Was he supposed to let death hold them in its grasp? In that case, what good was it for God to have created them in the first place? It would have been better for them not to have been made, than to be made and then be abandoned to die.

It was simply impossible that God should permit the human race to be carried away into corruption. Such a thing would be unfitting, and unworthy of God's goodness.

Athanasius switches to the perspective of Christ the Logos . . .

The Logos saw the rational human race being destroyed. He saw death reigning over us through our corruption. He saw, too, how the threatened punishment from the original Transgression had inextricably bound corruption to us. Yet he also saw how unthinkable it would be for the law of death to be repealed without being fulfilled.[27] In other words, he saw that the events coming to pass were completely unacceptable! The very ones whom he had created were disappearing.

Furthermore, he could plainly see the excessive wickedness of men, and how, slowly but surely, they had piled up sins against themselves to an intolerable level. He saw that everyone is responsible for their own deaths. And so he had mercy on our race. He felt compassion for us in our weakness. He came down to us in our corruption. The Logos was unable to bear that death should gain the victory, that his creatures should perish, and that the work of his Father in mankind should come to nothing. That is why he took to himself a body—a body which is in every way the same as our own.

Now Athanasius focuses on the Crucifixion and Resurrection . . .

Jesus Christ made the creation itself abandon its silence. What a wondrous thing! In his death, or rather, in that triumphant monument of his death—I am referring to the cross—all creation confessed that he who was revealed in a body and who suffered was not just a mere man, but was the Son of God and the Savior of everyone. The sun was turned away [by darkness], and the earth quaked, and the mountains were shattered, and all creatures crouched down in awe. These things showed that Christ on the cross was God, and that all creation was his servant. In its fearful response, the creation was bearing witness to the presence of its Master.

Every person owed an outstanding debt that had to be paid. For as I have already said, everyone was due to die. This is above all why Christ came to live with us. His purpose was this: after he had proved his divinity from his works, he went on to offer a sacrifice on behalf of all, handing over his [bodily] temple to death in our place. He did this for two reasons. First, he wanted to free us and make us no longer liable to the original Transgression. Second, he wanted to show that he is stronger than death. In his own body he demonstrated that he is imperishable, and that he is the firstfruits of everyone's resurrection!

8

JOHN CHRYSOSTOM

Words have great power. They teach. They please. They persuade. The right words can delight us. As the book of Proverbs says, "A word fitly spoken is like apples of gold in a setting of silver" (Prov. 25:11). On the other hand, words can wound. King Solomon reminds us that "Death and life are in the power of the tongue, and those who love it will eat its fruits" (Prov. 18:21). The Apostle James gives us similar wisdom when he tells us the tongue is small yet powerful—like a bit which can control a horse, or a rudder which can control a ship. "No human being can tame the tongue," James writes. "It is a restless evil, full of deadly poison. With it we bless our Lord and Father, and with it we curse people who are made in the likeness of God" (James 3:8–9). The power of the spoken word is immense—for good or ill.

In modern times no one has wielded words more powerfully than Sir Winston Churchill, the heroic prime minister who led Great Britain through the dark days of World War II. Today he is regarded as the greatest orator of the twentieth century. In a time of crisis, Churchill's words steadied a nation. When Hitler's armies forced

France to surrender in 1940, his evil eye turned to the shores of England. The Nazis hoped a devastating blow to the Royal Air Force would bring England to its knees. British courage was faltering; many were calling for appeasement. Into that tenuous situation stepped Winston Churchill. He delivered speeches in Parliament and on the BBC that prepared England for war. Instead of bargaining with Hitler, he urged his countrymen to stand and fight with their blood, toil, tears, and sweat.

In the summer of 1940, Hitler's *Luftwaffe* was preparing to rain down destruction on southern England. But the new prime minister stood in the House of Commons on June 18 and offered the immortal words,

> The battle of France is over. I expect that the battle of Britain is about to begin. Upon this battle depends the survival of Christian civilization. Upon it depends our own British life, and the long continuity of our institutions and our Empire. The whole fury and might of the enemy must very soon be turned on us. Hitler knows that he will have to break us in this island or lose the war. If we can stand up to him all Europe may be free and the life of the world may move forward into broad, sunlit uplands; but if we fail, then the whole world, including the United States, and all that we have known and cared for, will sink into the abyss of a new dark age made more sinister, and perhaps more prolonged, by the lights of a perverted science. Let us therefore brace ourselves to our duty and so bear ourselves that if the British Commonwealth and Empire lasts for a thousand years, men will still say, "This was their finest hour."[1]

German bombers were over England in a matter of weeks after Churchill's speech. The long-running aerial engagement now bears the name he coined: the Battle of Britain. It was a decisive turning point in World War II. Though outmanned, the Royal Air Force stood firm and turned back the Nazi onslaught. Perhaps more importantly, the English people found their nerve. All who lived through those days remember the courage that was infused into their veins by their prime minister's stirring speeches. It was not just the power of guns and planes, but the power of words, that saved England in 1940.

Like twentieth century England, the ancient church drew strength from its own great orators. But these Christian orators were not political statesmen who stood in the Roman Forum to address the toga-clad aristocrats of the Senate. Rather, they were preachers who filled the great churches of the empire with their powerful sermons. Chief among these ancient preachers was the bishop of Constantinople, John Chrysostom (usually pronounced "Chris-SOS-tum"). His nickname means "Golden Mouth," for indeed that is what he had. Born around AD 349, John was educated under Libanius, the most outstanding orator of his day. A professor of rhetoric in Athens, Constantinople, and Antioch, Libanius reminds us of many modern university professors: brilliant, humane, learned—and hostile to the Christian faith. Libanius looked with disgust at the rise of Christianity. This background makes the deathbed quotation attributed to him all the more remarkable. When asked which of his students should succeed him in his professorship of rhetoric, Libanius replied, "It ought to have been John, had not the Christians stolen him from us."[2] John Chrysostom must have been a great communicator to have impressed his pagan teacher so much. Yet to Libanius's dismay, John used his speaking skills for the name of Jesus Christ.

In this chapter we will meet a church father whose "golden mouth" helped him rise to the highest ranks of the ancient church. John loved the Bible and preached it with passion to the adoring masses. Yet we will also discover that his bold and prophetic words got him in trouble with the political authorities. John Chrysostom was a complicated man. Though he served as a bishop in the splendid churches of the newly Christianized Roman Empire, he reserved his highest esteem for the lifestyle of the solitary hermit who contemplated God in simplicity. Though John would eventually become the most beloved of all the eastern church fathers, in his own day he was banished to die alone in exile. It is not easy to put John Chrysostom into a box. As we get to know him in this chapter, we'll gain insight into several facets of the ancient church in the fourth century. We will learn about its new monasticism, its scriptural interpretation, and its developing architecture. But most of all, we will learn about the power words command when they are marshaled by a master preacher like John the Golden Mouth.

Competing for the Prize

John was a widow's son. Even so, he was a son of privilege, for his father had been a high-ranking army administrator who left his family a substantial estate in Antioch. John's mother Anthusa, a devout Christian, resolved not to remarry even though she was only twenty when she was widowed. John later reported how difficult it was for such a young single mother to manage the family's property. To add to her troubles, the expense of John's education became a heavy burden. Nonetheless, this exceptional woman made sure her son received the best training available. When Libanius inquired one day about John's mother, and learned she was now forty and had lived without a man for two decades, he exclaimed, "Heavens! What women there are amongst the Christians!"[3]

John's fine education and public speaking skills would have opened many doors for him to pursue a distinguished career in the civic bureaucracy of Antioch. But this was not the life John had in mind. His deep spiritual interests drew him inexorably toward ministry in his local church. The bishop Meletius noticed this promising young man of eighteen and drew him into his inner circle. John received baptism and was named to the important position of *lector*, the reader of scripture in the ancient church service. Because he wanted to live the most godly life possible, John met regularly with other young men to read the Word, fast, pray, and hold each other accountable in temptation. They considered themselves to be spiritual brothers who had entered into a "contract with Christ."[4] Yet even as he expe-

rienced the joy of heightened devotion, John found himself longing
for something more. Finally he decided he must turn his back on
the busy life of the city to pursue solitude and ascetic rigor in the
craggy mountains above Antioch.[5]

For four years, John sojourned in the wilderness under the guidance of a spiritual mentor who lived with great self-discipline. High
on Mt. Silpius, overlooking the city below, John battled against his
flesh in order to defeat its desires.[6] In particular he struggled with
sexual temptation. During this period of his life, he believed avoidance of women was the only way to keep from sinning.[7] After John
had learned the basics of the ascetic life, he went off by himself for
two more years to live alone in a cave. He studied so much scripture
that he was able to memorize vast portions of the Old and New Testaments. Yet his lifestyle had become so austere that he began to do
physical damage to his body. John's ancient biographer wrote, "He
never relaxed for that two-year period, not in the days nor at night,
and his gastric organs became lifeless and the proper functions of the
kidneys were impaired by the cold."[8] In fact, for the rest of his life
John had digestive troubles. In Greek icons he is always depicted as
exceedingly slim, even gaunt. What could possibly drive a man to do
this to himself? Such asceticism is almost always misunderstood by
modern evangelicals. Too often, our outlook has more in common
with the American dream of "life, liberty, and the pursuit of happiness" than with a biblical view of bodily self-mortification. Perhaps
this a good place to talk about what the early church appreciated in
its monks and ascetics.

The word "monasticism" refers to a lifestyle of spiritual retreat
from the cares of the world to focus solely on God. Sometimes it was
pursued in solitude, and other times in a community. In addition
to worship, prayer, study, and Christian service, the monastic life
normally required *asceticism*: the disciplining of the body against
its fleshly desires.[9] In the ancient church we can discern a very early
monastic expression in the widows who lived together, devoted to
prayer and good works, as outlined in 1 Timothy 5. We also find

individuals in the second and third centuries who remained in their homes while practicing personal asceticism and celibacy. Origen is a good example of this. Alternatively, there were unmarried women and men who lived together under the same roof like spiritual brothers and sisters. It was a convenient arrangement, since there were certain social roles each could perform for the other (e.g., financial provision in exchange for domestic service). However, the church frowned on these arrangements due to the obvious temptations and lack of propriety they presented.[10] Such early ascetic tendencies crystallized into a more structured monastic movement in the fourth century. This was because, after the rise of Constantine, martyrs were no longer being made. The age of persecution had passed. So, monasticism became the new vehicle for expressing one's total devotion to Christ. The tears of repentance replaced the blood of the martyrs.

The earliest monastic movements blossomed in the deserts of Egypt and Syria. One by one, Christians experienced an irresistible call to spiritual retreat in lonely places. The most famous of these first monks was St. Anthony, whom we met in chapter 7. Athanasius had celebrated the life of this holy man by writing a biography which enjoyed wide approval in the ancient church. Due to writings like this, the ascetic life became extremely popular in the fourth century—especially among young people who were sold out for Christ and wanted to live boldly for him. At other times in church history, such passion for God has resulted in missions, evangelism, or aid to the poor. The ancient church was by no means devoid of these things. But for many early Christians, spiritual revival resulted in an ascetic way of life. As we consider this fact, we might be tempted to believe those monks should have chosen a vocation with more "practical" results. Let's think about that idea for a minute. Perhaps it's based on presuppositions we ought to question.

I have found that evangelical Christians often suffer from certain prejudices against monasticism. We suspect it was about spiritual showmanship, or Pharisaic legalism, or abandoning the world so as to become useless to the church. But the early Christians did not see it that way. They believed monks who were devoted to praying full-time did a great service for the body of Christ.[11] Would you criticize the feeble shut-in grandmother in your church because her time is spent in fervent prayer, seasoned with the Word, instead of in the many activities our churches offer? I wish that every church could have an army of prayer warriors like these! You don't have to be active and busy to have an impact for God. The shining example of godly saints can spur on many imitators. Of course, a shut-in grandmother does not have a choice about her form of ministry; her frailty dictates it. In contrast, the ancient ascetics adopted their lifestyle on purpose—often in the prime of their lives. In our comfortable homes, surrounded by our many luxuries, we can easily ask ourselves: why would the monks choose such a difficult path? The answer has to do, not with meritorious works, but with biblical commands.

I often tell my Christian college students that if they had lived in a different era, many of them—both male and female—would have been monks. This surprises them, for their image of monasticism has been colored by the decrepit form it took in the time of the Protestant Reformation, when it rightly became a target of criticism. In contrast to this corruption, the original spirit of monasticism in the ancient church was marked by a very biblical outlook on the spiritual disciplines. Perhaps our cozy Christianity has made us forget that the Bible often speaks of bodily renunciation.[12] Too often, we associate divine blessing with material possessions, whereas scripture calls us to a hard road of discipleship. The Apostle Paul wrote in 1 Corinthians 9:24–27, "I discipline my body and keep it under control." This translation of the original Greek is not inaccurate, but I think it is much too tame. Literally the text says, "I mistreat my body and make it my slave." Why does Paul do this? He reminds us, "Every athlete exercises self-control in all things. They do it to receive a perishable wreath, but we an imperishable." In other words, Christians are urged toward a life of asceticism to win an eternal prize. Scripture constantly tells us that the flesh can only be defeated through hard effort. In one of the best books I have ever read on this subject, my former pastor Kent Hughes calls it "spiritual sweat."[13] When we put monasticism into a biblical perspective, there is much about it we can appreciate. It is not really about works salvation or earning credit with God through self-imposed ordeals. In the ancient church, asceticism usually emerged from a concern to take scripture seriously when it says, "Those who belong to Christ Jesus have crucified the flesh with its passions and desires" (Gal. 5:24).

If the ancient monks were not driven by outward religious duty, what motivated them? Let me draw an analogy from my teaching experience. Whenever I address monasticism in the classroom, a few students invariably tell me later that they deeply resonated with what I was saying. I once had a student stay after class to disclose with tears in her eyes that she longed to pursue Jesus with such a heightened level of devotion (and later she was honored by God with great suffering). My theory is that young people connect so well with monastic ideals because they are in the process of sorting out their loves. In my ministry among college students, I have often observed the little glances, the shy smiles, the teasing flirtations that occur between the sexes. Perhaps this is perfectly innocent for the unattached. But what happens when you make an exclusive commitment? Then those things must cease; for if they continue they will undermine your fidelity to your beloved. The ancient ascetics understood with great clarity what every boyfriend or girlfriend instinctively knows: that competing loves must be put away, or they will seduce you and crowd out your devotion to your one and only. Applied on the spiritual plane, the ancients perceived that a passionate, mystical love for God will be injured when the desires of the flesh vie for attention. I suggest this message is not only for college students in the throes of infatuation, but for all who know something about the sacrifice involved in true love.

With this in mind, I hope we are now in a better position to understand John Chrysostom. Some Christians might fault him for not taking proper care of his "temple" in those cold Syrian caves. I'm not sure I'm qualified to pass judgment on that matter. But I do know we should not fault John for the passionate love of God he possessed. At its best, monasticism in the ancient church was a vehicle for growing closer to the Lord and taking one's spiritual life to the next level. It afforded ample time for prayer, contemplation, silence, and worship—as well as something else that a learned man like John could pursue: the reading of scripture. In the pages to come, we will discover that John had a distinctive approach in his handling of God's Word.

"Theorizing" with Scripture

After six years at the mountain top, John came back to earth. His health was simply too poor to remain among the monks in their high huts and caves. After a period of time to regain his strength, John resumed his duties as lector in the church of Antioch. A few years later he was made a deacon. But it was not until eight years after his descent from the mountain that John was called to become an ordained presbyter. As such, he now took on the responsibility of public preaching. This was to be John's greatest calling—as well as his downfall. Over nine hundred of his sermons still survive, while many more have been lost to history. There is scarcely any biblical book, moral topic, theological point, or issue of his day, that John Chrysostom did not tackle. His sermons provide us a wealth of insight into the power of the preacher in the ancient church. Such power could bring great benefit; yet it could make enemies too.

In his sermons John reveals his deep devotion to the Bible. The man with the golden mouth used the power of his words to unleash the power of the Word. Today we would call him an "expositor" of the scriptures. At times his homilies sound more like Bible commentaries, as he provides verse-by-verse exposition of the sacred text.[14] But there is something important we should note here. When John interpreted the Bible, he used a very different method than what we have already seen in Origen. Origen's "Alexandrian" method of allegorization had a long history among the ancient Greeks, who used it to reinterpret their embarrassing mythology to find a more profound meaning. In the early church, Origen applied some of the same principles to the text of scripture. Yet not everyone agreed with what the great scholar of Alexandria had done with the Bible. A school of thought arose in opposition to allegorical exegesis, and this school was centered in the Syrian city of Antioch. Therefore, modern scholars of early Christianity make a distinction between the "Alexandrian" and "Antiochene" approaches to biblical interpretation.[15] While we have discussed the Alexandrian method in chapter 6, we have not yet looked at the Antiochene approach. This we must do if we are to understand John Chrysostom.

During the time John lived in Antioch prior to his ascetic withdrawal to Mt. Silpius, he had come under the influence of a teacher named Diodore (who eventually went on to be the bishop of Tarsus, the hometown of the Apostle Paul). Diodore's role in Antioch was to provide spiritual oversight for the earnest young men who had entered into sacred brotherhood.[16] John Chrysostom was greatly affected by the time he spent at Diodore's feet. The fact that he later delivered a sermon called *Commendation of Diodore* demonstrates the esteem in which he held his master. The same could be said for John's good friend and fellow-student Theodore, whose destiny was to become the bishop of Mopsuestia.[17] These three men—Diodore of Tarsus, Theodore of Mopsuestia, and John Chrysostom—are known today as leading figures in the "Antiochene" school of biblical interpretation.

Diodore's writings have come down to us rather incompletely. Yet we are fortunate to have his commentary on the Psalms, in which he lays out the differences between Alexandrian and Antiochene exegesis. Basically, the dispute is over the meaning of the word *allegory*. Diodore wrote,

> Holy Scripture knows the term "allegory" but not its application. Even the blessed Paul uses the term: "This is said by way of allegory,

for they are two covenants" [Gal. 4:24]. But his use of the word and his application are different from that of the Greeks. The Greeks speak of allegory when something is understood in one way but said in another.[18]

Diodore then provides an example. In Greek mythology, Zeus calls the goddess Hera his sister and his wife. Because a literal reading would imply that the father of the gods had intercourse with his sister, the Greeks allegorized the text to make it speak instead about certain natural elements which have different affinities and can be mixed in different ways. Of course, earth science was not the point intended by the original author. But through allegory, a more acceptable symbolic meaning could be discovered—though admittedly, it bore little relation to the original intent of the narrative. For Diodore, such illegitimate reinterpretations were what the Christian allegorists were doing when they found new meanings in scripture:

> Those who pretend to "improve" Scripture and who are wise in their own conceit have introduced allegory because they are careless about historical substance, or they simply abuse it. They follow not the apostle's intention, but their own vain imagination, forcing the reader to take one thing for another.[19]

In this way, the Antiochene school sought to rein in some of the wild speculations they found in Alexandrian exegesis.

So what method did the Antiochenes propose instead? If they abhorred what they saw as Alexandria's allegorical fancy, how did they proceed to interpret scripture? Diodore was faced with a difficult balancing act. On the one hand, he had to find spiritual meaning in the Bible. He could not interpret the text only according to "the letter" as the Jews were said to do. If the literal/historical meaning were the only meaning, then the Bible (and Diodore is thinking of the Old Testament here) would become nothing more than a history book for the Jews. It would have no prophetic or christological significance for the church. On the other hand, Diodore wanted to

avoid the extravagance he perceived in the Alexandrians, for whom
the literal sense could be left behind. In fact, the Alexandrians sometimes even regarded the literal reading as an intentional error inserted
by God as a divine stumbling block to prompt a search for the spiritual meaning! To reach a middle ground between the literal and
the spiritual, Diodore and the other Antiochenes offered the term
theoria to explain their methodology. He wrote,

> Scripture does not repudiate in any way the underlying prior history
> but "theorizes," that is, it develops a higher vision (*theoria*) of other
> similar events in addition, without abrogating history.[20]

> One thing is to be watched: *theoria* must never be understood as
> doing away with the underlying sense; it would then be no longer
> *theoria* but allegory. For whenever anything else is said apart from
> the foundational sense, we have not *theoria* but allegory. Even the
> apostle [Paul] did not discard history at any point, although he could
> introduce *theoria* and call it allegory.[21]

Therefore, for the Antiochene exegetes the literal sense served as the
essential foundation for any spiritual meaning that might be discovered.[22] This was their basic difference from the Alexandrians.

When John Chrysostom came to the biblical text, it was the Antiochene method he put into practice. Commenting on Galatians
4:24 (the key verse which mentions allegory), John asserted that Paul
had used the term *allegory* in a way that was "contrary to usage."[23]
Paul did not intend to leave behind the historical sense, as Greek
allegory often did. Rather, he created a typology in which certain
events in the lives of Hagar and Sarah were able to speak "somewhat
farther" into the future, to describe the old and new covenants that
Christians can discern. John compares typology to a man who has
drawn a picture of a king.[24] The outline sketch will be recognized for
what it is, so that the viewer will say, "Lo, there is the king." However,
once the outline has been painted in full color, the bare lines are
no longer visible, and the picture is now comprehended in much

greater detail. In the same way, the Old Testament must be read in light of the fuller revelation that Christ has brought. Like the Alexandrians, John insisted that spiritual truths were to be drawn from the original narratives. Both John and Origen were willing to seek a higher meaning in the text of scripture. To fail to do so would be to turn the Bible into a history book instead of the church's book. Yet John's exegesis avoided the speculative leaps that the Alexandrians often made. He argued that any higher meaning must correspond to what the text literally said in its original setting.

A New Rise to New Heights

John's preaching in Antioch proved extremely popular with the Christian masses. He had a knack for making the literal meaning of scripture relevant to his congregation's needs. His illustrations were colorful, his topics timely and pertinent. The people of Antioch thronged to his church—often to be entertained by his speaking skills as much as to be edified by his content! In any era, such a gifted preacher will be sought by other congregations. One day in AD 397, John received an imperial order to appear at a martyr's church outside the northern gate of Antioch. From there he was whisked away in a carriage and given some stunning news. He was to be made a bishop—and not just any bishop, but the *bishop of Constantinople*, the eastern capital of the Roman Empire![25] John's time of fruitful pastoral ministry at Antioch had come to an end. It had been a period relatively free from political intrigue. Unfortunately, John would soon find himself fighting for his political life (and even his physical life) at Constantinople.

A nasty web of imperial and ecclesiastical politics was being spun around John Chrysostom as he journeyed toward the capital city. Much of the ugliness that would ensue can be traced to the long-standing rivalry between Alexandria and Antioch. The two cities had always been competitors, ever since their founding in the wake

of Alexander the Great's conquests three centuries before the time
of Jesus. In Christian times, theology had become the weapon of
choice. Athanasius of Alexandria, for example, had been opposed
by the Syrian Arians. Likewise, we have just seen how biblical interpretation could be a source of contention between the rival cities.
And in chapter 10, we will discover that the doctrine of Christ's
person will once again cause a theological war between Antioch
and Alexandria.

In the age of Imperial Christianity, church controversies were
not fought solely through scathing pamphlets and Sunday morning
diatribes. They inevitably involved behind-the-scenes conniving to
gain the support of the political powers. This is exactly what we find
in the case of John Chrysostom. When Constantinople's previous
bishop had died, the bishop down in Alexandria, named Theophilus, immediately recognized an opportunity to seize political influence. He had a favorite protégé whom he wanted to install in the
vacancy. Perhaps you can imagine Theophilus's frustration when he
found out that, not only had his candidate been rejected, but that
John Chrysostom—an Antiochian!—was to be given this powerful
position.[26] From that day, Theophilus became John's sworn enemy.
He was an ambitious schemer who wanted to advance Alexandria's
power against Antioch or Constantinople. This was the ugly world
John entered as a brand-new bishop in the imperial capital.

But it was also a splendid world into which John had come. We
can hardly underestimate the grandeur of this ancient city, which
at the time was being hailed as the New Rome. Founded more than
a thousand years earlier by migrating Greeks as the little village of
Byzantium (from which we get the term "Byzantine Empire"), the
settlement had grown into a sizeable town due to its strategic location. Two continents, Europe and Asia, meet there. Even today,
modern Istanbul's bridges connect West and East in a very tangible
way. The city guards a narrow intercontinental waterway called the
Bosporus, through which all ships from the Black Sea must pass
to gain access to the wider Mediterranean. Emperor Constantine

had recognized precisely this strategic value of Byzantium when he chose it to become New Rome, or as it came to be called, *Constantinou polis*—the City of Constantine. In AD 330 he rededicated the city, quadrupled its size, and began to adorn it with new imperial buildings and stout walls. He also gave free bread to all its citizens to ensure their prosperity. But then Constantine did something no previous emperor had done. He decreed that several grand churches be erected in his new Christian capital. Let's pause for a moment to get a sense of the spectacular new architecture that had developed in John Chrysostom's time.

The story of Christian art and architecture is conveniently divided into pre- and post-Constantinian periods. Prior to Constantine, Christian art tended to be simple. It was the art of the common person, carried out in a rather primitive style—as seen, for example, in the ancient burial catacombs around Rome. Though beautiful in its own way, such early efforts cannot be called "high art." The necessary economic resources were not yet available for Christians to create lavish artistic works or to build on a large scale. Therefore, virtually no Christian buildings have survived from before the fourth century.[27]

Everything changed with Constantine's rise to power. Across the empire, he financed the construction of many new churches. Among them was a new cathedral in Constantinople called the Great Church, later known as the Church of Hagia Sophia, or Holy Wisdom.[28] Today the resplendent building on this site is not the one Constantine ordered to be built, for it burned down in a riot when John Chrysostom was sent into exile. The Hagia Sophia we see today was dedicated in AD 537. No contemporary visitor to Istanbul should bypass this magnificent edifice. It is a world-class monument to the splendor of the Byzantine Empire. Yet even in John's day, his congregation marveled at the grandeur of his timber-roofed cathedral.[29] The Great Church was eclipsed only by another stunning building in the city: the Church of the Holy Apostles. When John preached from there, he was preaching from the church that not only held the bodily remains of Emperor Constantine in its mausoleum, but also what were believed to be the bones of Luke, Andrew, and Timothy. Although today we cannot visit these original churches where John Chrysostom ministered, we can gain a sense of their beauty from a description recorded by Eusebius. Speaking about the Church of the Holy Apostles, he wrote:

> This building [Constantine] carried to a vast height, and brilliantly decorated by encasing it from the foundation to the roof with marble slabs of various colors. He also formed the inner roof of finely fretted work, and overlaid it throughout with gold. The external covering, which protected the building from the rain, was of brass instead of tiles; and this too was splendidly and profusely adorned with gold, and reflected the sun's rays with a brilliancy which dazzled the distant beholder. The dome was entirely encompassed by a finely carved tracery, wrought in brass and gold.[30]

When we picture John Chrysostom preaching from a shining church like this, we can only be amazed at how far he has come from his cave on Mt. Silpius!

Yet in another sense, we must recognize that John never really left the monastic experience of his youth. It was his unwillingness to compromise with worldly standards that had first driven him to the mountains of Antioch. Now, having arrived at the summit of imperial power and ecclesiastical prestige, John once again refused to compromise. Dressed in the fine robes befitting his office, and surrounded by the grandeur of architectural masterpieces, the man at the center of it all remained a monk at heart. The values John had learned in the wilderness—disdain for sensual pleasures and the trivial pursuits of a vain society—were the same values he advocated from his episcopal chair. Seated before his standing congregation, his sermons thundered forth with righteous anger. However, unlike at Antioch, John now had political enemies with the power to defeat him.

The new bishop embarked on a radical course of reform, based on the austere principles he had embraced all his life. For example, he instituted stricter standards for the corrupt clergy he found in the city, purging out the bad apples (such as two deacons who had been charged with murder and fornication).[31] He sold many church treasures to fund hospitals for the sick and for lepers. And he quickly put an end to the extravagant banquets his predecessors had been accustomed to offer. John believed the church's money should be spent on the poor, not on expensive parties thrown by bishops. Such actions caused the social elite in Constantinople to resent their new pastor, whom they viewed as something of a spoilsport. When John ate his meager meals alone in his private quarters, the grumbling among the aristocrats couldn't be stifled.

But despite strong actions like these, it was John's public words that got him in the most trouble. When he decried the corruption and sensuality he saw in the imperial court, powerful forces began to stir against this reformer. Theophilus of Alexandria, who had been watching and waiting for the right moment, now saw his chance. He seized upon an ill-chosen expression in one of John's sermons. Preaching against imperial opulence, John had apparently referred to the emperor's wife as "Jezebel," the harlot queen of the Old Testament. Making the most of this opportunity, Theophilus used a church council (pertaining to a completely different issue) to trump up charges of sedition against John. The many people whose morality John had criticized over the years now leapt at the chance to get revenge. The final outcome was dire: John was banished from his congregation and sent to a remote village in the cold, bandit-infested mountains. There the exiled bishop—much loved by his people but resented by the rich and powerful—lived out his remaining years in cheerless desolation. He spent the long hours writing poignant letters to his friends back in Constantinople. And so the great ascetic, who had always revered the monastic life, died in a place of lonely isolation. It was intended to be a shameful punishment. But perhaps there was no better place for John Chrysostom to end his earthly sojourn than in suffering and solitude, away from the busy capital with its opulence and power.

Reflections on John Chrysostom

In coming to terms with John Chrysostom, we are inevitably struck by the power of words. Here was a man who preached with passion and conviction. For all Christians, the words spoken by the pastor standing in the pulpit as God's man for the hour constitute a holy treasure. When based on diligent scriptural preparation and the Spirit's empowerment, the preacher's choice words can become a divine call to a higher standard. Who hasn't been deeply moved by a sermon that celebrated the sacrifice involved in foreign missions? Who hasn't cringed with heartfelt repentance at a prophetic denunciation of sin? Who hasn't been led by a preacher's vivid imagery into the warmth of God's all-encompassing love? The pastor who expounds the Word of God before his people holds an awesome power within his mouth. His words can be a source of golden treasure.

Yet John Chrysostom also reminds us that words can injure. We can see this in his scathing remarks about the Jews. In his day (unlike our own) Judaism constituted a significant threat to Christianity. John had seen many in his congregation at Antioch be drawn to the ancient and revered rites of the Jews, which undercut the church's standing.[32] Ever since the time of Ignatius of Antioch, this had been a problem in the city. To mitigate this threat to his flock, John resorted to highly inflammatory words against the Jews. His attacks on the Chosen People do not deserve to be defended. It is unfortunate but true that John Chrysostom plays a large role in the history of Christian anti-Semitism. I mention this not to leave us with a bad impression of John, but to remind us of the power of words—for good or ill.

Despite his faults, the early church's foremost preacher demands our respect. Our spiritual ancestor John Chrysostom died with his dignity intact. The powerful authorities who banished him kept insisting that he be pushed further into isolation. They even offered the cruel soldiers a pay bonus if he were to die in transit. For three months, poor John was forced to travel in the pouring rain or with the hot sun beating on his bald head. John's emaciated body, already weakened from his years of asceticism, began to shrivel like "an apple turning ripe in the sun on the topmost branch of a tree."[33] At last, on a forced march, John collapsed in the road after only a few miles. He was taken to a nearby martyr's shrine, where he changed into clean white robes. There he partook of his final communion, marked himself with the sign of the cross, and lifted his feet onto the bed to be received by Christ. John Chrysostom's last recorded words were, "Glory to God for all things."[34] The celebrated orator, who had poured forth his golden speech in some of the greatest churches of the Roman Empire, never uttered anything more profound.

Provocative Questions

1. How has reading this chapter changed your view of monasticism? Describe a time you have experienced spiritual refreshment through a retreat from the everyday world. Or imagine you could take one week to be completely alone for the purpose of sacred contemplation. Where would you go? How would you spend your time? Would you fast? In what ways do you think it would be difficult? What temptations might you face? Read Matthew 4:1–11 and Luke 4:1–13. What do you notice in these texts that gives you insight into Jesus's own experience of spiritual retreat and temptation?

2. In chapter 6 you encountered Alexandrian biblical interpretation, and now you have read about the Antiochene method. Which one attracts you more? Why? How do you know when a spiritual truth is valid? How do we avoid reading our own ideas into the text of scripture? Consider a sample text such as the Song of Songs (the Alexandrians and Antiochenes both wrote commentaries on this book, but came to very different conclusions about it). What kind of truths does it intend to teach us today?

3. How do you feel about spending large sums of money on architecture or decorations for a church? Assuming we all recognize that the church is the *people*, not the *building*, does that mean the building is therefore irrelevant? In your opinion, when does architectural splendor go too far? How do you balance practical needs such as serving the poor with the need to make a place of worship visually appealing? Does Matthew 26:6–13 address this issue? In what ways does your church incorporate art into its communal life? Is art a form of worship? Is beauty inherently God-pleasing?

4. Describe a time you have been powerfully affected by a sermon. To what do you attribute the impact it had on your life? Did the sermon spur you to action? Can you think of a word picture a preacher has described so vividly you can still recall it today? What point was the preacher trying to illustrate? In your church, is the sermon the focal point of the service? What kind of "preaching style" does your pastor tend to use? Is your pastor a teacher? An expositor? A colorful storyteller? An orator? What themes are emphasized in your pastor's sermons? What does your pastor do that grabs your attention and draws you in?

5. Have you ever experienced the impact of hurtful words? What kind of words were they? Lies? Slander? Gossip? Criticism? Flattery? Harshness? Have you ever hurt someone deeply with your words? What wisdom does James 3:1–12 offer us about the use of words among Christians?

Good Books to Dig Deeper

Many of John Chrysostom's works can be read in the *Nicene and Post-Nicene Fathers*, First Series, volumes 9–14. Two other sources for his prolific output are the series *Fathers of the Church* (Catholic University of America Press) and *Ancient Christian Writers* (Newman Press).

An ancient biography of John Chrysostom, written by his contemporary Palladius, can be read in:

Meyer, Robert T. *Palladius: Dialogue on the Life of St. John Chrysostom.* Ancient Christian Writers. Vol. 45. New York: Newman Press, 1985.

By far the best overview of John Chrysostom's life, combining scholarly detail and delightful readability, is:

Kelly, J. N. D. *Golden Mouth: The Story of John Chrysostom: Ascetic, Preacher, Bishop.* Grand Rapids: Baker, 1995.

A very good but much shorter biography, along with an excellent selection of primary texts, can be found in:

Mayer, Wendy and Pauline Allen. *John Chrysostom.* New York: Routledge, 2000.

A Taste of John Chrysostom

Homily on the Statues 17.9–10, 12

During the Easter season of AD 387, the whole city of Antioch cowered in fear of Emperor Theodosius. A new imperial tax had been announced in the city, and in the protest that followed some rioters had pulled down or defaced the bronze statues of the emperor and his family. Everyone knew such an affront to the statues was an insult to the emperor himself. High treason like that could only call down his immediate wrath. Theodosius was indeed prone to handing out harsh punishments for rebellion. In fact, a few years later he ordered the massacre of 7,000 citizens at Thessalonica for a riot there. The Antiochians had every reason to fear swift retaliation from the Roman government for their riotous behavior (see Acts 19:40 for a similar situation).

As John's congregation fretted about the impending consequences of the riot, he preached a series of Lenten sermons that have come to be called the "Homilies on the Statues." Soon the imperial verdict was handed down. City councilmen were executed, bread distribution to the poor was suspended, and the theater, horse track, and public baths were closed. But worst of all, the city was stripped of its prestigious status as a "metropolis." John's "Homily 17" used this punishment as an opportunity to define for the Christians of Antioch the true basis for their city's greatness. Notice his rich imagery, his use of scripture, and his stern yet loving pastoral exhortation.

Certainly the emperor's decree hurts. But really, these things aren't so burdensome. They've actually brought great benefit to us! Tell me: What is so grievous about what has happened? That the emperor has closed the theater? That he's made the horse-racing track out of bounds? That he's plugged up and buried these fountains of wickedness? May they never be opened again! It was from them that the roots of evil grew out into the city. From them came the men who bring down our city's reputation. They sell their voices by cheering on the erotic dancers, and drunkenly hand over their salvation to them for three cents! Those men turn everything upside down. My beloved, is this why you're upset? These things should instead make you rejoice and be glad. You ought to express gratitude to the emperor because his punishment has become your correction, his penalty your education, and his anger your instruction . . .

Are you grieving that our city's dignity has been stripped away? Well it's time to learn a lesson about what gives a city true dignity. Then you'll clearly understand that so long as the inhabitants themselves don't give it up, no one else will be able to remove our city's honor. It's not about having the rank of metropolis, nor being filled with large and beautiful buildings. It's not about being adorned with many columns and spacious porticoes and covered walkways.[35] It's not about being publicly celebrated by other cities. Rather, greatness comes from the virtue and piety of its inhabitants. That's what gives a city its dignity and ornamentation and security. If these things aren't found, then even if the city were to enjoy countless honors from emperors, it would be the most worthless place of all.

Do you want to learn about the dignity of your city? Do you want to discover its heritage? I'll tell you precisely what it is—not just so you can know about it, but so you can strive for it too. What's the greatest honor of our city? "It was in Antioch that the disciples were first called Christians" (Acts 11:26). No other city throughout the world can make this claim—not even the city of Romulus itself![36] This is why Antioch can look the whole world in the eye: because of that love for Christ, that boldness of speech, that manly courage [displayed by the first Christians].

Do you want to hear of another honor and praise for the city? One time a very severe famine was approaching, and the inhabitants of Antioch decided, as much as each one was able, to send an offering to the saints in Jerusalem (Acts 11:27–30). Behold this second honor: kindness in the midst of famine! The hard times didn't hold them back, nor did the expectation of disaster make them hesitate. At a time when people are normally trying to gather up something from others, the Antiochians freely gave out of their own means—not only to those nearby, but to those far away! Can you see their faith in God and unconditional love for their neighbors?

Perhaps you want to learn still more about the honor of this city? Certain men came down from Judaea to Antioch who were muddying the gospel by introducing Jewish rituals (Acts 15:1). The Antiochians couldn't bear this innovation in silence or keep quiet. So they came together and formed a council. They sent Paul and Barnabas to Jerusalem, making sure that the apostles disseminated pure doctrine throughout the whole world, freed from all Jewish disease. *This* is the honor of a city! *This* is its privileged position before all! *This* is what makes it a metropolis—not on earth, but in heaven! All other honors are perishable and fleeting. They pass away with our present life. In fact they often come to an end even before our life does, as has happened now. To me, a city whose citizens don't love God is more worthless than any country village, and more dishonored than any cave! . . .

If you're a Christian, you don't have a city on earth. God himself is "the designer and builder" of our city (Heb. 11:10). Even if we were to possess the whole world, we would still be "foreigners and travelers" in every land (Heb. 11:13). Our names are engraved in heaven. Our citizenship is there. So let's not be like little children, who overlook what is truly great, and admire what is of no account. Remember: it is not the prominence of our city, but the virtue of our souls, that provides our true adornment and security!

9

AUGUSTINE

In 1990 a young man named Chris McCandless set out on a journey of self-discovery.[1] As a recent college graduate from an affluent suburban home, he was like many middle-class youth in wanting to experience the freedom of the open road. What made Chris different was the extreme restlessness within his soul. Heading west from Atlanta in a beat-up Datsun, Chris charted a course into the unknown. Eventually the blazing heat of an Arizona summer killed his car. Yet he did not despair; for as the layers of security on which modern people depend were peeled back, Chris felt an exhilaration in his newfound freedom. He buried his worldly possessions in the sand and ceremoniously burned the only money he had to his name. Now the true journey began.

Chris wholeheartedly embraced the life of the wanderer. In fact, he would later give himself the name "Supertramp." He meandered across the majestic western landscape, hiking in national parks, canoeing the Colorado River all the way to Mexico, and working occasionally in no-name towns when he needed a little cash. His travels brought him extraordinary hardship and peril: he lived on plain rice for days at a time, and endured exposure to the harsh elements. The suburban boy from Virginia fell in among the drifters and derelicts who populate the homeless underworld of the American West. Through it all, Chris always kept moving. His wanderlust never seemed to be satisfied. Though he sometimes entertained the idea of abandoning his tramping lifestyle, his "itchy feet" inevitably got the best of him, carrying him off to somewhere new.

In time Alaska began to sound its siren's call. To Chris, the last frontier was the ultimate destination for the ultimate wanderer. In a cryptic postcard to one of his few friends, he wrote, "It might be a very long time before I return South. If this adventure proves fatal and you don't ever hear from me again, I want you to know your [*sic*] a great man. I now walk into the wild." And that is exactly what he did. Having hitchhiked up through the Yukon Territory, Chris found himself in the rugged foothills around Alaska's Mt. McKinley. Snow was still on the ground one April day when Chris said goodbye to the stranger who had given him a lift. Then he walked off the edge of the world.

Hiking deep into the wilderness, Chris stumbled across the shelter that would be his home for 113 days—and then would become his tomb. He found an old abandoned bus that had served as a makeshift refuge for hunters. Now Chris moved in. Exhilarated at the prospects of his grand adventure, he scrawled a manifesto on a piece of plywood in his new home:

> Two years he walks the earth. No phone, no pool, no pets, no cigarettes. Ultimate freedom. An extremist. An aesthetic voyager whose home is the road. Escaped from Atlanta. Thou shalt not return, 'cause "the West is the best." And now after two rambling years comes the final and greatest adventure. The climactic battle to kill the false being within and victoriously conclude the spiritual pilgrimage. Ten days and nights of freight trains and hitchhiking bring him to the Great White North. No longer to be poisoned by civilization he flees, and walks alone upon the land to become lost in the wild.

Perhaps you can sense this young man's palpable longing for spiritual rest. He was wandering the earth, trying to find ultimate meaning and fulfillment. Instead he found disaster. Though he was able to subsist for several months on berries, roots, and small game, Chris began to grow weak on such a meager diet. Then he made a fatal mistake: he ate some poisonous seeds that rendered him too sick to hunt. With his body already in starvation mode, he went downhill quickly. In desperation he penned a heartbreaking plea: "S.O.S. I need your help. I am injured, near death, and too weak to hike out of here. I am all alone, this is no joke. In the name of God, please remain to save me. I am out collecting berries close by and shall return this evening. Thank you, Chris McCandless. August?" But help did not arrive in time. Three weeks later, some hunters discovered the pitiful note. And inside the bus they found the emaciated corpse of the Supertramp.

In this chapter we will meet an ancient church father who, like Chris McCandless, was a restless wanderer. Both of them were in spiritual turmoil. Both roamed far and wide, trying to find peace in various sources. But unlike the modern-day voyager, Augustine of Hippo found rest during his lifetime. The motif of the restless wanderer is a central theological concept for Augustine. In a famous expression at the beginning of his autobiography, he cried out to God, "Our heart is restless, until it rests in you."[2] He was describing the fundamental spiritual longing which many try to satisfy in inferior ways, but which God alone can truly satisfy. Augustine eventually discovered what the Supertramp never did: that real peace only comes from knowing God through Jesus Christ.

Yet Augustine of Hippo always remembered what it was like to be a restless wanderer. In fact, two of his most significant writings use the image of the wanderer to articulate their main points. In his *City of God*, Augustine pictured the Christian as an alien or exile in the world. Believers must wander far from their heavenly home while sojourning temporarily in the City of Man. And in his *Confessions*, Augustine used the concept of restlessness to narrate the story of his own life's journey. Certainly he discovered through firsthand experience that the human heart is restless until it rests in God.

So let's take this opportunity to journey with Augustine on his spiritual odyssey. By God's grace, his story does not end in tragedy like that of Chris McCandless, but in victory through Jesus. Augustine has offered us a window into his soul by writing his autobiography, the *Confessions*. The work is a treasure of church history that no Christian should fail to read at some point. What did Augustine mean by "confession"? The Latin word *confessio* had connotations that may be unfamiliar to the modern reader. When we think of "confession," we think of owning up to our sins. The person who "confesses" is either a criminal who admits his crimes before the authorities, or on a more spiritual level, is a Christian who seeks forgiveness from a faithful and just God. Certainly Augustine showed himself willing to confess his sins. His work is a masterpiece of transparency with respect to his evil deeds and the darkness of his heart. But it is much more than this. A "confession" in the Augustinian sense is also a "testimony."[3] It is the act of bearing witness to the unfathomable greatness of divine grace in the midst of human sin. Today we often ask our fellow Christians (especially if they were infamous sinners) to "share their testimony." We do this because we want to hear God's goodness rehearsed in our presence, witnessing the transforming power of his mercy and grace. That is exactly what Augustine's spiritual autobiography sought to do. It was written as a prayer: a spiritual offering poured out through pen and ink before the Heavenly Father. As we get to know Augustine through his *Confessions*, let's journey alongside him as he shares his testimony with us.

A Restless Wanderer

Augustine was born in sin. This is a point he makes right at the beginning of his *Confessions*. (It's also a theological conviction whose defense occupies much of his later life; but more on that in a moment.) He remarks that even as an infant he was selfish and demanding, bawling loudly to get his way. Though he obviously cannot recall those days, Augustine views such childish behavior as evidence that all people are sinners from birth. "The feebleness of infant limbs is innocent," he writes, "not the infant's mind."[4] Augustine has observed babies who cannot yet speak, but who still express furious jealousy when their siblings receive their mother's milk. "If 'I was conceived in iniquity and in sins my mother nourished me in her womb' (Ps. 51:5), I ask you, my God, I ask, Lord, where and when was your servant innocent?"[5] The implied answer is, "Never." We must understand Augustine's starting place if we are to understand his story. The great bishop was painfully aware of his alienation from God due to sin. It was precisely this alienation that caused him to search for answers in all the wrong places during the early years of his life.

Augustine's birthplace was the Roman African town of Thagaste (modern Souk Ahras, in Algeria). Back then, as today, it was a non-descript town of little consequence. His father Patrick was a man of modest means who had to scrape together enough money to send Augustine to school. For most of his life Patrick was not a Christian, and he disappears off the scene rather quickly. The figure from Augustine's home who had the greatest influence on him was his devout Christian mother Monica. In fact, we might say her influence on her son, which continued into his adulthood, bordered on unhealthy codependency. Despite that awkward dynamic, Monica appears to have played a large role in Augustine's eventual conversion by her godly example and earnest prayers.

As a teenager Augustine wanted nothing to do with Christ. So he embarked on his first real attempt to satisfy the restlessness in his soul: through sex. Monica had warned him to avoid fornication and especially adultery, but he ignored her and rushed headlong into sexual sin, not only from lust, but also to boast about his exploits (real and imagined) to his friends. He writes,

> I refused to satisfy my internal hunger with your spiritual food, my God, and I was unaware of any need . . . My soul was sick and cov-

ered in sores, and it rubbed up against material things in a desperate attempt to relive the itching . . . To love and be loved in return was what excited me, especially if I could enjoy my lover's body. So I polluted the stream of friendship with the filth of lust and obscured its brightness with foul passions.[6]

Later Augustine would comment on this phase of his life by extolling the satisfaction he had finally found in God:

Sexual caresses are intended to arouse love, but there are no softer caresses than yours and no object of love is more beneficial than your truth, which is more beautiful and radiant than all other things . . . So the soul fornicates when it turns from you and seeks what is pure and unadulterated elsewhere, yet the search is futile while it is away from you.[7]

Though Augustine could look back on his youth from such a wise perspective, as a restless teenager he had not yet come to appreciate the beauty of God.

Nevertheless, Augustine did begin to realize his sexual habits were a form of slavery. Sex was a compulsion that did not truly satisfy. So as a young man he decided to look to human philosophy to assuage his guilt and provide him with the meaning of life. The particular philosophy he embraced was called Manicheism (pronounced Man-ih-KEE-ism). Manicheism was a Persian religious system that had recently migrated into the Roman Empire. Its main teaching was a radical dualism of light and darkness, or good and evil. The Manichees taught that in a great cosmic battle, the good side had been defeated by evil; so now the world was a mixture of both principles. Adam and Eve were created by the evil side through the mating of demons. This meant human beings are the product of an evil force, and are naturally wicked. Yet within humanity's corrupt physical bodies, light particles are trapped. Only the priests of the Manichees, called the "Elect," could release the light. Perhaps you can see why this philosophy appealed to Augustine. First of all, it gave him a clear conscience with respect to his sexual addiction. He could claim that his fleshly body had overpowered the good inclination within him, so he just couldn't help sinning. His true self was the "good soul" inside of him, which remained untainted by his outward moral failings.[8] Furthermore, Manicheism provided a fairly undemanding process for dealing with sin. Simply by becoming a member of the Manichean community and providing for the Elect's food and daily needs, Augustine was promised reincarnation with the hope of eventual salvation.

But Augustine was too much of an intellectual to remain with the Manichees for long. Eventually their trite platitudes became apparent to him, and their superficial answers to perplexing questions turned him off. At the same time, Augustine found that his career prospects were skyrocketing. So he turned to yet another means to satisfy his restless longings: worldly success. As his education had progressed, Augustine had discovered he was a very talented public speaker. In the Roman world, skill in the art of rhetoric was a sure ticket to prominence. At age twenty-two Augustine took his first teaching post in the great city of Carthage. (This is the city where Tertullian had displayed his own eloquence nearly two centuries before, and where the martyr Perpetua had given her ultimate testimony to Christ.) From Carthage, Augustine moved up to Rome. Then, at the height of his career, he was nominated for a prestigious professorship of rhetoric in Milan, which meant he would be an official orator in the imperial court. His job was to give speeches in honor of prominent officials and to promote the state's agenda. The new position offered Augustine the chance to mingle with the aristocratic elite. Suddenly the provincial thirty-year-old from an African backwater found himself on the brink of greatness. A regional governorship loomed as a distinct possibility if he played his cards just right. After his rambling years, Augustine was about to begin—to borrow the words of Chris McCandless—his "final and greatest adventure."

Milan in the late fourth century was the perfect place for an up-and-comer like Augustine. The Roman Empire had been split into two halves, and Milan housed the western emperor's palace and its affiliated governmental apparatus. Situated in northern Italy with access to strategic Alpine passes, Milan had become the capital of the West like Constantinople in the East. The city of Rome was in serious decline and had ceased to function as the administrative center of the empire. So it was not Rome but Milan that lay at the center of a vast mosaic of imperial bureaucracy and cronyism. At this time, the Roman Empire was based on a system of political patronage (the vestiges of which can still be seen today in the Italian Mafia). Rich and powerful senators tapped the chosen few to ascend the ranks of political office. Aspiring young men attached themselves as loyal clients to their patrons. Advancement often required strategically placed bribes. In this environment, Augustine soon realized he needed something he didn't have: a respectable marriage to a well-connected heiress, along with the wad of cash she would provide.[9] Such necessities confront us with one of the most disgraceful deeds Augustine ever committed (a deed which also takes some of the shine off saintly Monica). With his mother's help, he arranged a marriage to an upper-class girl—and in so doing, left great pain in his wake.

Augustine had been living with a lover since he was about seventeen years old. We do not know who she was, for he never tells us her name. It is generally believed she was a slave, or at least from a lower class than he. Augustine remained sexually faithful to his concubine for a decade and a half. One of the misconceptions many people have about Augustine is that he was a complete profligate until his conversion. Actually, except for a few wild teenage years, he had only shared his bed with this one woman. Yet she was not his wife, and Augustine knew full well he did not intend to remain committed to her or to raise a family with her. In Roman society, the practice of concubinage was widely accepted. Even the Christian church was prepared to accommodate it as a kind of common law marriage so long as there was lifelong fidelity. But Augustine understood he was merely using this woman temporarily for her body: "With her

I learned how wide a difference there is between the partnership of marriage entered into for the sake of having a family, and the mutual consent of those whose love is a matter of physical sex."[10] When the time came for him to "marry up," the partner who had been exploited as a sexual object could be cast aside.[11]

Augustine contracted an engagement to a ten-year-old girl from a wealthy family. This was accomplished partly through Monica's efforts because she believed a good marriage would cause her son to settle down and get baptized as a Christian. Of course, the engagement meant that Augustine's concubine would have to be dismissed. In a poignant reminder of the consequences of sin, Augustine later confessed:

> Meanwhile my sins multiplied. The woman with whom I habitually slept was torn away from my side because she was a hindrance to my marriage. My heart which was deeply attached was cut and wounded, and left a trail of blood. She had returned to Africa vowing that she would never go with another man.[12]

In the meantime, Augustine procured another lover to sate his desires until his fiancée would reach the marriageable age of twelve. Yet he still lamented his break-up:

> But my wound, inflicted by the earlier parting, was not healed. After inflammation and sharp pain, it festered. The pain made me as it were frigid and desperate.[13]

To make matters worse, Augustine kept with him in Milan the teenage son he had fathered with his concubine. So imagine the fate of this poor woman: utterly rejected after a long-term, exclusive relationship, she was ripped from the man to whom she had given her best years, and was separated forever from her only son. She returned home to Africa penniless and ashamed, while Augustine got engaged to a rich preteen to further his career. Indeed it is a tragic and sordid affair.

This is the Augustine we find in Milan in AD 386. He was experiencing great success in his job. All his prospects were bright. But on the inside he was torn with anxiety and ridden with guilt. He was horribly unhappy. On the day of an important, high-pressure speech, he found himself envying the merry, drunken beggar he chanced to encounter in the street. Apparently the carefree happiness Augustine so desperately sought could be achieved by begging a few coins to buy wine. The rat race life seemed utterly futile. But God was at work in Augustine's misery. "I aspired to honours, money, marriage, and you laughed at me. In those ambitions I suffered the bitterest difficulties; that was by your mercy."[14] The Manichean philosophy had proved hollow, the prospect of career success held no lasting appeal, and sex had become a source of relational pain. In the face of such spiritual restlessness, Augustine turned to the one person in Milan who seemed to possess an abiding peace: the great bishop Ambrose, whose preaching would soon light a fire in Augustine's soul.

Rest at Last

Ambrose was fifteen years older than Augustine, and he came from a much different background. Whereas Augustine had to claw his way up the social ladder from the fringes of the empire, Ambrose was reared with privilege. Educated at Rome, the son of a highly-placed father, Ambrose pursued a career in law until a governorship opened up for him in northern Italy. With a family whose heritage in the church was longstanding and well known, Ambrose was widely respected as a godly Christian statesman. So perhaps it is not surprising that when the Arian and Nicene factions were rioting over who should replace Milan's deceased bishop, and Ambrose had to intervene to restore order in the church, somebody (according to tradition it was a small child) realized the politician standing in front of them might be the right man for the job! The crowd demanded Ambrose by acclamation. When it became clear he could not evade this unexpected pastoral call, he was hurriedly baptized, and so became a bishop.[15] In fact, he would be the greatest bishop Milan has ever seen.

When Augustine arrived in the city, Ambrose had been a revered figure in the Milanese church for over a decade. Having donated his great wealth to charity, Ambrose had become famous for his devotion to the Bible and his powerful preaching. These were two important factors in Augustine's conversion. One of the main reasons Augustine had rejected Christianity (despite being raised with Monica's constant evangelism) was his intellectual disdain for the scriptures. Trained to appreciate the eloquence and stylistic perfection of Cicero, he found the Latin translations of the Bible to be grammatically inferior and full of crude stories. Like so many unbelievers, he thought the Word of God was utterly simplistic and could not stand up to rational scrutiny. Augustine failed to realize that "the Bible is composed in such a way that as beginners mature, its meaning grows with them."[16]

In his pride, Augustine had rejected the scriptures many years earlier. But now in Milan he began to attend Ambrose's church services—not to be edified by the content, but just to pick up some rhetorical techniques from the famous preacher. Nevertheless, the Word of God began to do its work in Augustine's heart:

> Above all, I heard first one, then another, then many difficult passages in the Old Testament scriptures figuratively interpreted, where I, by taking them literally, had found them to kill (2 Cor. 3:6). So after several passages in the Old Testament had been expounded spiritually, I now found fault with that despair of mine, caused by my belief that the law and the prophets could not be defended at all against the mockery of hostile critics.[17]

Through Ambrose's learned sermons and allegorical exegesis, Augustine began to realize the Christian faith is intellectually defensible after all. Looking back, he perceived this to be God's work in his life. "I now began to believe that you would never have conferred such pre-eminent authority on the scripture, now diffused through all lands, unless you had willed that it would be a means of coming to faith in you and a means of seeking to know you."[18] The intellectual restlessness that had driven Augustine to the emptiness of Manicheism was now driving him toward the church. His search for a philosophy that would provide him with rest was almost over. Yet he was not quite ready to take the plunge.

Augustine also had to be confronted with the utter futility of his career aspirations. At the pinnacle of his professional success, he encountered some moving testimonies of great men who had put away their secular ambitions for the sake of Christ. One of them was an African named Marius Victorinus, the most prominent scholar of his day. He was so brilliant that the Senate had honored him by erecting a statue of him in the Forum, the very heart of Rome. Throughout his life Victorinus had been an ardent worshiper of the pagan gods. But in his old age he had come to realize, through long philosophical contemplation, especially in the thought of Plato, that Christianity was the true way. (Recall that in chapter 2 we saw this same pattern of conversion in Justin Martyr.) For a while, Victorinus kept his faith in Jesus secret. But when he was challenged on this point by a godly evangelist, Victorinus decided he needed to go public with his beliefs.[19] "He was afraid to offend his friends, proud devil-worshippers," Augustine says. But then "he became ashamed of the emptiness of those rites and felt respect for the truth."[20] Having offered himself for Christian baptism, he was given the opportunity to recite the creed in private. This he refused to do. When Victorinus strode to the front of the church to boldly proclaim his newfound faith in Christ, the stunned congregation burst forth with gasps of joy. The people marveled that such an eminent pagan could be converted. Of course, when the pagans heard the news of his defection from their ranks, they "gnashed with their teeth and were sick at heart" (Ps. 112:10).[21]

Around the same time that Augustine heard about Victorinus, he received a visit from his friend Ponticianus, a high-ranking court official who was also from Africa. During the visit he happened to pick up and read a book lying on Augustine's table. He was surprised to find it was the Apostle Paul. Augustine explained that he had been ruminating on scripture lately. Ponticianus was pleased to hear it, for he was already a committed Christian. As the conversation continued, he shared with Augustine the story of the Egyptian monk named Anthony whose biography had been recorded by Bishop Athanasius. Having never heard of Anthony, Augustine was astonished to hear about the monk's heroic self-denial. Ponticianus went on to share a personal story. He told Augustine how one day he was walking with some friends in a garden when they came upon a monastic house. There they found a copy of Athanasius's book, the *Life of Anthony*. One of Ponticianus's friends was deeply moved as he read it. He discerned that he was wasting his life in secular pursuits. "Tell me, I beg of you, what do we hope to achieve with all our labours?" he cried out in frustration. "What is our aim in life? What is the motive for our service to the state?"[22] Touched in his spirit, he turned to his other friend and declared, "As for myself, I have broken away from our ambition, and have decided to serve God."[23] His friend felt the same way. That very day, both of them quit their jobs and broke off their engagements, dedicating themselves full-time to God's service. Their two fiancées decided to do the same. This amazing testimony, like that of Victorinus, made a profound impact on Augustine. He understood that other people were making the kind of hard decisions he was still hesitating to make. Could he not follow their example?

Having grappled with his besetting sins of prideful intellectualism and careerism, only one obstacle remained. Yet for Augustine it was the hardest one to surmount: his attachment to his carnal appetites. He was well aware of the high standards of holiness required for the followers of Jesus. In contrast, when he looked in the mirror he perceived himself as "twisted and filthy, covered in sores and ulcers. And I looked and was appalled, but there was no way of escaping from myself."[24] He confessed,

I was an unhappy young man, wretched as at the beginning of my adolescence when I prayed to you for chastity and said, "Grant me chastity and continence—but not yet." I was afraid you might hear my prayer quickly, and that you might too rapidly heal me of the disease of lust which I preferred to satisfy rather than suppress.[25]

Greatly disturbed in his soul, Augustine fled outside to a quiet garden. He was torn in two. On the one hand, he knew exactly what he wanted to do. Yet his old loves, the sins of the flesh, called out to him, saying, "Are you getting rid of us? From this moment we shall never be with you again!" As he struggled with the cost of discipleship, Augustine felt that Lady Chastity appeared to him as a serene and noble woman. She appealed to the example of great saints. "Are you incapable of doing what these men and women have done?" she asked. "Do you think them capable of achieving this by their own resources and not by the Lord their God?"[26]

Augustine now burst into tears. As he sobbed in agony, he heard a child's voice telling him to "Pick up and read!" It didn't sound like any children's game he knew. Perhaps it was a divine command? Augustine rushed over to his book of Paul's letters and read the first words upon which his eyes fell: "Not in orgies and drunkenness, not in sexual immorality and sensuality, not in quarreling and jealousy. But put on the Lord Jesus Christ, and make no provision for the flesh, to gratify its desires" (Rom. 13:13–14). It was all he needed to hear. At that moment, Augustine gave his life to Christ. Finally, he had found rest.

Theologian of Grace

On Easter Eve, the night of April 24 in the year AD 387, a band of Christians in rough robes approached the New Basilica of Milan with its nearby baptistery.[27] They were hungry, for they had been fasting through Lent; yet their souls were full of the divine food provided by their bishop Ambrose. Each day during the previous week, Ambrose had instructed the catechumens in the creed of the faith. Now by the golden glow of oil lamps they observed a nocturnal vigil in the church. The sound of chanted hymns heightened the aura of mystery and wonder. As dawn approached, they discarded their robes, were anointed with oil, and renounced Satan and all his works. Then they descended into the baptismal pool, an octagonal marble font fifteen feet across with special channels to deliver the water. (Today the ancient place can still be visited underneath Milan's medieval cathedral, the Duomo.) Bishop Ambrose performed baptism by immersion in the name of the Father, Son, and Holy Spirit. When the Christians emerged from the font, he offered them clean linen robes, confirmed them with oil, and then did something unusual: he washed their feet to become their humble servant. As morning dawned in splendor that Easter Day, Augustine was among those who rejoiced in the knowledge that his sins had been washed away by the risen Christ. Once again, the tears flowed down his cheeks—but these were tears of joy at God's amazing grace.[28]

Augustine headed home to Africa, intending to lead a life of quiet contemplation and celibacy (he never did marry the girl to whom he had been engaged). Unexpectedly, a series of tragedies struck in a short span. His devout mother Monica died, and so did his teenage son Adeodatus, as well as another very close friend. Perhaps Augustine could have sunk into lonely despair. But even if that were possible, he was never given such an opportunity; for soon a new and unwanted duty was forced upon him: he was called to a congregation.[29] Augustine did not aspire to be a pastor of a church. In fact, he had avoided visiting any place where there was a vacancy, lest the multitude press him into service. But one day he was visiting the coastal city of Hippo Regius to recruit a friend to his monastic lifestyle. The place had a bishop already, so Augustine felt quite safe going to church there. However, the bishop knew a good thing when he saw it. In a sermon before the gathered faithful he underscored their need for a new assistant pastor. The crowd began to shout Augustine's name and push him forward. Suddenly he found himself—like Ambrose before him—called into pastoral ministry when he least expected it. Believing the call to be from God, Augustine acquiesced to the people's desire. He went on to serve the Christians of Hippo as a presbyter and then as a bishop for the next four decades.

Hippo Regius was the second most prominent city in Roman North Africa after Carthage. Today among the ancient ruins in Annaba, Algeria, the outline of Augustine's church can still be seen. It was located in the Christian quarter, across the street from the best villas in town, on what was then the Mediterranean coastline. Immediately next to Augustine's church is a small baptistery with a waist-deep font. The church itself is of moderate size, not built on a grand scale like the churches John Chrysostom was preaching in over at Constantinople. Nor was it so lavishly decorated, though pieces of green and white mosaic can still be seen on the floor of Augustine's church. In the semicircular apse the modern visitor can sit in the place where the bishop's chair, or *cathedra*, was situated. From this spot Augustine preached to his flock, instructing them in righteousness and warning them against theological errors. Although ancient Hippo could never have claimed to be at the center of things like the great cities of the empire, Augustine nonetheless made his presence widely felt. Through his doctrinal treatises, numerous letters, and attendance at church councils in the nearby metropolis of Carthage, Augustine soon became one of the great churchmen of his age. There was no theological dispute in which he was not involved.

In his theology, Augustine emphasized the utter necessity of divine grace, for he knew we are sinful and helpless people. There were two major groups in his day that tended to downplay grace. On the one hand, there were the Pelagians, who said human beings were not born into sin. Pelagius was a British ascetic who, along with some other thinkers, began a theological movement that has come to bear his name. Pelagianism taught that no one has inherited the guilt of Adam's sin. Adam certainly was a bad example, but he did not pass a sin nature to his descendants. So the human will is completely unconstrained. We can freely choose to sin, or we can be righteous. In fact, it is possible (though not many people can actually accomplish it) to live a perfect life and earn salvation through good works or law-keeping.

Around AD 402, Pelagius reacted negatively to a text he found in Augustine's *Confessions*. Augustine had written, "Command what you will, but grant what you command." He was saying: "Lord, you have the right to make any moral precept you want, but then you must provide the help we need to keep your commands." In other words, Augustine believed no one can please God apart from a prior and distinct work of grace. It is "not possible not to sin," and that's exactly why grace is needed. But the Pelagians insisted God has made it possible for us to earn salvation by choosing and being good. Grace serves as a helping hand that makes obedience easier for us, but we don't absolutely have to have it. We're not sinners who need God's saving intervention, but free people who only need to do our best. Augustine directed all his considerable theological firepower against this pernicious teaching. Largely due to his influence, Pelagianism was condemned at several councils in Africa, and was finally defeated at a major council at Ephesus in AD 431. Today it is regarded as a heresy which denies the biblical teaching (found especially in Romans 5) that all people are born into the original sin of Adam, and so need God's grace to receive salvation.

The other major group with a deficient view of grace in Augustine's time was an African counterchurch movement called Donatism.[30] For much of Augustine's life, this alternate expression of Christianity was stronger and more vigorous in Africa than the catholics whom he led. Yet in the end, Augustine and the catholics prevailed. The Donatists were extremely rigorous and exclusive—the most morally demanding people you could imagine. They believed only the most righteous, the most devoted, the most purified people could be called true Christians. Some zealous Donatists even roamed the countryside as bands of thugs who took it upon themselves to enforce their strict legalism through beatings with clubs. Twice Augustine avoided being ambushed by them only because he accidentally took the wrong road. Often these fanatics committed suicide to prove their willingness to go to "martyrdom."[31]

In its origins, Donatism was a breakaway movement that began in Carthage in the days of the Great Persecution of AD 303. When that ordeal ended, a deacon named Donatus and his followers insisted that no one who had capitulated under the threat of torture could be considered a faithful Christian. They were unwilling to extend grace to church leaders who had been weak in the face of persecution. Baptisms performed by such leaders were declared invalid. And so the Donatists founded a schismatic church under new bishops who rebaptized their adherents. In Augustine's day, a century later, this breakaway movement was still going strong, even though the age of persecution had long since passed. The Donatists continued to view the catholics as "polluted."

Augustine opposed Donatism because he believed it had a faulty doctrine of the church. Whereas the Donatists considered the church to consist only of the "pure," Augustine advanced an ecclesiology called the "mixed church." He said the church is composed of sinners and saints. As anyone who has ever darkened the door of a church knows, good people can do bad things. There are varying levels of sanctification within the body of Christ. If we make the church into a country club for the spiritually elite instead of a "hospital for sinners," we have misunderstood the very nature of God's grace. Augustine fought hard against the legalism and pride of the Donatists. His own profound experience of grace had taught him all he needed to know about its importance for the Christian life. By the time he died, Donatism was well into decline. Yet it managed to hang on for a couple more centuries until it was finally destroyed in North Africa (along with the catholic Christians there) by the rise of Islam. Perhaps the tenacity of Donatism can serve as a reminder of how easy it is to become an elitist church that withholds grace from the broken among us. Of all people, Augustine, the Theologian of Grace, would not have wished us to do so.

Reflections on Augustine

At the end of this chapter on Augustine, I am left with the sense that there is so much more we could have said. We have barely scratched the surface. Do you wish to get to know Augustine a little better? Then here is what I recommend. To understand this saint you must do more than read books *about* him. You must even do more than read books *by* him—though I do suggest the *Confessions* is a must-read for every believer! But to truly understand Augustine, you must get to know the God who was his all-encompassing passion.[32]

Augustine's theology was a theology of God's abounding love. This divine love is so deep that it inspires a holy awe in the hearts of those on whom his grace has been lavished. Only when we recognize the sin into which we are born, and the sin which we ourselves commit, can we appreciate the profundity of God's love. It awakens in us a mystical passion to behold his own beauty ever more. Humanity's highest good is to contemplate the face of God. "For me to cleave to God is good" (see Ps. 73:28). The ability to love God with such great fervor is a gift shed abroad in our hearts by the Holy Spirit. There are only two kinds of people in this world: those who love themselves, and those who love God. Augustine asks us never to forget we are the people who love the Lord our God!

In the year that Augustine died, AD 430, barbarian invaders from beyond the empire were poised to vandalize his city of Hippo. They were besieging its walls even as he lay dying on his bed. But Augustine was not too concerned about them. What preoccupied his mind in the last moments of a well-lived life? His biographer records that Augustine asked to have the penitential psalms of David written on sheets of paper and hung about his room. Then he asked for absolute privacy with no disturbances. For ten days he prayed and wept and communed alone with God; and then he died. Here are some of the words from Psalm 51 upon which Augustine meditated during his last days in the earthly city. Truly they are words for the sinner who is journeying home toward the City of God:

Have mercy on me, O God,
according to your steadfast love;
according to your abundant mercy
blot out my transgressions.
Wash me thoroughly from my iniquity,
and cleanse me from my sin!

For I know my transgressions,
and my sin is ever before me.
Against you, you only, have I sinned
and done what is evil in your sight,
so that you may be justified in your words
and blameless in your judgment.
Behold, I was brought forth in iniquity,
and in sin did my mother conceive me.

Behold, you delight in truth in the inward being,
and you teach me wisdom in the secret heart.
Purge me with hyssop, and I shall be clean;
wash me, and I shall be whiter than snow.
Let me hear joy and gladness;
let the bones that you have broken rejoice.
Hide your face from my sins,
and blot out all my iniquities.

Create in me a clean heart, O God,
and renew a right spirit within me.
Cast me not away from your presence,
and take not your Holy Spirit from me.
Restore to me the joy of your salvation,
and uphold me with a willing spirit.

Then I will teach transgressors your ways,
and sinners will return to you.
Deliver me from bloodguiltiness, O God,
O God of my salvation,
and my tongue will sing aloud of your righteousness.

O Lord, open my lips,
and my mouth will declare your praise.

Provocative Questions

1. Do you have a story of aimless wandering before you came to Jesus? Compare your experience with Augustine's. Did you have a sense of spiritual restlessness like him? What did it feel like to be a spiritual seeker? What steps brought you to faith in Christ? Were there strategic people involved? Did you ever have a "garden of Milan" crisis experience?

2. Augustine struggled with a temptation universal to all people: sex. In what specific ways does sexual sin offer temptations in our culture today? Why is this an area of such difficult struggle for so many? Read 1 Corinthians 6:12–20 and 1 Thessalonians 4:1–8. What hints does the scripture offer to help us avoid sexual sin? What have you learned from Augustine about sexuality?

3. Augustine tried to find inner peace through his career. Do you struggle with the same issue? In what ways do you seek significance in the workplace, or in your life's calling? What is the essential attraction offered by career success? Augustine encountered some key people who had renounced their worldly aspirations for the sake of God. Is there anyone whom you admire in this regard? Assuming that work is inevitable for all of us, what would a biblical perspective on work look like? See Genesis 3:17–19; Proverbs 10:2–5; Ecclesiastes 2:17–26; Ephesians 4:28; Colossians 3:17, 22–25; and 2 Thessalonians 3:10–12. Do any other relevant texts come to your mind?

4. Augustine's baptism marked a very significant transition in his life. Ancient baptism was a profound, life-altering event. It was accompanied by spiritual and theological preparation, fasting, liturgy, and celebration. Describe your own bap-

tism, if you can. How is baptism practiced in your church? Consider Romans 6:1–11. What theology is baptism supposed to express? How could a church properly express that theology? Can you imagine your church having a baptismal service like the one Augustine experienced? Why or why not?

5. We have called Augustine the "Theologian of Grace." In contrast, the Pelagians said we don't need a special work of grace, since we are not born sinners. Where do you see this kind of theology being advocated today? See Romans 3:9–20 and 5:12–19 for a biblical perspective. In a similar way, the Donatists diminished God's grace by excluding all "sinners" from their midst. What can go wrong when we fail to show grace to the broken sinners among us? Does being graceful mean we must coddle sin? What is the right balance here? Share a story about a time you (or someone you know) experienced the grace of God. Was the grace mediated through another believer?

Good Books to Dig Deeper

There are many English translations of Augustine's *Confessions*. One very good and widely available edition is:

Chadwick, Henry. *Saint Augustine: Confessions.* Oxford: Oxford University Press, 1991.

Although some newer studies of Augustine's life have appeared, I cannot recommend them. In my opinion the best biography is still:

Brown, Peter. *Augustine of Hippo: A Biography. A New Edition with an Epilogue.* Berkeley: University of California Press, 2000 (orig. 1967).

For a quick overview of Augustine's life and thought, see:

Chadwick, Henry. *Augustine*. Past Masters. Oxford: Oxford University Press, 1986.

Cooper, Stephen A. *Augustine for Armchair Theologians*. Louisville: Westminster John Knox Press, 2002. (Ignore the juvenile illustrations; the content is solid.)

Knowles, Andrew and Pachomios Penkett. *Augustine and His World*. Downers Grove, IL: InterVarsity Press, 2004. (A pocket edition, lavishly illustrated with art, color photos, and graphics.)

A very handy reference work, with detailed articles on virtually every Augustinian subject, is:

Fitzgerald, Allan D., ed. *Augustine through the Ages: An Encyclopedia*. Grand Rapids: Eerdmans, 1999.

A Taste of Augustine

Confessions VIII.xi.26–xii.29

Here is Augustine's famous conversion experience in the garden of Milan. He agonizes over the costly demands of discipleship and struggles with the besetting sins of the flesh. Finally he hears a divine word and gives himself to God. This is one of the most spiritually moving scenes in all of Christian literature.

Empty frivolities, "vanities of vanities," my long-standing loves—these things held me back. They plucked at the robe of my flesh and softly murmured, "Are you sending us away? Shall we no longer be with you? Not ever? From now on, shall such-and-such be forbidden to you forever and ever?" And what deeds were they suggesting in what I've called "such-and-such"? My God, may your mercy make their suggestions repugnant to the soul of your servant! Such filth they proposed—such vile things! Yet now I heard those voices as diminished whispers. They did not confront me boldly out in the open. It's as if they were muttering behind my back. They furtively snatched at me as I walked away, trying to get me to look over my shoulder. Admittedly they did slow me down a bit. I hesitated to break away, to shake loose from them, to leap across to where I was being called. Meanwhile my domineering sexual habit was saying to me, "Do you think you can possibly live without these things?"

At last the heat of those voices began to cool. From up ahead, in the place I was facing but was afraid to cross over to, the pure and dignified figure of Chastity appeared to me.[33] She was serene, and vivacious without being flirtatious. In an entirely wholesome way she coaxed me to come forward and waver no more. To receive and embrace me she held out her holy hands, in which she held a host of good examples. There were many boys and girls, a great throng of young adults, and people of all ages, dignified widows and elderly virgins. In all of them I could see that Chastity was by no means infertile, but was the "joyous mother of children" (Ps. 113:9), fruitful in you, Lord, her husband. She was smiling at me with a daring smile, as if to say, "Can't you do what these men have done, and these women? Or do you truly think they could do it by themselves, apart from the Lord their God? It was the Lord their God who gave me to them! Why do you try to stand in your own strength, only to find yourself slipping? Cast yourself on him! Don't be afraid. He won't draw back and allow you to fall. Make the leap with confidence. He will catch you and heal you."

But I blushed with great shame, for I was still listening to the murmuring voices of those vanities. Hesitant, I hung in the balance. Then a second time Chastity seemed to speak to me: "Close your ears to those immoral parts of your earthly body, and so put them to death. They may whisper sweet delights to you, but they have nothing to do with the law of the Lord your God." A struggle raged in my heart in which I was pitted against myself!

Without even knowing what I was doing I flung myself down beneath a nearby fig tree and opened the floodgates of my tears, which flowed like rivers from my eyes as an acceptable sacrifice to you (Ps. 51:16–17). Not in these exact words, but in this sense, I cried out to you over and over: "But you, Lord, how long? How long, Lord? Will you be angry forever? Do not remember our sins of the past" (Ps. 79:5, 8; 89:46). For my old sins made me aware that I was still in their grip. So I burst forth with miserable cries: "How long? How long will I say, 'Tomorrow! Tomorrow!' Why not right now? Why not end my perversion right this minute?"

These are the things I was saying as I wept in most bitter sorrow within my heart. Suddenly I heard a voice from a nearby house— maybe a boy or a girl, I'm not sure—singing a chant over and over: "Pick it up and read! Pick it up and read!" Right away my expression changed, and I started thinking as hard as I could about whether children normally sing something like that in a kind of game. But I couldn't remember ever having heard such a thing anywhere. So when I had gotten control of my gushing tears, I stood up. I could interpret this voice as nothing other than a divine command which ordered me to open my Bible and read the first chapter I should find . . . I grabbed it, opened it, and silently read the first passage on which my eyes fell: "Not in reveling and drunkenness, not in fornication and impurity, not in quarreling and jealousy; but put on the Lord Jesus Christ, and make no provision for the flesh in its desires" (Rom. 13:13–14).

I had no desire to read any further. There was no need. For as soon as I reached the end of this verse, the light of assurance flooded into my heart. All the dark shadows of my insecurity were scattered in every direction.

10

CYRIL OF ALEXANDRIA

Everyone knows there is a special bond between twins. They often dress alike, or have the same tastes in books, music, or food. Sometimes it even appears they can read each other's minds. When they exchange a look, seeming to possess an intuitive contact we outsiders can't comprehend, they simply shrug and say with a smile, "It's a twin thing." Social science researchers have tried to document this supposed "telepathic" connection. In a 1997 experiment before a live audience for a TV show, two teenaged twins, Evelyn and Elaine Dove, apparently communicated with each other despite being physically separated.[1] Evelyn was taken into one studio and hooked up to lie detector equipment. In another studio, Elaine was seated in front of a large pyramid, completely isolated from her sister. The host spoke to her in soothing words to induce a state of relaxation. Suddenly the pyramid (which had been created by special effects technicians) exploded with a bang and a shower of sparks and colored smoke. This gave Elaine quite a scare. Amazingly, over in the other studio, Evelyn's polygraph monitors shot off the chart. Though she had absolutely no idea what was going on in Elaine's room, the spike in her graph at the exact moment of the explosion seemed to indicate she was somehow in touch with her twin subconsciously. Whatever we are to make of such events, my point is that twins share a common bond. They partake of a unity by virtue of their close relationship. At the same time, they remain separate and distinct individuals. Thus they are "two" and simultaneously "one," in a certain manner of speaking.

At this point you might be asking yourself, "What do twins have to do with the ancient church fathers?" I bring up the subject because one of the most contentious theological debates of the early church concerned the issue of reconciling duality and unity. I am referring to the argument over Jesus Christ, who is both human and divine at the same time. But how exactly should we explain this theological truth? Perhaps we might think of him as a "divine person" who shares many attributes with a "human person"? Like a pair of twins, there would be two subjects here. So this would be a solution which emphasizes *duality*. Any shared unity between them would be a matter of association, not equivalent identity.

I don't mean to suggest the church fathers actually used the analogy of twins.[2] But they definitely did struggle to explain Jesus's simultaneous humanity and divinity. No less than three major councils were called to adjudicate the matter. And the idea which I've just illustrated by twins—that the Son of God might be considered as two distinct beings who share a common bond—was one of the many options on the table. Yet it was an option vehemently rejected by the man who is the subject of this chapter, Cyril of Alexandria. As we get to know Cyril, we'll learn why the *unity of Christ* was so important to him. It was a truth he spent his life defending, for it is absolutely essential to the theology of salvation. In the fractious christological debates of the fifth century, Cyril ended up as the winner. To achieve this victory he proved himself an able heir to the Alexandrian tradition of lofty theological thinking—as well as gritty political maneuvering. We'll discover both intellectual brilliance and stubborn intransigence in this powerful Alexandrian bishop.

An Heir of Alexandria

In chapter 8 we followed John Chrysostom's rise to power in Constantinople and his downfall at the hands of Theophilus of Alexandria. When Theophilus trumped up charges against John at a biased synod and brought accusations that led to his exile, a twenty-five-year-old assistant stood approvingly at his uncle Theophilus's side. This nephew was the young Cyril. Born around AD 378 and educated in Alexandria's fine schools, Cyril was already a *lector* (reader) in the church with a bright future in ministry. He had a real knack for theology and deep devotion to Christ. But as we can see, Cyril was also exposed at an early age to the rough-and-tumble world of ecclesiastical politics. Although he eventually repudiated his initial rejection of the great John Chrysostom,[3] Cyril continued to boldly confront those he found heretical. Many historians have even viewed his behavior as harsh, opportunistic, or devious. For example, his failure to speak out against the murder of a female pagan philosopher by a frenzied Christian mob has earned him criticism.[4] But Cyril wouldn't have viewed his actions as anything other than the zealous defense of vital truth. We must recall he lived in a world where truth mattered and accurate theology was essential.[5] Bishops were expected to use every means at their disposal to protect their flocks from wolves (Acts 20:28–30). Perhaps Cyril was only following the advice he got from Augustine, who once wrote to him urging, "Correct [the heretics] with your pastoral care and with your fatherly gentleness, or even with remedial severity, if there is need . . . We are doing this, however, so that we may not be saddened by the loss of anyone but instead may rejoice, as far as possible, over the salvation of all."[6]

When Bishop Theophilus died in AD 412, Cyril was made the next bishop of Alexandria—though not without controversy. The imperial politicians favored a candidate who was likely to be more docile than Cyril. So they sent in troops to enforce their will. But Cyril had his own sort of troops: the crew of strong young men whose job it was to carry the sick on stretchers to the Christian hospitals. Although

Cyril emerged victorious after three days of fighting, the incident foreshadowed the turbulence that would characterize his ministry tenure. To be a bishop in Alexandria required a certain dogged tenacity (the kind we've already seen in Athanasius's stance "against the world"). Unfortunately, a good measure of political scheming was also needed, as Theophilus had demonstrated. It can fairly be said that Cyril exemplified both tenacity and duplicity during his years at the helm of the Alexandrian church. In any case, as one historical observer put it, "Cyril came into possession of the episcopate with greater power than Theophilus had ever exercised."[7] This was power he was not afraid to use.

But Cyril did not only inherit the down-and-dirty politics and surreptitious power plays of the Alexandrian church. He was also an heir to Alexandria's rich intellectual and theological tradition. Since its very beginnings, the city had been home to many eminent philosophers. Its library, we've already learned, was a jewel of the ancient world—though the ancients actually were more impressed with the harbor's lighthouse. Just as that bright light shone forth to beckon sailors from distant seas, so the city's intellectual renown served as a beacon for the Mediterranean's greatest thinkers. Soon Alexandria garnered a reputation for its distinguished Christian theologians, such as Origen and Athanasius. The theologians of Alexandria did their theology in a particular way: they focused their attention on the divine and ethereal realm of the unknowable God, who lives far above the mortal plane. On this point, Cyril was no exception. He found a holy and awesome God in the pages of scripture.

In historical treatments of Cyril's life, the emphasis is usually placed on his role as a polemicist who defended a certain christological view. What often goes overlooked is his deep commitment to the Bible. Cyril was a prolific commentator on the Word of God. Meditations on scripture's inner meaning poured from his pen. Today his exegesis fills seven bulky volumes of a modern edition with tiny, dense Greek print.[8] In biblical commentary that often went verse-by-verse, Cyril lavished loving care on the Pentateuch,

Isaiah, the Minor Prophets, Luke, and John. He wrote much more than this, but not all of it has survived. Even if Cyril had not won fame for his role in the fifth-century christological controversies, he would be noteworthy as a profound exegete. In all his reflection on scripture, he always found a way to uncover the mystery of Christ.[9] Cyril possessed a deep appreciation, as did other Alexandrians before him, that the Bible is a Christian book through and through. However, he sometimes needed to be reminded that God's revelation to the Jews was more than just types and shadows of things to come.[10] The Chosen People still belong to God; they are not repugnant to him. Cyril's rarified Alexandrian environment tempted him to overlook the fact that the real-world, historical Jesus came to earth as the Jewish Messiah.

In the great melting pot of the ancient church, two main traditions came to be mixed together. On the one hand, there was a Jewish element which cherished the Hebraic roots of the faith. Recognizing that God is a God of history (as seen especially in Old Testament Israel), this theological perspective emphasized the earthly, the historical, and the human. On the other hand, there was a Greek element which valued the Platonic ideal of pure, unchanging truth in a realm far above us. Theologians of this type tended to emphasize the heavenly, the transcendent, and the divine aspects of Christianity. Generally speaking, we can characterize the former as the view of Antioch, and the latter as the view of Alexandria. Perhaps you've already noticed this divide. When we examined patristic biblical interpretation, we saw that Antiochene exegesis tended to be grammatical and historical, while Alexandrian exegesis was allegorical and spiritual. This is not to say the Alexandrians ignored grammar, or that the Antiochenes ignored spiritual truth. Yet if we are making generalizations, it's safe to say there were different theological approaches in each of these rival cities. Alexandria's "spiritual" viewpoint dramatically affected Cyril's solution to the great crisis of his day: how to explain the divine and human natures of Christ.

One Son or Two?

Let's think back to the theological issues we discussed in chapter 7. The Council of Nicaea in AD 325 had declared Jesus Christ to be *homoousios*, or "of the same substance" with the Father. Athanasius and the three Cappadocians were the primary defenders of this point, against the heresy of the Arians who said Christ was an inferior creation. Thus the Nicene doctrine of the Trinity, which was worked out during the fourth century, insisted that Christ was fully God in every way. But now, in the fifth century, the pump was primed for a new debate: how exactly is the man Jesus of Nazareth to be considered a divine being? Or to put it another way: since Nicaea has declared Jesus is God, what is the precise relationship between his humanity and divinity? The debate moved from Trinitarian questions to christological ones.

In Christology there are two tendencies which, if followed to their extremes, will lead to heresy of one kind or another. The first tendency is to overemphasize Jesus's humanity. Some ancient thinkers even viewed him as a "mere man," not a divine figure at all. To explain his divine titles and works, they said he was simply a man who had been "adopted" by God and given the empowering presence of the divine Logos within. These so-called Adoptionists argued that the godly human named Jesus, at a specific point in time (usually his baptism), became God's special son. He was filled with heavenly power just like the Old Testament prophets, only more so. Yet the man who was adopted, Jesus of Nazareth, remained separate from the Logos who did the empowering. As you can see, this is a theology of *duality*. It makes a distinction between the Logos who indwells flesh, and the man whose flesh is indwelt.

Today we call Adoptionism heresy. Jesus was much more than a good man singled out by God for special empowerment. But in ancient times, some theologians in and around Antioch were attracted to this general idea because of their real-world focus. If any of them went so far as to call Jesus a "mere man" infused with divinity, they were rejected as Adoptionist heretics. Yet many Antiochene theologians (such as John Chrysostom's friends Diodore of Tarsus and Theodore of Mopsuestia) tended toward a Christology that overemphasized Christ's humanity. Though they were not outright Adoptionists, they did distinguish between the Logos who assumed a body, and the Man whose body was assumed by the Logos. In their attempts to do justice to the real man Jesus who walked the dusty roads of Galilee—the man who hungered, thirsted, suffered, and died—the Antiochene theologians assigned human frailties to the man, and sort of bracketed off the Logos as something entirely different. They didn't want the Logos (i.e., the eternal pre-incarnate Christ) to diminish the real human growth and struggles of Jesus on earth. Unfortunately, this made it seem the divine Logos and the man Jesus weren't truly unified. While the Antiochene theologians certainly did the church a favor by insisting Jesus was a true human being, their earthly focus and pronounced christological dualism needed to be balanced by the other side.

The Alexandrian theologians provided the necessary counterbalance—and they in turn had to be kept from extremes by Antioch. The christological tendency at Alexandria was to think of the Logos as so all-encompassing that Jesus, the earthly man, basically disappeared. In its most extreme form, the Alexandrian theology did not even consider Jesus to be a true man at all. He was not exactly like us in every way. Rather, he had a special kind of super-soul which ruled the body with complete mastery. The Alexandrians were so keen to elevate the heavenly, other-worldly aspect of the Logos that they often disregarded or downplayed Jesus's earthly life. To them he was a great mystical power, totally in control all the time—not a man who truly suffered and felt weakness, a man with whom we can identify. Some Alexandrians eventually lapsed into the error of saying that Christ only had a single nature (the divine one). His human nature was so inconsequential it was like a drop of honey dissolved in the ocean: entirely dissipated, and altogether insignificant. As an Alexandrian theologian, Cyril always felt inclined to elevate the divine nature of Christ. While he was not an out-and-out denier of Jesus's real humanity, he tended to emphasize the *unity* of Christ and his awesome deity. So he definitely needed the counterbalancing weight of the Antiochenes' very human Jesus to prevent him from going too far with his emphasis on the heavenly Logos.

The fifth-century debates over Christology came to a head under a man now viewed as a heretic: Nestorius, the bishop of Constantinople. He was trained in Antioch, so when he ascended to one of the most powerful bishoprics in the empire in AD 428, he made it his business to advance Antiochene theology.

The spark that set the controversy alight had to do with the proper way to refer to the Virgin Mary. Nestorius rejected the title "God-Bearer" as a designation for the mother of Jesus.[11] In strong and uncompromising language, he endorsed the Antiochene separation between the human and the divine in Christ. Nestorius famously said, "I hold the natures apart, but unite the worship."[12] In this way he expressed his reluctance to assign human attributes to the divine nature of Jesus. Therefore, God could not be born of a woman. Mary only gave birth to a man. To this man, divinity was somehow conjoined (an idea very close to Adoptionism, if you think about it). For the Nestorian party, Mary could be called the "Man-Bearer" or "Christ-Bearer," but she could not be considered the mother of God. The being in her womb was just a man, with whom there was a divine "association" of some kind. Jesus was given the title "God" only because of this vague association. Such erroneous doctrine falls far short of the mystery of the incarnation, in which Mary did indeed give birth to God in the flesh. Jesus is fully God *and* fully man from the moment of his virginal conception.

When Cyril found out what his fellow bishop in Constantinople was teaching, he was shocked into action. If one "holds the natures apart" as Nestorius did—bracketing off certain things such as physical birth into the human nature alone—then obviously Jesus was not a single person. To Cyril's way of thinking, there would be two individuals here! This is what I illustrated above in the concept of twins:

two distinct beings who are merely joined by an affinity or association. Cyril cursed this doctrine. He accused Nestorius of believing
in two sons: the son of God and the son of Mary. Urging Nestorius
to recant, Cyril wrote a letter instructing him in the correct view:

> It was not the case that initially an ordinary man was born of the
> holy Virgin and then the Word simply settled on him—no, what is
> said is that he underwent fleshly birth united from the very womb . . .
> In this way we shall confess one Christ and Lord, not worshipping
> a man 'along with' the Word . . . but worshipping one and the same
> Christ because the Word's body is not dissociated from him.[13]

We can see that Cyril's primary concern was for the *unity* of the
God-Man. But Nestorius did not respond to Cyril's concerns. He
viewed Cyril as a typical Alexandrian bishop, always trying to undermine the eastern capital of Constantinople. Now things began
to snowball. A great theological controversy was coming to a head.
In the battle to come, Cyril owned one distinct advantage: the support of the bishop of Rome. Before we can finish our account of the
fifth-century christological controversies, we must say a word about
the role of the Roman pontiff at this time.

The Rise of the Papacy

In the summer of AD 430, Cyril wrote to the bishop of Rome
about the controversy he was having with Nestorius. He mailed a
packet of Nestorius's problematic writings, contrasting them with
a carefully-arranged dossier of testimonies from earlier church
fathers. In the cover letter, Cyril pulled no punches: "Since the
longstanding custom of the churches persuades us to communicate
with your Holiness, then I write of necessity to point out that even
at this moment Satan is [through Nestorius] confounding all things,
raging against the churches of God, and trying to seduce people
everywhere, who once were walking on the right path of faith."[14]

Cyril then drove home his appeal: "If we have been entrusted with
the dispensation of the word and the safe-keeping of the faith, then
what could we say on the day of judgment if we had kept silent
about such matters?"[15] Such a provocative letter was bound to get
a response in a place like Rome. The pope immediately sent off
the packet for evaluation by a respected theologian named John
Cassian, who returned a negative verdict on Nestorius's doctrine.
Interestingly, Cassian dedicated his treatise refuting Nestorian-
ism to his good friend, a man who will figure prominently in this
ongoing saga. His name was Leo. Though he was only a deacon in
the Roman church at the time, he would go on to become a pope.
We know him today as Leo the Great.

Leo the Great marks the beginning of a change in the status of
the bishop of Rome. The Roman church had always been respected
in early Christian circles. Along with the other great cities of the
empire—such as Constantinople, Alexandria, Antioch, Ephesus, or
Carthage—it shone brightly in the constellation of Christian congregations. Rome was the old imperial capital, the largest and most
populous city in the world, the natural place to look for leadership.
With its connection to Peter and Paul, its reception of a Pauline letter, its long-standing theological orthodoxy, its many martyrs, and
its reputation for piety, Rome could not help but carry weight in the
ancient church. But in Leo's time, such informal prestige began to
evolve into something more. Playing on the connection with Peter
(who ended his life at Rome and whose tomb was still revered there),
Leo began to preach sermons and write letters elevating the role
of the pope as the living voice of Peter, to whom Jesus said, "You
are Peter, and on this rock I will build my church" (Matt. 16:18).[16]
Historically speaking, many scholars consider Leo the first identifiable "pope" in the strict sense of the word. In his letters he gave
a special connotation to the Latin word *papa*, referring it only to
himself.[17] Of course, drastic changes did not occur overnight. Yet
when Leo died in AD 461, he had definitely advanced the position
of the Roman pontiff.

Looking back with the benefit of hindsight, we can see that Pope Leo was laying the foundations of the medieval papacy. However, we must not jump ahead too much along the historical timeline. We are not in the age of Martin Luther here. The Christians of the fifth century such as Leo, Augustine, or Cyril lived in the sunset of the ancient world. Though the Middle Ages were about to dawn, the early church fathers remained people of the Greco-Roman era. As we learned in the introduction to this book, their church was catholic, but not yet Roman Catholic. Let's not treat them anachronistically. It was the specific trials of the ancient period that drove their actions. For example, one of the distinctive aspects of Leo's pontificate was his role as a civic leader for Rome. In addition to being the spiritual shepherd of a Christian congregation, he was forced to take on new political roles—something not traditionally associated with ministry. Perhaps this repulses the modern reader, especially if we are picturing the power-hungry medieval bishops who ruled as decadent Italian princes. But we should be careful not to read later history back into earlier times. Leo became something like the *de facto* mayor of Rome out of sheer necessity. He lived in the age of what historians call the Barbarian Invasions. What is meant by this term?

In the early days of republican Rome, before the mantle of imperial glory had settled on her shoulders, the aggressive little city-state in Italy started carving out new territorial holdings by warring with the indigenous peoples in various lands. These non-Roman "barbarians" remained on the fringes of the republic and then the empire, kept at bay by the disciplined Roman legions. To the north, the "barbarians" included people of Germanic origins. They were rough tribal warriors who dwelt across the Rhine and Danube rivers, which traditionally marked the northern frontier. For centuries Rome ruled the barbarians with an iron fist, holding them off or conquering them when new lands were needed. But inevitably, the decline and fall of the Roman Empire began to set in. Institutions decayed; economics shifted; Christianity introduced a merciful ethic. Whatever the reason (and historians have no shortage of them), in the fifth century the Roman army could no longer hold back the barbarian tide.[18]

In AD 410, Alaric the Goth and his hordes descended on Rome. He didn't actually do much damage, but the psychological blow was enormous. A foreign enemy sacking the Eternal City! It had been exactly 800 years since it had last happened. Such was the tumultuous age in which Pope Leo lived. Though Augustine died just in time to miss seeing his city fall to a foreign enemy (the Vandals), Leo was unable to escape that fate. The government and the emperor's court had long since fled to the safety of Milan, and from there to Ravenna's protective marshes. Rome was now a shadow of her old self. So in AD 452 when Attila the Hun was advancing toward the city with conquest in mind, the bishop of the Christian church was one of the few men with enough public standing to go out and parley with him. While the exact nature of those events is uncertain, we do know that Leo took on unprecedented responsibilities during his ministry. He found himself functioning like a politician: bargaining with invaders or engaging in a flurry of diplomatic correspondence with the imperial courts at Ravenna and Constantinople. He wasn't trying to become a despotic medieval pope; he simply had no other choice. No one else was left to do the job.

Only fifteen years after Leo died, the Roman Empire in the western lands came to an inglorious end as the barbarians finally took over. But Leo couldn't afford to give in to his fears during those chaotic times. There were Christians in the city who needed their pastor to stand firm. This was true not only in the realm of war and statecraft, but also in the realm of theology. Leo the Great was going to play a pivotal role as he joined forces with Cyril to defeat the Nestorian heresy. Theirs was an age of great theological achievement amidst precipitous societal decline. Though they didn't know it, these later church fathers were living in the twilight of a dying civilization. What kind of Christianity would be handed on to the Middle Ages? What kind of Jesus would be bequeathed to future generations? These were the vital questions Leo and Cyril were trying to answer.

Victory for Orthodoxy

After the Roman church had had a chance to evaluate Cyril's dossier on Nestorius, they sided completely with the Alexandrian bishop. The Italian contingent met and repudiated Nestorius's doctrines, then wrote to Cyril asking him to enforce this decision on their behalf. He was only too happy to oblige. As it turns out, a major council was in the works. Originally it was Nestorius's idea, for he had hoped Cyril would be discredited. But soon things began to spin out of his control. The council's location was moved from Nestorius's own backyard in Constantinople to the city of Ephesus. This was a major blow for several reasons. For one, the bishop of Ephesus did not like Constantinople's interference in the affairs of Asia Minor, so he was not inclined to be friendly to Nestorius. But even worse, Ephesus was a focal point of Marian devotion, since it was the traditional location where John had taken Jesus's mother to live out her old age. (Mary is still venerated at Ephesus; I was once harangued at her supposed house by an insistent nun extolling the glories of the Virgin.) The Ephesian locals did not look favorably on Nestorius's refusal to call Mary the "God-Bearer." With these new developments, things did not bode well for Nestorius.

Cyril's Egyptian party arrived in Ephesus to find that Nestorius had been coolly received. He had not been allowed to preside at communion in any of the city's churches. At this point Cyril took charge. He had the right to do so, not only as the senior bishop from Alexandria, but also because the Roman delegation had appointed him their representative until they could arrive. Although many of the bishops had been delayed in transit, Cyril made his move. He convened the council in the city's cathedral, the Church of Mary the God-Bearer (the impressive remains of which are still visible today on the way out of the archaeological site). In a single day, Nestorius was declared a heretic and his ideas were condemned. Though later wrangling continued, Cyril clearly had won a great victory. The people of Ephesus celebrated in the streets, as did the Alexandrians when their bishop eventually returned home in triumph.

However, as important as the Council of Ephesus was, it did not bring final resolution to the christological debates in AD 431. It took another major council two decades later to produce an authoritative christological creed. This council took place at Chalcedon, a small town across the water from Constantinople. The Definition of Chalcedon still stands today as the hallmark of orthodoxy. All evangelical Christians hold to the theology taught at Chalcedon as the standard of biblical faith. When this council met in AD 451, Cyril had already died. Nevertheless, his theology lived on in the words of the creed. Cyril's key watchword was "union." He had coined the term "hypostatic union" to express his view. This theological term meant that Christ is one person (or *hypostasis*) who possesses two natures, divine and human.[19] He is not two persons, or two sons. He is not a man who is "associated" somehow with the Logos. He is not a man chosen and infused with divine power. Rather, he is a complete unity, a single individual, God in the flesh. In him, full deity and full humanity are perfectly united; and this has been the case ever since the virginal conception. For Cyril, such theology is no mere abstraction. Jesus Christ had to be divine and human in order for salvation to be possible.[20] Human beings are saved as they are lifted up into divine life by the one who is able to span the great divide between heaven and earth. Salvation requires a single God-Man to join us as men and bring us to God.

In the Definition of Chalcedon, Cyril's Alexandrian emphasis on the unity and deity of Christ was counterweighted by language that affirmed Christ's true humanity and his dual natures. Pope Leo the Great played a strategic role here. He had written a christological treatise known as the *Tome* which nicely balanced the two sides in the debate. This work was read at the council and served, along with Cyril's writings, as a touchstone for the participants. When all the dust settled, the orthodox creed of Chalcedon affirmed that Christ is "in two natures, without confusion, without change, without division, without separation; the distinction of natures being in no way annulled by the union, but rather the characteristics of each nature being preserved and coming together to form one person and *hypostasis*."[21] So here we find the absolute *unity* Cyril had always demanded, along with the Antiochenes' recognition of the *duality* of natures. The two natures of Christ cohere harmoniously in a single person without any unnatural admixture. The Chalcedonian Definition also affirmed that Mary is the "God-Bearer" or "Mother of God." This is an essential truth for Bible-believing Christians—not because it says something about Mary, but because it means the Son she bore was always God himself. At Chalcedon, Jesus's full deity and full humanity were delicately balanced.

Was the great christological debate finally over now? Not really. The extreme Alexandrian party, with their unity emphasis, did not like Chalcedon's reference to "two natures." So they never did accept the Definition as authoritative. They became known as "Monophysite" churches (from a Greek term that means "one nature"). They still exist today as the Oriental Orthodox Churches.[22] On the other hand, the radical Antiochenes found just enough language in the creed of Chalcedon to make them happy. The wording was ambiguous enough for them to accept. They could claim the "union" of Christ's natures referred to the loose kind of union they envisioned. To clarify matters, these so-called Nestorian churches were eventually repudiated at a third major council in AD 553. Nevertheless, they, too, still exist today, known as the Assyrian Church of the East.[23] In fact, the supreme patriarch of this church ministers in north Chicago not far from where I teach. It's a little startling to think that such ancient controversies have resulted in divisions which can still be seen in our world!

However, we should not think that either the Monophysites or the Nestorians represent the mainline of Christology. These groups are not Roman Catholics or Eastern Orthodox; they are distinct communions with non-Chalcedonian views of Christ's person. They represent extreme opinions that were rejected during the ancient church period. Therefore, only one group was left standing in the middle: the centrist perspective of Cyril and Leo. Having benefited from their avoidance of the ends of the spectrum, these thinkers arrived at the balance that is so necessary for proper Christology. They knew Jesus Christ is no conjoined twin, no mere man, no adopted son. He is a unity, and he is God. Yet this does not mean we can ignore his dual natures. In Christ, both God and Man were perfectly united in hypostatic union. Cyril bequeathed this doctrine to the Greek East, just as Leo did to the Latin West. Today the Christology of these church fathers is held by Eastern Orthodoxy and Roman Catholicism alike. And despite the problems evangelical Christians would have with many doctrines emanating from those churches, on matters of Christology we are precisely in step with them. We hold to the faith of Chalcedon because men like Cyril, poring over scripture to discern the Christ presented there, found the right balance in the fifth century. Aren't you glad he did the hard work of blazing this difficult theological trail?

Reflections on Cyril of Alexandria

Cyril stands at the end of an era. He lived in what scholars call "Late Antiquity," a time when the Roman Empire was weakening like an old man whose glory days were long past. Indeed it isn't too much to say that the ancient world was ending, and the medieval world was about to begin. This is especially true if we are talking about the western half of the empire—Italy, North Africa, Gaul, Britain—since those regions suffered more of the barbarians' depredations. But even in the East, where the Byzantine Empire would preserve the flame of old Rome until as late as 1453, times were nonetheless changing. What can we say about Christianity in the age of Cyril?

The Christian church of AD 500 stood poised between the splendor of its Greco-Roman past and the promise of its medieval destiny. It was the only institution to survive the transition from the ancient world into the Middle Ages, where it would become the unifying faith of a Christendom on the rise. When a little baby was born of a virgin in Bethlehem during the reign of Caesar Augustus, no one could have predicted a new religion was about to take over the world. But that is exactly what happened. While we believe in the guidance of a divine hand and the working of the Holy Spirit, we must also recognize that the triumph of Christianity came about through historical means. It took real people, living in the real world, expressing their faith in tangible ways, to establish the early church. Once it was on firm footing, the church was ready to move with confidence into the Middle Ages and beyond. The ancient church fathers began the journey which you and I travel today.

Cyril of Alexandria serves us well as a capstone for this book. In him, we see many of the book's themes come together in a coherent way. Recall the introductory chapter, where we discovered three common misconceptions evangelicals often have about early Christianity. Now that we've gotten to know the church fathers a little bit, perhaps we can see how wrong our preconceived notions often are. The first misconception is that *the church fathers were not biblical.* But Cyril has shown us that he stands within a rich tradition of scriptural exegesis at Alexandria. Of course, Cyril represents only one side of a two-way conversation with Antioch. While ancient interpretive methods differed from our own, it was the early Christians' reflection on the Bible that shaped their lives at every point. Each figure in this book has been shown to have engaged the Word of God in a serious fashion, albeit in ways appropriate to their respective times and places.

The second misconception is that *the ancient church fathers were Roman Catholics.* But Cyril's political maneuvering reveals precisely the opposite: Rome, though an important center of Christian life, was not the dominant head of a single church hierarchy that always did its bidding. It was only after the time of Leo, about AD 500, that a true papacy was established. Before the Roman Catholic Church existed under the clearly recognized authority of the pope, there was the "lowercase-c" catholic church of the ancient period. It

possessed a great sense of its universal nature, but no sense whatsoever of singular control. While the prestige of the church at Rome
was always very high, it was by no means the preeminent capital
of ecclesiastical life. Rather, Christianity flourished in all the great
cities of the empire.

We have encountered some of these cities in this book. Ignatius
gave his life to save divided Antioch; Justin Martyr apologized for
the faith in Ephesus and Rome; Irenaeus missionized provincial
Lyons in Gaul; Tertullian, Perpetua, and Augustine exemplified
rigorous Carthage and North Africa; Origen, Athanasius, and Cyril
did their theology in cerebral Alexandria; while John Chrysostom
preached amid the splendors of Constantinople. One of the main
purposes of this book has been to introduce you to these places—
places whose memories of mighty deeds from long ago are not quite
extinguished even today. You can still go to these lands. I hope you
will make time to visit them someday. And when you do, you just
might catch on the wind the whispering voices of bygone peoples
and their ancient civilizations. If you listen hard enough, you can still
hear the clashing of arms on epic battlefields, the roar of the crowd
in ruined amphitheaters, or the resonant preaching and sonorous
chanting in crumbling basilicas. Lands long drenched in blood and
demonism desperately needed to find a new Lord. A thoroughly
pagan culture yearned to acquire a Christian mind. This was the
daunting task facing the first believers.

In light of this, we can now see the error of the third misconception: that *the church fathers represent the "fall" of Christianity*. If it were
true that devastating and irreversible apostasy arose under Emperor
Constantine, then we really shouldn't be teaching the patristic legacy
of Chalcedon as orthodox Christology. Yet it is precisely the doctrine
of the church fathers (not just on this point but in numerous areas
of theology) that modern evangelicals still embrace today. Far from
becoming stagnant, the church reached a theological high-water
mark in the late ancient era. Furthermore, Cyril represents more
than just a doctrinally vibrant church. He also shows that there had

been no collapse in the church's faithfulness to Christ the Lord. The absolute necessity of the God-Man as the only possible means of human salvation was the very principle to which Cyril committed his whole life. Is this not the same testimony to which the martyrs had borne witness? Would Ignatius, Polycarp, Justin, Blandina, Sanctus, Perpetua, Felicity, or Origen have died for a mere man? The truth that the martyrs defended with their lives—the centrality of the risen Jesus—is the same truth the apologists such as Justin, Irenaeus, and Tertullian, and the theologians such as Athanasius, Augustine, and Cyril defended in their writings. No sooner had the threat of persecution ended with Emperor Constantine, than the new threat of theological heresy arose. But the church did not "fall" in those tumultuous days—at least no more than it has fallen in our own time. It simply adapted to unaccustomed realities with renewed determination.

Admittedly, new challenges and temptations emerged in the post-Constantinian era. A different relationship to human government had to be forged, one that contained inherent pitfalls. But through this whole process of readjustment, faithful Christians like those profiled in this book continued to live out their faith responsibly. Far from representing the church's fall, figures like Cyril represent a triumphant church. Even though they no doubt committed the sins that entangle every generation of believers, the early church fathers have given us a profound theological inheritance. The Christology hammered out by Cyril in the fifth century bequeathed to orthodox believers of later generations a Jesus who is to be worshiped as fully God and fully man.

Yet that's not all. The early Christians also gave the church a doctrine of the Trinity. They discerned the boundaries of the canon of scripture. They interpreted the Word of God. They organized themselves into an ecclesiastical structure that could defeat the danger of Gnostic heresy. They defended grace in the face of legalism. They pursued bodily self-denial in ways that put us to shame today. They produced a great rhetorical tradition of powerful preaching of the Word. And many of them gave their lives for their Lord amidst horrendous suffering. When you consider the hostile environment into which Christianity was born, the legacy the church fathers have passed down to us is astounding. As they would be the first to say: *Soli deo gloria.*

Provocative Questions

1. The Council of Chalcedon attempted to balance two important points in theology: the humanity and divinity of Christ. Extreme opinions led to heresy. Each side needed to be moderated by the other to find a mediating viewpoint. Are there other theological issues like this today? Do you see a spectrum of beliefs on certain topics, in which the balanced position in the middle is probably the correct one? Name some of these issues. What are some issues on which no compromise is possible?

2. In what ways do you see the humanity of Christ overemphasized in churches today? Is Jesus's image softened in popular evangelical culture? Is he "watered down" to be a man just like us? What does scripture have to tell us about his manhood? See Matthew 4:1–11; Mark 14:32–42; Philippians 2:5–11; and Hebrews 4:15–16.

3. In contrast, where do you see the deity of Christ being overemphasized today? Is Jesus ever presented as "remote" from his people? What is the difference between that and a proper appreciation for his awesome glory? See Mark 4:35–41; Colossians 1:15–20; Hebrews 7:26; and Revelation 19:11–16 for some biblical discussions of Christ's majesty. Does 2 Corinthians 8:9 bring together the themes of weakness and glory?

4. Which of the ten church fathers profiled in this book did you like the most? The least? Was there a particular one whose story you identified with in a special way? Why?

5. Before reading this book, what did the term "church fathers" mean to you? What names or people would you have associated with that term? Did you have any of the "misconceptions" listed above? Has your understanding of the early church now changed at all? Name a couple of things you will take away from reading this book.

Good Books to Dig Deeper

One of Cyril's most mature theological works is available in:

McGuckin, John Anthony. *St Cyril of Alexandria: On the Unity of Christ.* Crestwood, NY: St. Vladimir's Seminary Press, 1995.

Three books which provide extensive background material, in combination with selected primary texts, are:

McGuckin, John. *Saint Cyril of Alexandria and the Christological Controversy: Its History, Theology, and Texts.* New York: Brill, 1994; repr. St. Vladimir's Seminary Press, 2004.

Russell, Norman. *Cyril of Alexandria.* New York: Routledge, 2000.

Wickham, Lionel R. *Cyril of Alexandria: Select Letters.* Oxford: Clarendon Press, 1983.

Cyril's exegesis may be profitably read in:

Smith, R. Payne. *Commentary on the Gospel of Saint Luke by Saint Cyril, Patriarch of Alexandria.* Astoria, NY: Studion Publishers, 1983.

Two studies which focus on Cyril's relationship to the Bible are:

McKinion, Steven A. *Words, Imagery, and the Mystery of Christ: A Reconstruction of Cyril of Alexandria's Christology.* Leiden: Brill, 2000.

Wilken, Robert L. *Judaism and the Early Christian Mind: A Study of Cyril of Alexandria's Exegesis and Theology.* Yale University Press, 1971; repr. Wipf & Stock, 2004.

A Taste of Cyril

On the Unity of Christ

Cyril wrote this work around AD 437, near the end of his life, and so with the ability to look back on his controversy with Nestorius. He composed it in the form of a dialogue between two unnamed interlocutors: A and B. Usually A provides the authoritative answers, and B simply responds agreeably to what is said or poses new questions.

In this selection we find Cyril making an important point: that Christology is intimately related to the doctrine of salvation. The reason Cyril insisted on the unity of Christ was to safeguard the truth that our Savior is simultaneously one with us and with God. In himself, Christ has made a bridge between God and Man. Cyril describes Christ as a Second Adam who undoes the work of the devil and our fall into sin through Adam. The Son of God's perfect obedience has reordered the human race back to the way it was supposed to be. By joining Christ in faith, we enter into his cosmic recapitulation.

You would not be mistaken if you caught overtones here from Athanasius (compare this text to the one translated in chapter 7). Cyril's understanding of salvation is consistent with a trend running through Athanasius all the way back to Irenaeus, in which salvation is a mystical participation in Christ and an elevation into divine life. This viewpoint, which has scriptural grounding, is very prominent in eastern theology.

A: We had become accursed because of Adam's sin, and had fallen into death's snare, forsaken by God.[24] But "all things have become new in Christ" (2 Cor. 5:17). Our situation has been restored to the way it was at the beginning. We desperately needed the Second Adam to come. I am referring to Christ, who is from heaven and is mightier than all sin. He is utterly undefiled and untouchable—the new firstfruits of our race. He came to deliver our human nature from punishment, and to call down upon us once again the gracious favor of the Father above, and to undo our forsakenness through his obedience and absolute submission. "For he committed no sin" (1 Pet. 2:22). But in him our human nature was enriched with such totally unassailable innocence, that we are now able to cry out with the bold words, "My God, my God, why have you forsaken me?" (Matt. 27:46). You should know that since the Only-Begotten had become a man, he uttered those words as one of us and on behalf of our whole human nature. It's as if Christ were saying:

"The first man had sinned. He lapsed into disobedience and ignored the commandment he had been given. He was snatched and carried off into this lawlessness by the serpent's trickery. Thus, with all fairness he was swept into ruin and came under punishment. But You [Father] have established me as a seedling to be a second beginning for everyone on earth. That's why I have been given the title, 'the Second Adam' (1 Cor. 15:45–47). In me You see man's nature cleansed, set aright in sinlessness, made holy and pure.[25] Now bestow the blessings of Your kindness; undo the forsakenness; rebuke the ruin; and put a limit on the consequences of wrath. I have conquered Satan himself, who used to reign of old. For he found absolutely nothing in me that belongs to him."

It seems to me that this was the meaning of the Savior's words. He was not calling down the Father's gracious favor on himself, but rather on us! For the consequences of [God's] wrath had passed down to human nature in its entirety. It was exactly like something being passed down in a plant from the original root—by which I mean Adam. "For death reigned from Adam to Moses, even over those who had not sinned in the manner of Adam's transgression" (Rom. 5:14). But in the same way, the things that come from Christ, who is our new firstfruits, will pass down once more to the entire human race. The very wise Paul guarantees this when he says, "For if by the transgression of one man, the many died, so much more" shall the many live through the righteousness of one man (Rom. 5:15). And Paul also says: "For just as in Adam all die, so also in Christ shall all be made alive" (1 Cor. 15:22).

B: So, would it therefore be foolish and utterly incongruous with the Holy Scriptures to think or say that it was [only] the assumed Man who used these human words—as if he were "forsaken" by the Word who had been conjoined to him?[26]

A: My dear friend, that would not only be ungodly, it would be proof of madness to the outer limits. But at any rate, that certainly seems appropriate for those who don't know how to think straight! For they bifurcate Christ's words and his acts, splitting them apart in every way. They have assigned some things to belong solely to the Only-Begotten, and others to a son who is different from him, born of a woman. In this way they've gone astray from the straight and unswerving path by which we can clearly comprehend the mystery of Christ.

Epilogue

Perhaps I may close this book with an illustration I use in my classes to describe the energizing effect that studying the Christian past can have. Twice I have been blessed to serve as a guest teacher on a Mediterranean cruise that toured various locations from early church history. The cruise ship was a very upscale sailing yacht known as the *Sea Cloud*. She has four masts and room for about 70 passengers, not counting the crew. Everything about the *Sea Cloud* speaks of luxury and the old-fashioned style of her wealthy socialite past (the ship was originally owned by cereal heiress Marjorie Merriweather Post and her Wall Street investor husband E. F. Hutton). One day I went forward to the front of the ship while she was at sea. I stood on the foredeck with the great bowsprit reaching toward the next port of call. The wind was blowing in my face and the waves were churning and parting beneath my feet. As I stood there, I was not at all taking a passive stance. I was active, braced, ready for action. I did not look backward, but forward into the future, contemplating the next destination at which I would soon arrive. At the same time, I did not impart any forward motion to myself. I was being carried along by the great ship, dwarfed by its massive weight, relying on it to propel me forward.

As I often tell my students, I believe my experience aboard that ship can serve as a metaphor for the history of the church. We certainly must not become mired in the historical past, longing to return to ports of call which we have already left behind. Our focus must be on the future. And yet our focus on the future must take into account the grand story of which we all are a part. If we would only wake up and take a good look at our surroundings, we would notice that our motion is not being imparted merely by our own efforts in our local churches in twenty-first-century America. We are small figures inevitably carried forward by the weight of the holy catholic church, whose sails are filled by the mighty wind of the Holy Spirit. The church of the Lord Jesus Christ is indeed a divine work. I hope this image will give you an exciting and refreshing perspective on your heritage in the faith.

As you get to know some of your fellow-sailors from ancient times, it is my prayer that your perspective on the value of church history will be widened. I hope you'll continue to carry out the tasks Jesus has assigned you to do, just as he had tasks for the ancient Christians as well. And as you go about your daily life, discharging all your God-given duties and responsibilities, I pray you will do so with an awareness that you're part of something much bigger than yourself. You are indeed part of the Church Universal: that great sweep of Christianity through the ages, with all its ups and downs, its twists and turns, its heroes and villains. This is your story, your family heritage. The fathers and mothers of the church are your spiritual ancestors.

Theologically speaking, there is only one body of Christ, into which all who believe in him are baptized. The true church is not represented by any one institution or denomination. It is rather his mystical body, which is spread throughout the world, and which penetrates down through the ages. You belong to it, if you're a Christian saved by grace; and this sense of belonging can energize your spiritual life in amazing ways. Perhaps on some level you have always known this to be true, and you're only now becoming fully aware of it. Or perhaps this is the first time you've ever thought of things in this way. Regardless, you will benefit immensely when you realize you're standing on the bow of a great ship of faith. To understand your solidarity with the fathers of the church—and indeed with all the heroes of church history—is to be lifted up from the mundane trivialities of the everyday world, and to conceptualize your life as a grand odyssey with your companions in Christ. So go ahead. Think of yourself in this way. Start running after the cloud of witnesses who have already run the race well. Fix your eyes on Jesus, just as they did in their day. Embrace your inner catholic, and see where it will take you!

NOTES

Introduction

1. Robert Louis Wilken, *The Spirit of Early Christian Thought: Seeking the Face of God* (New Haven: Yale Press, 2003), xiv.

2. For this association, see Angelo Di Berardino and Basil Studer, eds., *History of Theology, vol. 1, The Patristic Period*, trans. Matthew J. O'Connell (Collegeville, Minn.: Liturgical Press, 1996), 344–346.

3. Johannes Quasten, *Patrology*, vol. 1 (Westminster, MD: Newman Press, 1950; repr. Allen, Texas: Christian Classics), 1.

4. Irenaeus, *Against Heresies* 4.41.2. The quotation is taken from volume 1 of the 10–volume set called the *Ante-Nicene Fathers*. The ANF, along with the two series known together as the *Nicene and Post-Nicene Fathers* (NPNF), probably serve as the easiest way for the beginning reader to access the patristic sources. Most theological libraries have the entire 38-volume set of the ANF and NPNF, and it is also available online at www.ccel.org/fathers2/. The translations are antiquated and aren't based on the most up-to-date manuscript evidence. Nevertheless, the set is widely available, and for that reason I quote from it in this book whenever possible.

5. Clement of Alexandria, *Stromata* 1.1 (ANF 2:299).

6. Pamphilus set an example for Eusebius by dying as a martyr. His death is described in Eusebius's *Church History*, Martyrs of Palestine, 11 (NPNF ser. 2, 1:351–354). This document is appended to Book VIII of the *Church History*. Prior to Pamphilus's martyrdom, Eusebius visited him in prison for two years. His affection for his "father" is evident in the many warm things Eusebius had to say about him.

7. For this fourfold list, see for example Boniface Ramsey, *Beginning to Read the Fathers* (Mahwah, NJ: Paulist, 1985), 4–7; Christopher A. Hall, *Reading Scripture with the Church Fathers* (Downers Grove, IL: InterVarsity, 1998), 51–55; and also Hall's 2002 follow-up work *Learning Theology with the Church Fathers* (Downers Grove, IL: InterVarsity, 2002), 20–21.

8. Vincent of Lérins, *A Commonitory* 6 (NPNF ser. 2, 11:132).

9. Ibid., 72 (NPNF ser. 2, 11:152, slightly adapted for clarity).

10. Ibid., 77 (NPNF ser. 2, 11:154).

11. Ibid., 57 (NPNF ser. 2, 11:148).

12. We should recognize that the scholarly definition of "patristics" would certainly include other ancient figures who were deemed by later generations to be heretics. In an academic setting, all historical documents would be valid sources for inquiry into Christian beginnings. Scholars today do not attempt to pass judgment upon a given writer's "orthodoxy." In this book, however, we will be concerned more specifically with those figures whose lives and teachings are considered to be acceptable by the witness of historic, orthodox, and conservative Christianity.

13. For the history of these discussions, see Gabriel Moran, *Scripture and Tradition: A Survey of the Controversy* (New York: Herder and Herder, 1963); and Yves M.-J. Congar, *Tradition and Traditions: An Historical and Theological Essay*, trans. Michael Naseby and Thomas Rainborough (London: Burnes & Oates, 1966).

14. *Dei Verbum* 9. It is always best when discussing Roman Catholicism to work with what the Church's actual documents say and teach, instead of relying on Protestant characterizations. Today the proceedings of the Second Vatican Council provide the authoritative interpretation of all previous councils. Roman Catholic doctrine is nicely summarized in the Catechism of the Catholic Church (see § 80–83 on the subject of Scripture and Tradition). Both of these sources can be found online at www.vatican.va/archive/.

15. I know of one significant passage where "tradition" is used to speak of something not found in written scripture. The church father Tertullian wrote a treatise to Christians in the military, who traditionally refused to wear victory wreaths because they carried pagan religious significance (*The Chaplet* 1–4, ANF 3:93–95). By way of comparison, Tertullian mentioned other Christian rituals and habits that were not specifically discussed in the Bible, yet are to be followed based on "custom" and "usage" and "tradition." While Tertullian's idea of unwritten tradition here stands in contrast to the explicit written injunctions of scripture, we should note that he was not opposing the two entities as if they stood against one another. Rather, he was affirming the validity of certain longstanding Christian customs which in no way contradicted anything the Bible commands. In fact, they are consistent with scriptural principles and with reason. A modern example of something similar might be the use of steeples on our churches. The Bible does not mention this practice, yet it is not unbiblical, and is attested by common custom. The point is this: for the church fathers, tradition and scripture were in harmony, not competing entities.

16. Athanasius, *Festal Letter* 39 (NPNF ser. 2, 4:552).

17. Eusebius, *Church History* 6.23.2 (NPNF ser. 2, 1:271).

18. *Biblia Patristica* is a French work which uses Latin, so it is not very accessible to the non-technical reader. However, the volumes of the ANF and NPNF include

good scripture indices for each early church writer. These indices can be used to find patristic commentary on a particular Bible verse or passage. A couple of other very helpful tools for accessing patristic biblical exegesis are the *Ancient Christian Commentary on Scripture*, edited by Thomas Oden (InterVarsity Press), and *The Church's Bible*, edited by Robert Wilken (Eerdmans). See also Charles Kannengiesser, *The Handbook of Patristic Exegesis: The Bible in Ancient Christianity* (Leiden, the Netherlands: Brill, 2004).

19. Wilken, *The Spirit of Early Christian Thought*, xvii.

20. This is not to say that all contemporary Roman Catholic doctrines and practices are biblical or apostolic, but only that many Catholic teachings must be understood as continuous historical developments out of earlier thought. For example, though the theology has changed from biblical times, the breaking of bread and drinking of wine in the Mass is an evolution of the love feasts of the early Christians, for whom the elements represented the Savior's body and blood just as they still do for Catholics. Likewise, recitation of the Lord's Prayer is an ancient habit still practiced today. And there are not a few doctrines held by the Roman Church which every orthodox Protestant would hold as well, such as the Trinity or the two natures of the one person of Christ.

21. D. H. Williams, *Retrieving the Tradition and Renewing Evangelicalism: A Primer for Suspicious Protestants* (Grand Rapids: Eerdmans, 1999), 222.

22. Ibid., 226.

23. See for example J. M. Carroll, *The Trail of Blood Following Christians Down through the Centuries, or The History of Baptist Churches from the Time of Christ, Their Founder, to the Present Day* (Lexington: Ashland Avenue Baptist Church, 1931).

24. A contemporary example of this viewpoint, coming out of Brethren or Anabaptist life, is David Bercot's book, *The Kingdom that Turned the World Upside Down* (Tyler, TX: Scroll Publishing, 2003). Bercot argues that Emperor Constantine introduced a "hybrid" church in which the teachings of Jesus were forgotten and worldly values were embraced. Augustine supported this corrupted viewpoint, and so did the mainline reformers such as Martin Luther, John Calvin, and Ulrich Zwingli. Thus they did not preach the true gospel. Only the Anabaptists and some related movements understood the truth. One of the primary goals of Scroll Publishing Co. and of David Bercot's body of work is to advance a "fall" historiography. See http://www.scrollpublishing.com/.

25. D. H. Williams does an excellent job of detailing the historiography of "fallen" Christianity in chapter 4 of his book *Retrieving the Tradition and Renewing Evangelicalism*.

26. Eusebius is the first to provide us this account in his *Life of Constantine* 1:28–32 (NPNF ser. 2, 1:490–91).

27. Cornelius Dyck, "The Suffering Church in Anabaptism," *Mennonite Quarterly Review* 59 (1985): 5–23.

28. Martin Luther, "On the Councils and the Church," trans. Eric W. Gritsch, in *Luther's Works* 41, ed. Helmut T. Lehmann (Philadelphia: Fortress, 1966), 19–20. Luther goes on to borrow an image from St. Bernard in which studying the church fathers is compared to drinking from a clear brook: it is satisfying, but not as much as drinking from the actual fountainhead itself (the scriptures). Luther's approach to the church fathers was always selective. When he found them to be in harmony with scripture, he accepted them. When he believed them to be contrary to scripture, he felt the freedom to reject them on that point.

29. See Anthony N. S. Lane, *John Calvin: Student of the Church Fathers* (Edinburgh: T&T Clark, 1999).

30. John Calvin, "Calvin's Reply to Sadoleto," in *A Reformation Debate: Sadoleto's Letter to the Genevans and Calvin's Reply*, ed. John C. Olin (Grand Rapids: Baker, 1966), 62.

31. Ibid., 74.

32. Usually this idea is captured in the saying, "Those who cannot remember the past are condemned to repeat it," from George Santayana, *The Life of Reason: Introduction and Reason in Common Sense* (Scribners, 1905), 284.

Chapter 1 Ignatius of Antioch

1. http://www.tdcj.state.tx.us/statistics/deathrow/drowlist/cartrigt.jpg, accessed February 2007.

2. http://www.ccadp.org/uncensoredcartwright.htm, accessed February 2007. For Cartwright's final statement at his execution, see the Texas Department of Criminal Justice Web page, http://www.tdcj.state.tx.us/stat/executedoffenders.htm.

3. The image of a blazing meteor is not mine, but belongs to Michael Holmes in his updated edition of Lightfoot's classic work, *The Apostolic Fathers: Greek Texts and English Translations of Their Writings* (Grand Rapids: Baker, 1992), 129.

4. The Greek is ψυχή . . . τῷ θείῳ ζέουσα ἔρωτι. John Chrysostom's sermon on Ignatius may be read in NPNF ser. 1, 9:135–140.

5. Josephus, *The Wars of the Jews* 3.2.4. See William Whiston, *The Works of Josephus* (Peabody, MA: Hendrickson, 1987), 640. This text may be found online at http://www.ccel.org/j/josephus/JOSEPHUS.HTM.

6. For this argument, see in particular Raymond E. Brown and John P. Meier, *Antioch and Rome: New Testament Cradles of Catholic Christianity* (New York: Paulist, 1983), 45–72.

7. Scholars have vigorously debated the identity of Ignatius's opponents in Antioch. I take the position that there were two main groups: Jewish legalists, and docetists somehow connected with Gnostic belief. For an overview of this matter, see chapter 5 in Christine Trevett, *A Study of Ignatius of Antioch in Syria and Asia* (Lewiston, NY: Edwin Mellen Press, 1992).

8. Glanville Downey, *A History of Antioch in Syria from Seleucus to the Arab Conquest* (Princeton: University Press, 1961), 79–80.

9. Josephus, *The Wars of the Jews* 7.3.3 (Whiston, 753).

10. On the attractiveness of Judaism to the Antiochene Christians, see Wayne A. Meeks and Robert L. Wilken, *Jews and Christians in Antioch in the First Four Centuries of the Common Era* (Missoula, MT: Scholars, 1978), 31–36.

11. Ignatius, *Letter to the Magnesians* 10 (ANF 1:63). The editors of the *Ante-Nicene Fathers* series have chosen to print two different manuscript versions of the letters of Ignatius, which they call the "longer" and "shorter" versions. As you read, simply ignore the "longer" version, which has been determined by modern scholars not to be authentic. It is the product of a later theologian putting words into Ignatius's mouth. The "shorter" version printed in the left-hand column of the ANF is what Ignatius actually wrote.

12. For a good discussion of Ignatius's relationship to Jewish Christianity, including the relevant primary texts, see Oskar Skarsaune, *In the Shadow of the Temple* (Downers Grove, IL: InterVarsity, 2002), 214–217.

13. Ignatius, *Letter to the Magnesians* 8 (ANF 1:62).

14. Irenaeus, *Against Heresies* 1.23–27 (ANF 1:347–353). This author, the bishop of Lyons in Gaul, was a credible witness to the nature of Gnosticism in the East. He was born in Smyrna around the time Ignatius passed through, and grew up in the presence of Ignatius's friend Polycarp. It seems likely that Polycarp's church would have informed Irenaeus about Ignatius's martyrdom and the opponents he faced back in Antioch. We know that Bishop Polycarp made it his business to be familiar with various heresies. Irenaeus had also read some Gnostic texts, and used an anti-heretical work by Justin Martyr for further information. On Irenaeus's sources for his knowledge of Gnosticism, see Robert M. Grant, *Irenaeus of Lyons* (New York: Routledge, 1997), 11–12.

15. Downey, *A History of Antioch in Syria from Seleucus to the Arab Conquest*, 292–293, finds this hypothesis quite plausible. He notes that an earthquake is the explanation given for Ignatius's martyrdom in a sixth-century historical work.

16. Ignatius probably was martyred under the reign of Emperor Trajan, and today we possess a unique insight into his policy on Christianity. One of his provincial governors, Pliny the Younger, wrote to him about whether Christians should be punished merely for the "name," or for specific crimes. Pliny informed the emperor that his current policy was to inflict capital punishment upon anyone who admitted adhering to the name of Christ. Trajan wrote back with approval of this policy, although he advised Pliny not to seek out Christians or to put credence in anonymous accusations. The correspondence between the two may be found in Henry Bettenson and Chris Maunder, *Documents of the Christian Church* (Oxford: Oxford University Press, 1999), 3–5.

17. Ignatius, *Letter to the Ephesians* 1 (ANF 1:49).

18. Ibid., *Letter to the Romans* 5 (ANF 1:75).

19. The young Onesimus was highly praised by Paul and became like a son to him. With such endorsement, Onesimus would have been a likely candidate for eventual leadership in the early church several decades later. Where? Was it Ephesus? Colossians 4:9 connects Onesimus with the nearby town of Colosse. And if he can be equated with the figure of Onesiphorus, as some scholars suggest, then he has a connection to Ephesus as well (2 Tim. 1:16–18). The Onesimus of Ephesus from whom Ignatius received a visit, and the Onesimus whom Paul knew, may have been one and the same. But we cannot say for sure.

20. For this insight, see William R. Schoedel, *Ignatius of Antioch: A Commentary on the Letters of Ignatius of Antioch* (Philadelphia: Fortress, 1985), 10–12.

21. Ignatius, *Letter to the Ephesians* 4 (ANF 1:50–51, slightly adapted for clarity).

22. Trevett, *A Study of Ignatius*, delineates several different scholarly perspectives on the meaning of the church's attainment of "peace," 56–66.

Chapter 2 Justin Martyr

1. This account is based on Dr. Bright's article "The Beginnings of the Four Spiritual Laws" accessed February 2007 at http://www.retirementwithapurpose.com/lessons/tcintroduce2.html.

2. Eusebius, *Church History* 4.18.6 (NPNF ser. 2, 1:196). The city of Caesarea has also been suggested as a possible location where Justin lived for a time. See Thomas B. Falls, *St. Justin Martyr: Dialogue with Trypho*, revised by Thomas P. Halton (Washington, DC: Catholic University of America Press, 2003), xii.

3. We do know that before he was saved, Justin was quite impressed by the fortitude of the Christian martyrs. He wrote, "When I was delighting in the doctrines of Plato, and heard the Christians slandered, and saw them fearless of death and all other things which are counted fearful, I perceived that it was impossible that they could be living in wickedness and pleasure." *Second Apology* 12 (ANF 1:192). Justin's writings frequently reveal his interest in the subject of martyrdom. It seems reasonable that after becoming a Christian, he might have inquired at Ephesus about Ignatius, who had received a visit from the Ephesian bishop Onesimus.

4. Justin described his wanderings from teacher to teacher in a literary form reminiscent of other ancient depictions of a student's mishaps in various schools. For this reason some modern scholars have considered Justin's story to be satire, not a true autobiographical account. One advocate of this view is Erwin R. Goodenough, *The Theology of Justin Martyr* (Amsterdam: Philo Press, 1968), 58–59. However, there are other scholars who do understand Justin's story to be truthful—though certainly his comments about the various philosophical schools were intended to highlight their shortcomings. For this perspective see L. W. Barnard, *Justin Martyr: His Life and Thought* (Cambridge: University Press, 1967), 7–8. In my opinion the narrative has a ring of truth to it which signals its authenticity. Justin's personal testimony gives

us insight into the kind of restless search so many people embark upon as they grope about trying to find God.

5. Justin Martyr, *Dialogue with Trypho* 1 (ANF 1:194).

6. Ibid., 3 (ANF 1:195).

7. Ibid., 4 (ANF 1:196).

8. Ibid., 7 (ANF 1:198).

9. Ibid., 8 (ANF 1:198, slightly adapted for clarity). Another famous conversion experience in church history used similar language to describe a sudden warming of the heart. John Wesley, the founder of Methodism, wrote in his journal in 1738: "In the evening I went very unwillingly to a society in Aldersgate Street, where one was reading Luther's preface to the Epistle to the Romans. About a quarter before nine, while he was describing the change which God works in the heart through faith in Christ, I felt my heart strangely warmed. I felt I did trust in Christ, Christ alone, for salvation; and an assurance was given me that He had taken away my sins, even mine, and saved me from the law of sin and death." Like Justin Martyr, John Wesley went on to become an outstanding evangelist. You can read Wesley's Journal online at http://www.ccel.org/ccel/wesley/journal.toc.html.

10. Ibid., 142 (ANF 1:270).

11. Ibid., (slightly adapted for clarity).

12. Eusebius, *Church History* 4.11.8 (NPNF scr. 2, 1:184).

13. There is some debate about where exactly Justin lived. Some scholars argue he lived in "the house of one Martinus, above the Timotinian Baths." Others argue the evidence points to the existence of a Christian school somewhere along the Via Tiburtina. In supporting the latter conclusion, I follow Eric Osborn, *Justin Martyr* (Tübingen: JCB Mohr, 1973), 5–6.

14. *Second Apology* 3 (ANF 1:189).

15. Tatian, *Address to the Greeks* 19 (ANF 2:73).

16. *Second Apology* 3 (ANF 1:189).

17. The text, commonly known as the *Acts of Saint Justin*, is referred to as *The Martyrdom of the Holy Martyrs* by the editors of the *Ante-Nicene Fathers* set. It can be found in Volume 1, pages 305–306. Recall that this patristic series can be accessed online at http://www.ccel.org/fathers2/.

18. *Acts of Saint Justin* 4 (ANF 1:306).

19. Ibid.

20. In *Timaeus* 28c Plato wrote, "Now to find the maker and father of this universe is hard enough, and even if I succeeded, to declare him to everyone is impossible." This statement is often quoted by the church fathers. John M. Cooper, *Plato: Complete Works* (Indianapolis: Hackett, 1997), 1235.

21. Justin Martyr, *First Apology* 5 (ANF 1:164).

22. Ibid., 26 (ANF 1:171).

23. Goodenough, *The Theology of Justin Martyr*, 139, writes, "The Logos then in all circles but the Stoic, and often apparently even in Stoicism, was a link of some kind which connected a transcendent Absolute with the world and humanity. The Logos came into general popularity because of the widespread desire to conceive of God as transcendent and immanent at the same time; the Logos as variously described in the Schools made possible such a twofold and contradictory conception of God."

24. We should note that the patristic Logos Christology had a problematic tendency to subordinate the persons of the Trinity into a three-tiered hierarchy. For example Justin wrote, "we reasonably worship [Christ], having learned that He is the Son of the true God Himself, and [we hold] Him in the second place, and the prophetic Spirit in the third . . ." (*First Apology* 13, ANF 1:166–167). Because of this subordinating tendency, the Logos Christology will not be the final way that the early church came to express the doctrine of the Trinity (in which all three persons are equal). Nevertheless, Justin Martyr represents a first attempt at dealing with a very thorny theological problem. His effort was part of the church's biblical thought process through which orthodox doctrine was developed.

25. Justin even advanced the preposterous (though in his day, believable) argument that Plato had come across the writings of Moses, which formed the source of his own philosophic conception of God. In this way Justin tried to show that Christianity, with its roots in the Jewish prophets, predates even the ancient Greek philosophers. Today we find Justin's thesis fanciful, but it illustrates his goal of showing that Christian doctrine is the final completion of Greek philosophy. See *First Apology* 59–60 (ANF 1:182–183).

26. *Second Apology* 13 (ANF 1:193, slightly adapted for clarity).

27. *First Apology* 14 (ANF 1:167, slightly adapted for clarity).

28. Ibid., 46 (ANF 1:178). See also *Second Apology* 10 (ANF 1:191).

29. Justin is referring to the bishop, but he avoids using *episkopos* because his non-Christian audience would not understand that term. Instead he uses a more generic word for "leader" or "ruler."

Chapter 3 Irenaeus of Lyons

1. Bart. D. Ehrman, *The New Testament: A Historical Introduction to the Early Christian Writings*, 2nd ed. (New York: Oxford University Press, 2000), 17.

2. Ibid., 17–18.

3. This is not to say Irenaeus was an "evangelical" Christian as we use that term today, but only that his focus on the life, death, and resurrection of Jesus mirrors that of modern evangelicals. In other words, Irenaeus and a contemporary evangelical would both focus on the historical Jesus who died for sins, instead of viewing him primarily as an esoteric teacher of wise maxims.

4. Mary Ann Donovan, *One Right Reading? A Guide to Irenaeus* (Collegeville, Minn.: Liturgical Press, 1997), 3.

5. Ehrman details the literary battle for the legacy of Jesus in his masterful book *Lost Christianities: The Battles for Scripture and the Faiths We Never Knew* (New York: Oxford University Press, 2003). I do not agree with Ehrman's conclusion that these other "lost Christianities" were just as valid as (or maybe even better than) the form of Christianity that eventually triumphed. Nor do I agree that all these other groups deserve equal respect as legitimate expressions of the faith that Jesus intended to propagate. Ehrman stands in opposition to many viewpoints that an evangelical will hold dear. However, his book is an excellent survey of the diversity within the early Christian movement. Irenaeus is portrayed (among others) as a narrow-minded and mean-spirited ideologue whose "arsenal" consisted of "polemical treatises and personal slurs" designed to annihilate his Gnostic opponents. Obviously I do not agree with this assessment. I suggest you read a little of Irenaeus and decide for yourself how he should be regarded. See the "dig deeper" reading list at the end of chapter 3.

6. Eusebius has recorded for posterity Irenaeus's letter describing his childhood memories. It is found in *Church History* 5.20.5–7 (NPNF ser. 2, 1:238–239, slightly adapted for clarity). The building in which Irenaeus can so vividly picture Polycarp ministering is no longer in existence today. However, in the middle of urban Iznik, Turkey (ancient Smyrna) there is a Roman Catholic congregation called the Church of St. Polycarp which traces its origins all the way back to the second century.

7. Ibid.

8. Irenaeus, *Against Heresies* 1.preface.3 (ANF 1:316).

9. Eusebius, *Church History* 5.1.18 (NPNF ser. 2, 1:214).

10. Ibid., 5.1.19 (NPNF ser. 2, 1:214).

11. Ibid., 5.1.23 (NPNF ser. 2, 1:214).

12. Ibid., 5.1.24 (NPNF ser. 2, 1:214).

13. Ibid.

14. Pierre Nautin, *Lettres et écrivains chrétiens des IIe et IIIe Siècles* (Paris, 1961), 54–61.

15. Eusebius, *Church History* 5.4.2 (NPNF ser. 2, 1:219).

16. Ibid., 5.24.18 (NPNF ser. 2, 1:244).

17. Irenaeus, *Against Heresies* 1.9.4 (ANF 1:330).

18. Some of the brochure's striking statements include:

- "Christ's life story can be seen as representing the birth, crucifixion, and resurrection of the spirit in all of us as we make the spiritual journey described in Theosophical literature."

- "Theosophy, far from being inconsistent with the Christian Way, is in fact its other side. Theosophy merits consideration by all who wish to make their Christian faith both more intelligible to their minds and more alive in their hearts."

- "Every word in the Bible is not infallibly true in its literal meaning—the letter killeth, but the spirit giveth life (2 Cor 3:6)—but every word says something from which we can learn."

- "Those who take their stand in the eternal verities, on the inner or hidden aspect of Christianity, are like the man in the parable who 'had the sense to build his house on rock' . . . the house stands, for its occupants are no longer in bondage to the letter of the law. They hold to that hidden spiritual foundation of which external facts are but the sign and symbol. In possession of the Divine Wisdom, they know the truth which makes us free."

19. The precepts of The Church of Christ, Scientist, are summarized in the book *Science and Health with Key to the Scriptures* by Mary Baker Eddy. Among their beliefs are: God as Father-Mother (p. 332, line 4); Christ as an incorporeal being, who is separate from the man Jesus born of Mary (p. 332, line 9ff); rejection of the atoning blood of Christ for salvation (p. 25, line 6); and salvation through Jesus's revelation of knowledge (p. 315, line 30ff). We discover a truly gnostic view of salvation in Mary Baker Eddy's assertion that "Jesus came to seek and to save such as believe in the reality of the unreal; to save them from this false belief; that they might lay hold of eternal Life . . ." (*Miscellaneous Writings*, 63).

20. See www.gnosis.org/eghome.htm, and in particular look at the Gnostic Catechism. Information about the French group can be found at www.gnostique.org. You will not come away from these Web sites with the sense that Gnosticism died out in the time of Irenaeus.

21. Start at www.gnostic-church.org. This group considers itself to be an authentic modern expression of the Gnostic movement from ancient Christian times. Their primary texts are the Egyptian codices known as the Nag Hammadi Library, which are the main source today for our firsthand knowledge of Gnosticism. One of the most famous of these texts is the Gospel of Thomas.

22. Irenaeus, *Against Heresies* 3.2.2 (ANF 1:415).

23. Ibid., 4.28.1–2 (ANF 1:501). Note that the term "new covenant," which translates the same Greek word as "testament," was already in use to speak about the new salvific arrangement ushered in by Jesus (Luke 22:20; 2 Cor. 3:6). But Irenaeus appears to be the first Christian to use the term "New Testament" with reference to a collection of writings in sacred scripture. Though his meaning is not entirely clear, he apparently associated two sets of books with the two covenants of God. See Everett Ferguson, "The Covenant Idea in the Second Century," in *Texts and Testaments: Critical Essays on the Bible and Early Church Fathers*, ed. W. Eugene March (San Antonio: Trinity University Press, 1980), 144–51.

24. Two of the principal places where Irenaeus discusses the Rule of Faith (or Rule of Truth, as he more often calls it) are *Against Heresies* 1.10.1 and 3.4.2 (ANF 1:330–331 and 417).

25. The "big picture" I am describing here has come to be known in scholarly studies of Irenaeus as his "hypothesis" of the faith. See Philip J. Hefner, "Theological Methodology and St. Irenaeus," *Journal of Religion* 44 (1964): 294–309.

26. The central importance of the Rule of Faith for Irenaeus is clearly brought out in Donovan, *One Right Reading? A Guide to Irenaeus*, 11–17. The author shows how the Rule provides the underlying structure for *Against Heresies*.

27. Eric Osborn, *Irenaeus of Lyons* (Cambridge: Cambridge University Press, 2001), 216–219. Osborn argues that for Irenaeus the concept of "inherited guilt" was a prominent theme drawn directly from Romans 5:12. It leads to other theological images such as slavery and emancipation, birth and rebirth, debt and payment at the cross, and sickness and healing. However, another scholar has argued that Irenaeus's concept of sin is considerably weaker than Paul's own strong view of its power. See J. T. Nielsen, *Adam and Christ in the Theology of Irenaeus of Lyons* (Assen, The Netherlands: Van Gorcum, 1968), 75–76.

28. Again, on this point, see Osborn, *Irenaeus of Lyons*, 245–48.

Chapter 4 Tertullian

1. "Driving Cattle from Texas to Iowa, 1866: George C. Duffield's Diary," *Annals of Iowa*, Iowa State Department of History and Archives, Third Series, XIV (April 1924). Reprinted in Robert V. Hine and Edwin R. Bingham, *The Frontier Experience: Readings in the Trans-Mississippi West* (Belmont, Calif.: Wadsworth Publishing, 1963), 245–49.

2. These quotes are found respectively in *Prescription Against Heretics* 7 (ANF 3:246) and *Apology* 50 (ANF 3:55). The statement about martyrdom is often misquoted today as "The blood of the martyrs is the seed of the church," but what Tertullian actually said was simply: *semen est sanguis Christianorum*. The statement about Athens and Jerusalem is often used to show that Tertullian completely rejected philosophy. While he was perhaps not as comfortable in the mental world of the Greeks as some of the other church fathers may have been, Tertullian certainly knew ancient philosophy very well, and was heavily influenced by it, particularly by Stoicism. See Eric Osborn, "Was Tertullian a Philosopher?" *Studia Patristica* 31 (Louvain: Peeters, 1997), 322–334; and Justo L. Gonzalez, "Athens and Jerusalem Revisited: Reason and Authority in Tertullian," *Church History* 43 (1974), 17–25. The consensus seems to be that Tertullian was indeed a philosopher—but was an unwavering Christian one.

3. Some scholars today are calling this treatise "Prescriptions (plural) Against Heretics," for that is its name in some manuscripts. However, I have used the traditional title in the singular because it's used in the *Ante-Nicene Fathers* series. If you want to

read this text, I recommend you avoid the ANF because the wording is so difficult. Instead, see S. L. Greenslade, *Early Latin Theology*, Library of Christian Classics, vol. 5 (Philadelphia: Westminster, 1956).

4. Tertullian, *Prescription Against Heretics* 9 (Greenslade, *Early Latin Theology*, 37).

5. Ibid., 12, 14 (Greenslade, *Early Latin Theology*, 39–40).

6. Ibid., 14 (Greenslade, *Early Latin Theology*, 40).

7. A brief biography of Tertullian is offered, with several inaccuracies, by Jerome in his *Lives of Illustrious Men* 53 (NPNF ser. 2, 3:373). Cyprian's respect for his "master" is among the tidbits recorded there.

8. Classical scholar Timothy D. Barnes demolished what had been the accepted ecclesial portrayal of Tertullian in his book *Tertullian: A Historical and Literary Study* (Oxford: Clarendon Press, 1971, 2nd ed. 1984). See especially chapters 2 through 6. On the subject of Tertullian's legal training, see David J. Rankin, "Was Tertullian a Jurist?" *Studia Patristica* 31 (Louvain: Peeters, 1997), 335–342. Rankin argues Tertullian was not a "jurist," that is, a specialist in legal technicalities; but was an "advocate," or an orator who pleaded cases in court and was trained in rhetoric. Certainly, Tertullian's writings show us he knew how to argue!

9. Despite his harshness toward his opponents, Tertullian had some very tender things to say with regard to the married state. In a beautiful tribute to Christian marriage during a time of persecution, he writes:

> Where are we to find words enough to fully describe the happiness of that marriage which the Church cements, and the offering (of communion) confirms, and the benediction signs and seals, and angels carry back the news to heaven, and the Father considers to be ratified? . . . Both (spouses) are brethren, both fellow servants, and there is no difference of spirit or of flesh; nay, they are truly "two in one flesh." Where the flesh is one, one is the spirit too. Together they pray, together prostrate themselves, together perform their fasts—mutually teaching, mutually exhorting, mutually sustaining. Equally are they both found in the Church of God; equally at the banquet of God; equally in trials, in persecutions, in refreshments. Neither hides anything from the other; neither shuns the other; neither is troublesome to the other. The sick are visited, the indigent relieved, with freedom. Alms are given without danger of torment (from a disagreeable spouse); sacrifices (of the communion service) are attended without scruple; daily diligence is discharged without impediment . . . Between the two (spouses) echo psalms and hymns; and they mutually challenge each other as to which shall better chant to their Lord. Such things, when Christ sees and hears, He enjoys. To these He sends His own peace. Where two are, there He Himself is. And where He is, there the Evil One is not. (*To My Wife* 2.8, ANF 4:48, slightly adapted for clarity)

10. Tertullian, *Prescription Against Heretics* 36 (Greenslade, *Early Latin Theology*, 57).

11. One of the foremost scholars of North African Christianity is W. H. C. Frend. He makes the case that the African church's origins derive from Jewish life. See "Jews and Christians in Third Century Carthage," in *Paganisme, Judaïsme, Christianisme* (Paris: Éditions E. De Boccard, 1978), 185–194; reprinted in *Town and Country in the Early Christian Centuries* (London: Variorum Reprints, 1980), XVII.

12. *The Acts of the Scillitan Martyrs* 12 (ANF 9:285). When the Roman proconsul demanded to know what Speratus had brought with him in his case, he answered "books, and the epistles of Paul, a just man." That the "books" were the gospels is argued by Gerald Bonner, "The Scillitan Saints and the Pauline Epistles," *Journal of Ecclesiastical History* (1956): 141–46. This is possible, but Bonner may be reading too much into the evidence.

13. Ibid., 17. This benediction does not appear in every manuscript of the *Acts*.

14. Von Harnack accepts that Marcion was excommunicated by his father, but rejects the supposed reason for it given by the anti-heretical writer Hippolytus: that Marcion had seduced a young virgin in his home congregation. More likely he was excommunicated for heresy—which is a kind of metaphorical "seduction" of the virgin Church. Adolf von Harnack, *Marcion: The Gospel of the Alien God*, tr. John E. Steele and Lyle D. Bierma (Durham, NC: The Labyrinth Press, 1990), 16. On the other hand, Gerhard May sees the report of Marcion's excommunication as probably "legendary." "Marcion in Contemporary Views: Results and Open Questions," *The Second Century* 6 (1987–88): 135.

15. Justin Martyr, *First Apology* 58 (ANF 1:182, slightly adapted for clarity).

16. Irenaeus, *Against Heresies* 3.3.4 (ANF 1:416).

17. Tertullian, *Against Marcion* 1.2 (ANF 3:272, slightly adapted for clarity). The phrase "twin Clashing Rocks" refers to the mythological moving rocks in Marcion's own Black Sea, through which Jason and the Argonauts had to sail.

18. Winrich Löhr, "Did Marcion distinguish between a just god and a good god?" in *Marcion und seine kirchengeschichtliche Wirkung*, ed. Gerhard May and Katharina Greschat (Berlin: de Gruyter, 2002), 131–146.

19. Tertullian, *Against Marcion* 4.11 (ANF 3:360).

20. von Harnack, *Marcion*, 15.

21. Rather than seeing Martin Luther as a modern-day Marcionite, we might be inclined to give Adolf von Harnack that honor; for he once wrote, "To reject the Old Testament in the second century was a mistake which the Church rightly repudiated; to retain it in the sixteenth century was a fate which the Reformation could not yet avoid; but to continue to keep it as a canonical document after the nineteenth century is the consequence of religious and ecclesiastical paralysis." Quoted in John Barton, "Marcion Revisited," *The Canon Debate*, ed. Lee Martin McDonald and James A. Sanders (Peabody, MA: Hendrickson, 2002), 341–342.

22. Marcion accepted as authentic only ten of the thirteen Pauline epistles, excluding the Pastorals. He also believed Luke's gospel was not originally written by Luke. Rather, it had been penned by Jesus himself and was later corrupted. For this reason Marcion felt obliged to cut away portions of the received texts. Tertullian wrote, "Marcion openly and nakedly used the knife, not the pen, massacring Scripture to suit his own material." *Prescription Against Heretics* 38 (Greenslade, *Early Latin Theology*, 59).

23. In an earlier era, scholars viewed Marcion as nearly the sole impetus for the church's creation of its biblical canon. From this point of view, the catholics' canon would be a reaction to a heretic instead of something the church had been pursuing from the beginning. But today most scholars consider Marcion's influence on the canon, though notable, not to be absolutely determinative. The canonization process was already well under way in the mid-second century. While Marcion may have spurred some writers to be more concrete in their expression, he cannot be viewed as the main force behind the canonization process. See Barton, "Marcion Revisited," 354.

24. There are two places in the Bible where New Testament writings are accorded "scriptural" status. In 2 Peter 3:16, the letters of Paul are connected with "the rest of Scripture." In 1 Timothy 5:18, a gospel saying (Luke 10:7) is introduced by the phrase, "The Scripture says . . ." This evidence reveals that from a very early time, the gospels and Pauline epistles were highly regarded in the church. However, this is a long way from recognizing that there is a new, distinct entity called "The New Testament." Such recognition will not occur until around the time of Tertullian.

25. Everett Ferguson, "Factors Leading to the Selection and Closure of the New Testament Canon," *The Canon Debate*, 307–308. On Tertullian's canon more generally, see John F. Jansen, "Tertullian and the New Testament," *The Second Century* 2 (Winter 1982): 191–96.

26. Eusebius, *Life of Constantine* 4.36 (NPNF ser. 2, 1:549).

27. Eusebius, *Church History* 3.25.1–7 (NPNF ser. 2, 1:155–57).

28. See the chart in Appendix D of McDonald and Sanders, *The Canon Debate*, 591–597.

29. Lee Martin McDonald, "Identifying Scripture and Canon in the Early Church: The Criteria Question," *The Canon Debate*, 424–427.

30. Tertullian, *Against Marcion* 4.2 (ANF 3:347). On this subject, see Thomas P. O'Malley, *Tertullian and the Bible: Language, Imagery, Exegesis* (Nijmen: Dekker & van de Vegt, 1967), 72–73; and J. E. L. van der Geest, *Le Christ et l'Ancien Testament chez Tertullien* (Nijmen: Dekker & van de Vegt, 1972), 81–82.

31. Tertullian, *Against Marcion* 4.11 (ANF 3:361). The translation I use here is my own.

32. Tertullian, *Against Praxeas* 5 (ANF 3:600).

33. Ibid., 8 (ANF 3:603).

34. The verb used here can refer to sexual union, which reveals the intimate relationship Tertullian envisioned between the two Testaments.

35. Tertullian makes a pun here. The word "heretic" comes from the Greek word for "choice."

Chapter 5 Perpetua

1. Perpetua is recorded to be "about twenty-two years old." By our method of reckoning this means she was probably twenty-one. Precision with respect to age was not a high priority for the ancient Romans. Tim G. Parkin, *Old Age in the Roman World: A Cultural and Social History* (Baltimore: Johns Hopkins, 2003), 33–35.

2. Perpetua remarks that among all her relatives, only her father would be sad to see her suffer. This has been taken as evidence that the rest of her family were Christians who were quietly rejoicing in her martyrdom.

3. Carolyn Osiek, "Perpetua's Husband," *Journal of Early Christian Studies* 10:2, 287–290. The possibility that Saturus was Perpetua's husband provides the romantic angle in Amy Peterson's novel *Perpetua*.

4. There are some later patristic texts which seek to fill in some of the details, but scholars do not give them any historical credence in reconstructing Perpetua's life.

5. The text may be read in the *Ante-Nicene Fathers*, 3:699–706. It is included in this series among the works of Tertullian because earlier scholars thought he may have been the editor; but this is largely discounted today on stylistic grounds. See René Braun, "Nouvelles observations linguistiques sur le rédacteur de la Passio Perpetuae," *Vigiliae Christianae* 33 (1979): 105–117. However, another scholar does remark that there are certain rhetorical flourishes in the text which sound an awful lot like Tertullian's own handiwork (Timothy Barnes, *Tertullian: A Historical and Literary Study* [Oxford: Clarendon Press, 1971], 79–80). It is at least possible that Tertullian edited the account of the Carthaginian martyr he admired so much.

6. *The Passion of Saints Perpetua and Felicitas* 2.1 (ANF 3:700–701).

7. Putting babies to death by exposure to the natural elements was a common practice among the ancient Romans, applied more often to daughters than to sons. It is only with the Christian emperor Justinian that the laws were changed so that the punishment for killing an infant was the same as for any other homicide. Eva Cantarella, *Pandora's Daughters: The Role and Status of Women in Greek and Roman Antiquity* (Baltimore: Johns Hopkins, 1987), 135–136.

8. Cicero, *In Verrem* 2.1.112, quoted in Judith P. Hallett, *Fathers and Daughters in Roman Society: Women and the Elite Family* (Princeton, NJ: Princeton University Press, 1984), 96.

9. *Passion of Perpetua* 2.2 (ANF 3:701).

10. Jerome, *Letter 22, To Eustochium* 1 (NPNF ser. 2, 6:22–23).

11. *Passion of Perpetua* 1.2 (ANF 3:700, slightly adapted for clarity).

12. Ibid.

13. Ibid., 2.2 (ANF 3:701).

14. Ibid., 5.2 (ANF 3:703–704).

15. Ibid., (ANF 3:704, slightly adapted for clarity).

16. Ibid., 6.1 (ANF 3:704, slightly adapted for clarity). Martyrdom was often depicted as a "baptism of blood" in the early church. Like water baptism, martyrdom publicly identified the believer with Christ. Also, baptism was a means of washing away sins. Tertullian believed the martyr atoned for his sins by his death—certainly a problematic view.

17. In my opinion, Montanist themes are undeniably found in the work as it has come down to us today. At least one scholar (Weinrich) has rejected that conclusion, while others have debated whether the Montanism stems from the martyrs themselves or from the later redactor of the text. On this issue see Barnes, *Tertullian*, 77–79; William C. Weinrich, *Spirit and Martyrdom* (Washington, DC: University Press of America, 1981), 225–229; Cecil M. Robeck, *Prophecy in Carthage: Perpetua, Tertullian, and Cyprian* (Cleveland: The Pilgrim Press, 1992), 14–18; and Christine Trevett, *Montanism: Gender, Authority and the New Prophecy* (Cambridge: Cambridge University Press, 1996), 177–178.

18. While there may be some parallels between worship of Cybele-Attis and Montanism, many scholars now point instead to the apocalyptic and millennial outlook of the Book of Revelation as providing the kind of religious climate in which Montanism could develop. See D. H. Williams, "The Origins of the Montanist Movement: A Sociological Analysis," *Religion* (1989): 331–351.

19. Eusebius, *Church History* 5.14.1 and 5.16.7 (NPNF ser. 2, 1:229, 231).

20. There is some debate about whether the "Paraclete" was emphasized in earliest Montanism. See Trevett, *Montanism*, 62–66.

21. Trevett, *Montanism*, 135–137.

22. According to Tertullian, the Paraclete's higher standard of morality as revealed in the New Prophecy did not represent a fundamental change in Christian doctrine. Rather it was the addition of those things to which Jesus was referring when he said in John 16:12–13, "I still have many things to say to you, but you cannot bear them now. When the Spirit of truth comes, he will guide you into all the truth." *On Monogamy* 2 (ANF 4:59–60).

23. Robeck writes that Tertullian "never used these visions or oracles to establish doctrine per se; he merely introduced them as corroborating testimony to what he believed to be the legitimate teaching of Scripture" (*Prophecy in Carthage*, 201). "Tertullian was greatly concerned to demonstrate that prophetic manifestations in his day were assessed in relation to Scripture and the [Rule of Faith] . . . Tertullian argued for the supremacy of Scripture and the role of the Spirit in illumination" (204). Along the same lines, Trevett notes that Tertullian "used visions and Prophetic oracles as secondary, supportive and subordinate to teachings in Scripture and the [Rule of Faith] . . . The work of the Paraclete, said Tertullian, illumined and interpreted Scripture" (*Montanism*, 133). The

biblical approach adopted in Carthage stood in contrast to Montanism's original setting in Asia Minor, where the prophets believed their authority was equal to the writers of Scripture. As Montanus himself once said about himself, "I am neither angel nor envoy, but I the Lord God have come" (quoted in Williams, "Origins," 331).

24. The situation in Africa was somewhat different than at Rome, where a decision had already been made against the New Prophecy. Tertullian once castigated a heretic named Praxeas who had convinced the bishop of Rome to disavow his earlier acceptance of Montanism. Praxeas taught the heretical view that the Father and Son were actually the same being. So when he also opposed the New Prophecy, Tertullian accused him of a double error: "By this Praxeas did a twofold service for the devil at Rome: he drove away prophecy, and he brought in heresy; he put to flight the Paraclete, and he crucified the Father [by equating him with the Son]." *Against Praxeas* 1 (ANF 3:597).

25. *Passion of Perpetua* 1.3 (ANF 3:700). The translation I cite here is from Herbert Musurillo, *The Acts of the Christian Martyrs* (Oxford: Clarendon, 1972), 111.

26. Ibid., 3.2 (ANF 3:702). Notice that in both visions, the divine figure calls Perpetua his "child" or "daughter." This is significant when we consider what we have already said about Perpetua's renunciation of her earthly father.

27. The women are called prophetesses in Exodus 15:20; Judges 4:4; and Luke 2:36.

28. *Passion of Perpetua*, preface (ANF 3:699).

29. Ibid., 3.2 (ANF 3:702; quoted from Musurillo, *The Acts of the Christian Martyrs*, 119).

30. *The Martyrdom of Polycarp* 9 (ANF 1:41).

31. Pliny the Younger, *Epistle to Trajan*. Cited in Bettenson and Maunder, *Documents of the Christian Church*, 3.

32. W. H. C. Frend, *Martyrdom and Persecution in the Early Church* (New York: New York University Press, 1967), 90–93.

33. See also Acts 16:31; Romans 10:9; 2 Corinthians 4:5; Philippians 2:11; and Colossians 2:6 for the importance of the early Christian confession that "Jesus Christ is Lord."

34. *Passion of Perpetua* 6.1 (ANF 3:704).

35. Ibid., 6.3 (ANF 3:705).

36. Ibid., 6.4 (ANF 3:705).

37. Tertullian, *Apology* 50 (ANF 3:55, slightly adapted for clarity).

38. See for example Mary Ann Rossi, "The Passion of Perpetua, Everywoman of Late Antiquity," in *Pagan and Christian Anxiety* (Lanham, MD: University Press of America, 1984), 53–86; Frederick C. Klawiter, "The Role of Martyrdom and Persecution in Developing the Priestly Authority of Women in Early Christianity: A Case Study of Montanism," *Church History* 49 (1980), 251–261; and Brent D. Shaw, "The Passion of Perpetua," *Past and Present* 139 (1993): 3–45. The latter is a fine piece of historical scholarship, yet it betrays the classicist's all-too-frequent

disregard for the biblical and theological worldview that would have characterized a Christian woman like Perpetua.

39. Augustine of Hippo, *Sermon 280.1* (slightly adapted for clarity). Edmund Hill, *Sermons 273–305A On the Saints*, The Works of Saint Augustine: A Translation for the 21ˢᵗ Century, vol. 3, pt. 8 (Hyde Park, NY: New City Press, 1994), 72.

40. The gravestone, which is now in the Carthage National Museum, may well be the original one erected by Perpetua's father. But the inscription might instead belong to a girl from a later time who was named in Perpetua's honor. Archaeologists have also recovered fragments of the martyrs' collective grave marker from the Basilica Majorum, the great church built in Carthage after persecution of Christians ended. It was in this church that the martyr's remains were eventually collected, and were kept until being lost after the rise of Islam in the region. The inscription reads, "Here are the martyrs Saturus, Saturninus, Revocatus, Secundulus, Felicitas (and) Perpetua, who suffered on the 7ᵗʰ of March." See William Tabbernee, *Montanist Inscriptions and Testimonia: Epigraphic Sources Illustrating the History of Montanism* (Macon, GA: Mercer University Press, 1997), 105–112.

41. In the ancient world, loose or unkempt hair was a sign of mourning (see Lev. 10:6, NIV). "The practice of unbinding the hair in grief is particularly characteristic of women in Roman society, and dozens of textual and visual depictions of the practice survive." Anthony Corbeill, *Nature Embodied: Gesture in Ancient Rome* (Princeton, NJ: Princeton University Press, 2004), 83.

42. Gladiators in the Carthaginian amphitheater could exit by one of two gates: one for the living and another for the dead. Combatants spared by the crowd were taken out through the Porta Sanavivaria, or Gate of Life. Perpetua and Felicity's reprieve through this gate was, of course, only temporary.

43. Perpetua's words "Stand firm in the faith" are a quotation of 1 Corinthians 16:13. Her reference to "stumbling" may be an allusion to 1 Corinthians 1:23, where the crucifixion of Christ is called a "stumbling block."

44. The kiss of peace was commanded in Romans 16:16; 1 Corinthians 16:20; and 2 Corinthians 13:12. The ritual kiss was given on the lips in the early church and was exchanged between the sexes. The church fathers were aware of the possibility of temptation. For example, the writer Athenagoras warned against kissing a second time if it was found to be enjoyable. The kiss must be "very carefully guarded." Yet because it was commanded in scripture, it was deemed necessary, even if it might be a source of temptation. For a complete discussion of the kiss of peace, see Stephen Benko, *Pagan Rome and the Early Christians* (Indiana University Press, 1986), 79–102.

Chapter 6 Origen

1. C. S. Lewis, *The Lion, the Witch, and the Wardrobe: A Story for Children* (New York: Macmillan, 1950), 131–132.

2. Lewis was reluctant to see his stories treated as overly-literal allegories in which everything in Narnia had to sustain a one-to-one relationship with things in our world. He said, "You are mistaken when you think that everything in the books 'represents' something in this world. Things do that in *The Pilgrim's Progress* but I'm not writing that way. I did not say to myself 'Let us represent Jesus as He really is in our world by a Lion in Narnia': I said 'Let us suppose that there were a land like Narnia and that the Son of God, as He became Man in our world, became a Lion there, and then imagine what would happen.'" So it is not that Jesus is Aslan. Rather, Lewis wanted to communicate truth about Jesus through a narrative portrayal of Aslan. David C. Downing, *Into the Wardrobe: C. S. Lewis and the Narnia Chronicles* (San Francisco: Jossey-Bass, 2005), 64–65.

3. C. S. Lewis, *The Pilgrim's Regress: An Allegorical Apology for Christianity, Reason and Romanticism* (Grand Rapids: Eerdmans, 1933), 13.

4. Ibid., *The Allegory of Love: A Study in Medieval Tradition* (Oxford: Oxford University Press, 1936), 166.

5. David. C. Downing, *Into the Region of Awe: Mysticism in C. S. Lewis* (Downers Grove, IL: InterVarsity Press, 2005), 13.

6. The comparison between Origen and C. S. Lewis is noted in Anthony C. Thiselton, *New Horizons in Hermeneutics: The Theory and Practice of Transforming Biblical Reading* (Grand Rapids: Zondervan, 1992), 172. See also Gerald Bostock, "Allegory and the Interpretation of the Bible in Origen," *Journal of Literature & Theology* (March 1987), 42.

7. Origen spoke of his longing for spiritual intimacy when he wrote, "God is my witness that I have often perceived [Christ] drawing near me and being most intensely present with me; then suddenly He has withdrawn and I could not find Him, though I sought to do so. I long, therefore, for Him to come again, and sometimes He does so. Then, when He has appeared and I lay hold of Him, He slips away once more; and when He has so slipped away, my search for Him begins anew." R. P. Lawson, *Origen: The Song of Songs: Commentary and Homilies*, Ancient Christian Writers, vol. 26 (New York: Newman Press), 280.

8. Eusebius, *Church History* 6.2.11 (NPNF ser. 2, 1:250, slightly adapted for clarity).

9. Ibid., 6.2.10 (NPNF ser. 2, 1:250).

10. Roy MacLeod, *The Library of Alexandria: Centre of Learning in the Ancient World* (London: I. B. Tauris, 2000), 4–5.

11. Scholars generally agree that Origen was a Christian Platonist. That is to say, he used the ideas of Plato as an integral part of his system of Christian theology. For a discussion of aspects of Origen's thought that are opposed to Platonism, see Mark Julian Edwards, *Origen Against Plato* (Aldershot, England: Ashgate Press, 2002).

12. The classic exposition of the thesis that Gnostic Christianity was earlier than orthodoxy in Alexandria is found in Walter Bauer, *Orthodoxy and Heresy in Earli-*

est Christianity, ed. and trans. Robert Kraft, Gerhard Krodel, et al. (Philadelphia: Fortress Press, 1971), 44–60.

13. Eusebius, *Church History* 6.23.2 (NPNF ser. 2, 1:271).

14. Unfortunately, Origen's greatest work does not survive intact in its original Greek. The whole text is found only in a fourth-century Latin version by a monk named Rufinus. There are also some portions of the Greek text that have survived because they were quoted in another work. In volume four of the *Ante-Nicene Fathers*, the translation is supplied in two columns which represent the two textual sources. The definitive English edition is G. W. Butterworth, *Origen: On First Principles* (London: SPCK, 1936).

15. Origen, *First Principles* 4.9 (ANF 4:357, quoting the Greek, slightly adapted for clarity). For reasons unknown to me, the Web site www.ccel.org/fathers2 does not always provide both the Greek and the Latin translations of *First Principles*—a blemish on an otherwise masterful rendering of the ANF and NPNF volumes as online e-texts.

16. Origen normally built his interpretations off the literal sense as the foundation. But he believed sometimes the literal sense held little value except to prompt the reader to seek a more spiritual meaning. He wrote, "Divine wisdom provided that stumbling-blocks or interruptions to the historical meaning should occur by the introduction into the midst of the narrative certain impossibilities and incongruities. In this way the very interruption of the narrative might present an obstacle to the reader, whereby he might refuse to acknowledge the way which leads to the ordinary meaning; and being thus excluded and debarred from it, he might be recalled to the beginning of another way, in order that, by entering upon a narrow path, and passing to a loftier and more sublime road, he might lay open the immense breadth of divine wisdom . . . All this was done by the Holy Spirit in order that, seeing those events which lie on the surface can be neither true nor useful, we may be led to investigate the truth which is more deeply concealed, and to ascertain a meaning worthy of God in those Scriptures which we believe to be inspired by Him." *First Principles* 4.15 (ANF 4:364, quoting the Latin, slightly adapted for clarity). For more on this subject see Charles Scalise, "Origen and the Sensus Literalis," in *Origen of Alexandria: His World and Legacy*, ed. Charles Kannengiesser and William L. Petersen (South Bend, IN: University of Notre Dame, 1988), 117–129.

17. You can read the sermons in Gary Wayne Barkley, *Origen: Homilies on Leviticus 1–16*, Fathers of the Church, vol. 83 (Washington, DC: Catholic University of America, 1990).

18. Other biblical precedents that justified Origen's use of allegory were the rock that gave water to the Israelites, which signified Christ (Exod. 17:1–7; Num. 20:1–11; 1 Cor. 10:4–6), and the ox treading grain without a muzzle, which proved the apostles were worthy of their wages (Deut. 25:4; 1 Cor. 9:9–10; 1 Tim. 5:18). For a good discussion of the "scriptural basis of spiritual exegesis," see Henri Crouzel, *Origen: The Life and Thought of the First Great Theologian*, trans. A. S. Worrall (San Francisco: Harper & Row, 1989), 64–69.

19. One of Origen's sharpest critics in recent times wrote, "Where the Bible did not obviously mean what he thought it ought to mean, or even where it obviously did not mean what he thought it ought to mean, he had only to turn the magic ring of allegory, and—Hey Presto!—the desired meaning appeared. Allegory, in short, instead of ensuring that he would in his exegesis maintain close contact with biblical thought, rendered him deplorably independent of the Bible." R. P. C. Hanson, *Allegory and Event: A Study of the Sources and Significance of Origen's Interpretation of Scripture* (Richmond, VA: John Knox Press, 1959), 371.

20. Summing up the church's Rule, Origen speaks of one God the Creator, revealed in the Old Testament prophets, who sent his son to be born of a virgin, to die, and to rise again. The church now possesses the Spirit as she awaits rewards for the righteous and judgment for the wicked at the final resurrection. One item Origen adds to the Rule of Faith which we do not find explicitly stated in Irenaeus or Tertullian is allegorical exegesis of scripture. He lays it down as received Christian doctrine that "the Scriptures were written by the Spirit of God, and have a meaning not only such as is apparent at first sight, but also another, which escapes the notice of most. For those [biblical] words which are written are the outer forms of certain mysteries, and are the images of divine things. About this there is one opinion throughout the whole Church, that the whole law is indeed spiritual (Rom. 7:14). But the spiritual meaning which the law conveys is not known to all, but only to those on whom the grace of the Holy Spirit is bestowed in the word of wisdom and knowledge." *First Principles* Preface.8 (ANF 4:241, slightly adapted for clarity).

21. *First Principles* Preface.10 (ANF 4:241). The phrase I quote is from Butterworth, *Origen: On First Principles*, 6.

22. On the presence of the Logos in scripture, see Karen Jo Torjesen, *Hermeneutical Procedure and Theological Method in Origen's Exegesis* (Berlin: De Gruyter, 1985), 108–147.

23. Henri de Lubac, *Medieval Exegesis*: Volume 1: The Four Senses of Scripture, trans. Mark Sebanc (Grand Rapids: Eerdmans, 1998), 237–238.

24. By way of example, in his *Commentary on the Gospel of John* Origen prefaced a quotation of John 5:39 with the words, "Christ is written about even in the Pentateuch. He is spoken of in each of the Prophets, and in the Psalms, and as the Savior Himself says, in all the Scriptures. For he refers to them all when He says 'Search the Scriptures, for . . . they testify of Me.'" (ANF 9:347, slightly adapted for clarity). Origen was also fond of quoting John 5:46, "[Moses] wrote of me." He took this as biblical proof that the whole Bible is about Christ—not just the New Testament, which is obvious, but the Old Testament as well.

25. The concept of an interpretation being "worthy of God" was very important to Origen. See John Anthony McGuckin, ed., *The Westminster Handbook to Origen* (Louisville, KY: Westminster John Knox, 2004), 198–199.

26. On the discipleship aspect of an ancient school, see Robert L. Wilken, "Alexandria: A School for Training in Virtue," in *Schools of Thought in the Christian Tradition*, ed. Patrick Henry (Philadelphia: Fortress Press, 1984), 15–30.

27. Eusebius, *Church History* 6.3.4 (NPNF ser. 2, 1:251, slightly adapted for clarity).

28. Rowan Greer, *Origen: An Exhortation to Martyrdom, Prayer and Selected Works* (New York: Paulist Press, 1979), 42.

29. Eusebius, *Church History* 6.39.5 (NPNF ser. 2, 1:281).

30. A good summary of Origen's views about final judgment and rewards can be found in J. N. D. Kelly, *Early Christian Doctrines* (New York: Harper & Brothers, 1959), 469–474. See also the relevant articles in McGuckin, *Westminster Handbook to Origen*, such as "Apokatastasis," "Cosmology," "Demonology," "Hades," and "Resurrection."

31. On this subject see Elizabeth A. Clark, *The Origenist Controversy: The Cultural Construction of an Early Christian Debate* (Princeton, NJ: Princeton University Press, 1992).

32. Hanson, *Allegory and Event*, 363–365.

33. Henry Chadwick, *Early Christian Thought and the Classical Tradition: Studies in Justin, Clement and Origen* (Oxford: Clarendon Press, 1966), 95.

34. A quotation from Origen's *Commentary on Luke*, quoted in Butterworth, *Origen: On First Principles*, xiii (in the introduction to the Torchbook edition).

Chapter 7 Athanasius

1. Mary Mapes Dodge, *Hans Brinker, or, The Silver Skates: A Story of a Life in Holland* (New York: C. Scribners Sons, 1865, repr. Nelson Doubleday, 1954), 127–129. Strictly speaking, the boy in the story is anonymous. But in legend he has become associated with the title character, Hans Brinker.

2. The phrase was used by the evangelist and founder of Methodism, John Wesley, in a letter to anti-slavery crusader William Wilberforce. Wesley exhorted Wilberforce to stand firm against slavery as "Athanasius contra mundum." See Albert C. Outler, ed., *John Wesley* (Oxford: Oxford University Press, 1980), 85–86. Wesley appears to be quoting the earlier description of Athanasius by the sixteenth-century Anglican churchman Richard Hooker: "The whole world against Athanasius, and Athanasius against it." See *Laws of Ecclesiastical Polity* V.42.5, in W. Speed Hill, *The Folger Library Edition of the Works of Richard Hooker*, vol. 2 (Cambridge, MA: Belknap Press, 1977–1998).

3. Khaled Anatolios, *Athanasius* (New York: Routledge, 2004), 33.

4. Jerome, *The Dialogue Against the Luciferians* 19 (NPNF ser. 2, 6:329).

5. Eusebius writes, "Why need we mention the rest by name, or number the multitude of the men, or picture the various sufferings of the admirable martyrs of Christ? Some of them were slain with the axe, as in Arabia. The limbs of some were broken,

as in Cappadocia. Some, raised on high by the feet, with their heads down, while a gentle fire burned beneath them, were suffocated by the smoke which arose from the burning wood, as was done in Mesopotamia. Others were mutilated by cutting off their noses and ears and hands, and cutting to pieces the other members and parts of their bodies, as in Alexandria. Why need we revive the recollection of those in Antioch who were roasted on grates, not so as to kill them, but so as to subject them to a lingering punishment? Or of others who preferred to thrust their right hand into the fire rather than touch the impious sacrifice? Some, shrinking from the trial, rather than be taken and fall into the hands of their enemies, threw themselves from lofty houses, considering death preferable to the cruelty of the impious." *Church History* 8.12.1–2 (NPNF ser. 2, 1:332).

6. Ibid., 8.11.1 (NPNF ser. 2, 1:331–332).

7. The edict is recorded by Lactantius, *Of the Manner in Which the Persecutors Died* 48 (ANF 7:320, slightly adapted for clarity).

8. Though Constantine supported and professed Christianity, he did not immediately do away with pagan religion—either in his personal life or in the life of the Roman Empire. The outlawing of paganism and the official imperial endorsement of Christianity came under Emperor Theodosius, who reigned from AD 379 to 395.

9. Eusebius, *Oration in Praise of Constantine* 2.2 (NPNF ser. 2, 1:583, slightly adapted for clarity). *The Life of Constantine* may also be read in this volume.

10. On this subject, see Michael Grant, *Constantine the Great* (New York: Charles Scribner's Sons, 1993), 184–186.

11. The comment is found in Gregory of Nyssa's work *On the Deity of the Son and the Holy Spirit*. I do not know of an English translation of this work, but the Greek is available in *Patrologia Graeca*, vol. 46, 557B. The translation quoted is my own.

12. Gregory of Nazianzus, *Oration on the Great Athanasius, Bishop of Alexandria* 21.6 (NPNF ser. 2, 7:270–71, slightly adapted for clarity).

13. The origins of the Arian controversy are discussed by the ancient church historians Socrates Scholasticus (*Ecclesiastical History* 1.5–6, NPNF ser. 2, 2:3–6) and Sozomen (*Ecclesiastical History* 1.15, NPNF ser. 2, 2:251–252).

14. On the contributions of Origen to the Arian controversy, see R.P.C. Hanson, *The Search for the Christian Doctrine of God: The Arian Controversy* 318–381 (Edinburgh: T&T Clark, 1988), 61–70.

15. Language implying that the Son is not eternal can be found in a few Alexandrian writers prior to Arius. The most prominent example is Dionysius, bishop of Alexandria from 247 to 264, who wrote that "the Son of God is a creature" and "because he is a creature he did not exist before he came into existence" (Athanasius, *On the Opinion of Dionysius* 4, NPNF ser. 2, 4:177; cf. Hanson, 72–76). However, it seems that when Dionysius was confronted on these teachings by the bishop of Rome and others, he retracted or softened his views. It is safe to say that virtually all the church fathers agreed that Jesus Christ is eternal God. Even those writers (such

as Tertullian) who were reluctant to use the term "Son" as an eternal designation, nevertheless insisted that the Logos himself was eternal and had always been with God. It is the eternality of the Second Person of the Trinity that the orthodox fathers insisted upon, and Arius rejected.

16. Theodoret, *Church History* 1.6 (NPNF ser. 2, 3:43).

17. Eusebius, *Life of Constantine* 3.15 (NPNF ser. 2, 1:524, slightly adapted for clarity).

18. Athanasius, *Letter to Serapion*, concerning the death of Arius (NPNF ser. 2, 4:564–566). See also Timothy D. Barnes, *Athanasius and Constantius: Theology and Politics in the Constantinian Empire* (Cambridge, MA: Harvard University Press, 1993), 127.

19. Athanasius, *Defense before Constantius* 30 (NPNF ser. 2, 4:250).

20. Athanasius, *Defense of His Flight* 24 (NPNF ser. 2, 4:263–264).

21. Athanasius, *Life of Anthony* 69 (NPNF ser. 2, 4:214).

22. Arianism was not, of course, devoid of any emphasis on salvation. See Robert C. Gregg and Dennis E. Groh, *Early Arianism: A View of Salvation* (Philadelphia: Fortress Press, 1981).

23. Athanasius, *On the Incarnation* 54.3 (NPNF ser. 2, 4:65). Athanasius clearly did not believe, nor did he intend to imply, that we humans become little "gods," or that we can become equal to God in our being. Rather, his point had to do with growth in holiness. A better translation might be, "God became Man so that we might become godly." Athanasius was communicating a theology of sharing, in which God shares his life with us so we might become "partakers of the divine nature" (2 Pet. 1:4; cf. Ps. 82:6). In Christ, God and Man are joined. Therefore, in Christ our fallen human nature is renewed so that it might participate in the life that God has. Today the Eastern Orthodox Church still emphasizes this important doctrine, calling it "divinization."

24. Athanasius, *On the Incarnation: The Treatise* De Incarnatione Verbi Dei, anonymous translation, introduction by C. S. Lewis (Crestwood, NY: St. Vladimir's Seminary Press, 1944, repr. 1998), 3.

25. Ibid., 8.

26. Ibid., 9.

27. Athanasius points out that God could not abrogate his penalty for sin. He had decreed death for sin, so death was required. But in love, Christ is the one who took upon himself that death.

Chapter 8 John Chrysostom

1. Quoted in Roy Jenkins, *Churchill: A Biography* (New York: Farrar, Straus and Giroux, 2001), 621.

2. Sozomen, *Ecclesiastical History* 8.2 (NPNF ser. 2, 2:399). Quotation taken from J. N. D. Kelly, *Golden Mouth: The Story of John Chrysostom: Ascetic, Preacher, Bishop* (Grand Rapids: Baker, 1995), 8.

3. John Chrysostom, *Letter to a Young Widow* 2 (NPNF ser. 1, 9:122).

4. John wrote two letters to his friend Theodore, who had fallen in love and was considering abandoning the group of young celibates to enter into marriage. John warns Theodore: "You have blotted out your name from the list of the brethren, because you have trampled upon the covenant which you made with Christ." *Letters to the Fallen Theodore* 2.1 (NPNF ser. 1, 9:111). It appears these young men envisioned a high level of commitment for their ascetic fraternity.

5. The ancient Christians considered the city a tumultuous place of vice, whereas the wilderness was a quiet place of tranquility. For the contrast between the civic life and the ascetic life, see Aideen M. Hartley, *John Chrysostom and the Transformation of the City* (London: Duckworth Press, 2004), 23–25. In particular, John noted that homosexual abuse of boys by their teachers was very common in Antioch (though he does not admit to having had personal problems in this area). Entering into the monastic life could serve as a refuge from this civic evil. See Margaret Amy Schatkin, *John Chrysostom as Apologist* (Thessaloniki, Greece: Patriarchal Institute for Patristic Studies, 1987), 180–183.

6. The early monks often depicted their spiritual struggles as a battle against the flesh or the devil. Interestingly, a different kind of warfare occurred much later on the slopes of the very mountain where John had retreated. In the Middle Ages, the knights of the First Crusade fought a pitched battle atop Mt. Silpius as they attempted to wrest Antioch from the hands of the "infidels." See Thomas Asbridge, *The First Crusade: A New History* (Oxford: Oxford University Press, 2004).

7. John openly discussed his reluctance to serve in the clergy because of the temptations presented by life in the city. A woman's beautiful face, alluring movements, and seductive perfume and adornments "are enough to disorder the mind, unless it be hardened against them, through much austerity of self-restraint." Describing the relief he felt in his monastic isolation, he wrote, "Outrageous desires even now come over me, but they kindle only a languid flame, since my bodily eyes cannot fasten upon any fuel to feed the fire." He then offered an analogy. Vicious wild animals with full strength will be able to defeat those who fight them; but if the animals are starved and feeble, they can be subdued. John considered his asceticism to have a similar debilitating effect on the passions of his soul—weakening them so they could be overcome. *On the Priesthood* 6.2, 6.12 (NPNF ser. 1, 9:75, 80); cf. Kelly, *Golden Mouth*, 28–29, 84–85.

8. Robert T. Meyer, *Palladius: Dialogue on the Life of St. John Chrysostom*, Ancient Christian Writers, vol. 45 (New York: Newman Press, 1985), 35.

9. The term "asceticism" is difficult to define precisely, even for the scholars who populate the Society of Biblical Literature's academic study group on Ascetic Behav-

ior in Greco-Roman Antiquity. One suggested definition is: "a voluntary, sustained, and at least partially systematic program of self-discipline and self-denial in which immediate, sensual or profane gratifications are renounced in order to attain a higher spiritual state or a more thorough absorption into the sacred." On the difficulty of defining the term, and for an excellent overview of asceticism in ancient Christianity, see Elizabeth A. Clark, *Reading Renunciation: Asceticism and Scripture in Early Christianity* (Princeton, NJ: Princeton University Press, 1999), 14–42.

10. In addition to its great Trinitarian creed, the Council of Nicaea in AD 325 also passed various church laws, among them the following: "The great Synod has stringently forbidden any bishop, presbyter, deacon, or any one of the clergy whatever, to have a *subintroducta* [a female cohabitant] dwelling with him, except only a mother, or sister, or aunt, or such persons as are beyond all suspicion." *Canons of Nicaea* 3 (NPNF ser. 2, 14:11). Today it seems the height of foolishness for a man and woman, each trying to maintain their virginity, to live together alone. And so it seemed to John as well, for he wrote two treatises against the practice of so-called "spiritual marriage." He portrayed in vivid detail the conundrums that could arise: the monk who is supposed to be thinking about divine things would be going shopping and chattering idly with his 'sister'; they might meet each other at night by chance when their indecency would be exposed; or the monk would want to run ahead of the female nurses to care for his housemate's body in improper ways if she were to fall sick. Apparently some men justified this social arrangement by saying they were simply giving aid to a poor woman—to which John replied that there are plenty of old and maimed poor women to help, instead of only rescuing the pretty young ones! See Kelly, *Golden Mouth*, 49–51.

11. John Chrysostom believed one of the primary functions of a monk was to support the local church. He wrote, "Nothing more truly characterises the man who believes in and loves Christ than that he is concerned for his brothers and exerts himself for their salvation. Let all the monks who have withdrawn to the mountain peaks and have crucified themselves to the world heed these words. Let them back up the church's leaders with all the powers at their command, encouraging them by their prayers, their sympathy, their love. Let them realise that if, placed though they are so far away, they fail to sustain with all their efforts those whom God's grace has exposed to such anxieties and dangers, their life has lost all its point and their religious devotion has been shown up as useless." *On the Incomprehensible Nature of God* 6.2; see Kelly, *Golden Mouth*, 34–35. Recent scholarship has highlighted the intertwined relationship between the monastery and the urban congregation—a point which deconstructs the stereotype of the monk who lives behind cloistered walls and never has any contact with other believers. See Clark, *Reading Renunciation*, 36–37.

12. One scholar has aptly remarked, "It is surprising that Protestants, so given to the study of the Bible, overlook the ascetic dimensions of the New Testament itself" (Clark, *Reading Renunciation*, 20). The Greek word *askesis*, from which we get the

term "asceticism," originally referred to the bodily self-discipline needed to prepare for an athletic contest. The imagery of athletic training as a metaphor for the spiritual life can be seen, for example, in 1 Corinthians 9:24–27, 1 Timothy 4:7–8, and Hebrews 12:1–2. Other texts which speak of the dangers of the flesh or the need to "crucify" it are: Romans 6:6, 19; 13:14; 2 Corinthians 7:1; Galatians 2:20; 5:16–17; 5:24; Colossians 1:24; and 1 Peter 2:11. On the other hand, we are warned against the pride of false asceticism in Colossians 2:18–23. For more on this general subject, see Leif E. Vaage and Vincent L. Wimbush, *Asceticism and the New Testament* (New York: Routledge, 1999).

13. R. Kent Hughes, *Disciplines of a Godly Man* (Wheaton, IL: Crossway, 1991; repr. 2001), 14.

14. On the overlap between the genres of commentary and homily, see Hagit Amirav, *Rhetoric and Tradition: John Chrysostom on Noah and the Flood*, Traditio Exegetica Graeca 12 (Leuven: Peeters, 2003), 45–49. The author writes, "However different these genres are, the exposition of the Scriptures is their indisputable unifying basis," 45.

15. For further reading on the subject, see Manlio Simonetti, *Biblical Interpretation in the Early Church: An Historical Introduction to Patristic Exegesis* (Edinburgh: T&T Clark, 1994), and Robert M. Grant and David Tracy, *A Short History of the Interpretation of the Bible*, 2nd ed. (Philadelphia: Fortress Press, 1984).

16. An ancient source describes the scenario this way: "[John] determined to exercise himself in the sacred books and to practice philosophy according to the law of the Church. He had as teachers of this philosophy, Carterius and Diodore, two celebrated presidents of ascetic institutions. Diodore was afterwards the governor of the church of Tarsus, and, I have been informed, left many books of his own writings in which he explained the significance of the sacred words and avoided allegory. John did not receive the instructions of these men by himself, but persuaded Theodore and Maximus, who had been his companions under the instruction of Libanius, to accompany him," Sozomen, *Ecclesiastical History* 8.2 (NPNF ser. 2, 2:399). For a description of Diodore's responsibilities in presiding over the brothers, see Schatkin, *John Chrysostom as Apologist*, 161–163.

17. This is the same Theodore whom John had warned against leaving the brotherhood to enter into marriage (see note 4 above).

18. Karlfried Froelich, *Biblical Interpretation in the Early Church*, Sources of Early Christian Thought (Philadelphia: Fortress Press, 1984), 87.

19. Ibid., 86.

20. Ibid., 88.

21. Ibid., 85–86.

22. "In Alexandria, history was subjugated to a higher meaning; the historical referent of the literal level took second place to the spiritual teaching intended by the divine author. In Antioch, the higher *theoria* remained subject to the foundational

historia . . . [with the result that] deeper truth for the guidance of the soul took second place to the scholarly interest in reconstructing human history and understanding the human language of the inspired writers." Froelich, *Biblical Interpretation in the Early Church*, 21.

23. John Chrysostom, *Commentary on Galatians* 4.24 (NPNF ser. 1, 13:34).

24. John Chrysostom, *Homily X on Philippians* (NPNF ser. 1, 13:231).

25. Emperor Constantine had made the city the eastern imperial capital in AD 330. Furthermore, a major council at Constantinople in AD 381 had decreed that the city's bishop was to be the second most prominent bishop in the entire empire: "The Bishop of Constantinople shall have the prerogative of honor after the bishop of Rome; because Constantinople is the New Rome." *Canons of Constantinople* 3 (NPNF ser. 2, 14:178). Obviously, John Chrysostom was assuming a very important ecclesiastical position! Even today, the patriarch of Constantinople is honored as the spiritual head of the Eastern Orthodox Church, just as the pope is the head of the Roman Catholic Church (although the eastern patriarch has far less authority over Eastern Orthodox churches than the pope does over Roman Catholic churches).

26. Kelly remarks that the decision in AD 381 to give the bishop of Constantinople the second place of honor in the empire was an attempt "to cut Alexandria, traditionally accepted as the senior eastern see, down to size." It also fulfilled the emperor's wish "to secure for the bishop of his capital a position superior to that of all other eastern bishops" (*Golden Mouth*, 109). Theophilus of Alexandria correctly perceived the appointment of John Chrysostom as bishop of Constantinople to be a direct threat to his Egyptian power base in what had previously been the empire's second city. Of course, that does not excuse his behavior toward John. Theophilus's bad character is also illustrated by his later betrayal of the very candidate whom he had hoped to install at Constantinople. Theophilus used bribed witnesses to accuse him of engaging in homosexual liaisons.

27. One notable exception is the church at Dura-Europos in modern Iraq. This building was not originally constructed as a church. It was a personal home refurbished around AD 250 to serve as a place of worship. At that time, beautiful frescoes of biblical scenes were painted on the walls, a baptistery was installed, and a large assembly hall was created out of two rooms to allow for corporate gathering.

28. The normal early Christian practice was to have one church per city in which a bishop's chair (*cathedra*) was to be found. But the Great Church was not the only "cathedral" in Constantinople. Other prominent episcopal churches in the city were St. Anastasia, St. Eirene, and the Church of the Holy Apostles. See Wendy Mayer, "Cathedral Church or Cathedral Churches? The Situation at Constantinople (c. 360–404 AD)," *Orientalia christiana periodica* 66 (2000): 49–68.

29. Begun by Constantine and endowed in his will, the Great Church was completed by his son Constantius in AD 360. Twenty-one years later, Gregory of Nazianzus praised it as a "grand and renowned temple, our new inheritance." He compared

it to the Canaanite town of Jebus, whose inhabitants fought against King David until he conquered them and renamed the town Jerusalem (1 Chron. 11:4–9). Gregory was probably alluding to the fact that the Great Church, though built on the site of a former temple of Apollo, had now become the most prominent Christian church of all. He also remarked that all the smaller churches spread throughout Constantinople were inferior to this one in its great beauty. *"Last Farewell" Oration* 42.26 (NPNF ser. 2, 7:394).

30. Eusebius, *The Life of Constantine* 4.58 (NPNF ser. 2, 1:555).

31. Meyer, *Palladius*, 51.

32. The danger of Christian attraction to Jewish rites as the basis for John's anti-Semitic remarks is discussed in Robert L. Wilken, *John Chrysostom and the Jews: Rhetoric and Reality in the Late 4th Century* (Berkeley: University of California, 1983, repr. Wipf & Stock, 2004). See chapter III, "The Attraction of Judaism."

33. Meyer, *Palladius*, 73.

34. Ibid.

35. Antioch was known for its magnificent central avenue lined with colonnades (see chapter 1).

36. Legend says the city of Rome was founded by the twins Romulus and Remus in 753 BC.

Chapter 9 Augustine

1. My recounting of this story relies on the article by Jon Krakauer, "Death of an Innocent: How Christopher McCandless lost his way in the wilds," *Outside* (January 1993). The piece is available online at http://outside.away.com/outside/magazine/0193/9301fdea.html. Krakauer has also written a book about McCandless called *Into the Wild* (New York: Anchor, 1997).

2. *Confessions* I.i.1 (NPNF ser. 1, 1:45). There are numerous English translations of Augustine's *Confessions*, and virtually all of them are better than the NPNF. One of the most popular is Henry Chadwick, *Saint Augustine: Confessions* (Oxford: Oxford University Press, 1991). Today the series called The Works of Saint Augustine: A Translation for the 21st Century has quickly become the English-language standard for Augustine's writings. See Maria Boulding, *The Confessions*, The Works of Saint Augustine, ed. John E. Rotelle, part I, vol. 1 (Hyde Park, NY: New City Press, 1997). My quotations in this chapter will be from Chadwick's edition, except as noted. I will also give the reference in the NPNF.

3. On confession as a testimony, see Garry Wills, *Saint Augustine* (New York: Viking Penguin, 1999), xv-xvi.

4. *Confessions* I.vii.11 (Chadwick, *Saint Augustine: Confessions*, 9; NPNF ser. 1, 1:48).

5. Ibid., I.vii.12 (Chadwick, *Saint Augustine: Confessions*, 10; NPNF ser. 1, 1:48–49).

6. Ibid, III.i.1 (NPNF ser. 1, 1:60). The translation from which I quote here is the elegant edition of Carolinne White, *The Confessions of St Augustine* (Grand Rapids: Eerdmans, 2001), 28.

7. Ibid., II.vi.13–14 (NPNF ser. 1, 1:58). Again I quote here from White, *The Confessions of St Augustine*, 26–27.

8. Peter Brown, *Augustine of Hippo* (Berkeley: University of California Press, 1967; 2nd ed., 2000), 39–41. Augustine wrote about the attractions of Manicheism, "I still thought that it was not we who sin, but some alien nature which sins in us. It flattered my pride to be free of blame . . . I liked to excuse myself and to accuse some unidentifiable power which was with me and yet not I." *Confessions* V.x.18 (Chadwick, *Saint Augustine: Confessions*, 84; NPNF ser. 1, 1:86).

9. Brown, *Augustine of Hippo*, 52. At the height of his secular career ambitions, Augustine viewed a strategic marriage as his ticket to success: "Provided that we are single-minded and exert much pressure, it should be possible to obtain at least the governorship of a minor province. It would be necessary to marry a wife with some money to avert the burden of heavy expenditure." *Confessions* VI.xi.19 (Chadwick, *Saint Augustine: Confessions*, 106; NPNF ser. 1, 1:98).

10. *Confessions* IV.ii.2 (Chadwick, *Saint Augustine: Confessions*, 53; NPNF ser. 1, 1:68).

11. In a later treatise on marriage, Augustine seemed to acknowledge in a round-about way the sinfulness of his selfish treatment of his concubine: "If a man lives with one woman for some time, but only until he finds another worthier in terms of rank or advantages, he commits adultery in his heart, not against the one he wants to claim but against the one he lived with, even though they were not married." *On the Good of Marriage* 5.5, quoted in Wills, *Saint Augustine*, 18.

12. *Confessions* VI.xv.25 (Chadwick, *Saint Augustine: Confessions*, 109; NPNF ser. 1, 1:100).

13. Ibid.

14. Ibid., VI.vi.9 (Chadwick, *Saint Augustine: Confessions*, 97; NPNF ser. 1, 1:94).

15. The story of Ambrose's selection by the people of Milan may be read in Roy J. Deferrari, ed., *Early Christian Biographies*, The Fathers of the Church, vol. 15 (1952), 36.

16. *Confessions* III.v.9 (Chadwick, *Saint Augustine: Confessions*, 40; NPNF ser. 1, 1:62).

17. Ibid., V.xiv.24 (Chadwick, *Saint Augustine: Confessions*, 88; NPNF ser. 1, 1:88).

18. Ibid., VI.v.8 (Chadwick, *Saint Augustine: Confessions*, 96; NPNF ser. 1, 1:93).

19. The evangelist's name was Simplicianus. In addition to playing a key role in Victorinus's conversion, he was Bishop Ambrose's spiritual mentor, and succeeded him as bishop of Milan. Augustine also corresponded with Simplicianus from Hippo.

20. *Confessions* VIII.ii.4 (Chadwick, *Saint Augustine: Confessions*, 136; NPNF ser. 1, 1:118). Victorinus was eventually barred from his teaching position because of discrimination against Christians by the emperor Julian the Apostate.

21. Ibid.

22. Ibid., VIII.vi.15 (Chadwick, *Saint Augustine: Confessions*, 143–144; NPNF ser. 1, 1:123).

23. Ibid.

24. Ibid., VIII.vii.16 (Chadwick, *Saint Augustine: Confessions*, 144; NPNF ser. 1, 1:123).

25. Ibid., VIII.vii.17 (Chadwick, *Saint Augustine: Confessions*, 145; NPNF ser. 1, 1:124).

26. Ibid., VIII.xi.27 (Chadwick, *Saint Augustine: Confessions*, 151; NPNF ser. 1, 1:127).

27. Augustine's baptism is described in William Harmless, *Augustine and the Catechumenate* (Collegeville, MN: Liturgical Press, 1995), 79–105.

28. Augustine wrote about that holy moment, "During those days I found an insatiable and amazing delight in considering the profundity of your purpose for the salvation of the human race. How I wept during your hymns and songs! I was deeply moved by the music of the sweet chants of your Church. The sounds flowed into my ears and the truth was distilled into my heart. This caused the feelings of devotion to overflow. Tears ran, and it was good for me to have that experience." *Confessions* IX.vi.14 (Chadwick, *Saint Augustine: Confessions*, 164; NPNF ser. 1, 1:134).

29. He describes the incident in *Sermon* 355.2. See Edmund Hill, *Sermons 341–400 on Various Subjects*, The Works of Saint Augustine, part 3, vol. 10 (Hyde Park, NY: New City Press, 1995), 166. Other details of the event are provided by Augustine's ancient biographer Possidius. See Deferrari, *Early Christian Biographies*, 77–78.

30. The classic work on the subject is W. H. C. Frend, *The Donatist Church: A Movement of Protest and Reform in Roman North Africa* (Oxford: Clarendon, 1985). Among the important points made in Frend's book, which I do not have space to develop in our chapter, is the significance of the socio-political motivations behind the Donatist movement. It can be understood not only as a theological heresy or church schism, but as a grassroots movement pitting the indigenous Berber or Punic country-dwellers against the more wealthy, Romanized inhabitants of the cities and their surrounding estates.

31. From the perspective of comparative religious phenomena, there are obvious parallels here with certain practices found today in fundamentalist Islam.

32. On this point I can recommend the books of John Piper as a way to catch the great Augustinian vision of God's glory, grace, and love. Piper writes at the end of a long theological tradition whose roots include St. Augustine, mediated through John Calvin, the Puritans, and Jonathan Edwards. See http://www.desiringgod.org/.

33. Perhaps Augustine drew this image of personified chastity from his African predecessor Tertullian, whose treatise on monogamy spoke of "two Christian priestesses of holiness, Monogamy and Chastity."

Chapter 10 Cyril of Alexandria

1. Guy Lyon Playfair, *Twin Telepathy: The Psychic Connection* (London: Vega, 2002), 114–115. I am not asking my readers to accept any arguments made in Playfair's book, or to embrace the "paranormal." I am simply using the appearance of a striking affinity between twins to illustrate the concept of two individuals who possess a unifying bond.

2. None of the fathers used the word *didymos*, "twin," to describe Christ. But Cyril did explicitly reject the term *diprosopos*, "two-personned," as a christological term. See *On the Incarnation of the Only Begotten* 694e, in G. M. de Durand, *Cyrille d'Alexandrie: Deux Dialogues Christologiques*, Sources Chrétiennes 97 (Paris: Cerf, 1964), 240.

3. At the time of the synod in AD 403 (called "The Synod of the Oak"), Cyril was in full agreement with the charges brought by his uncle Theophilus against John. Later he begrudgingly admitted that John was not exactly unorthodox, but was more stubborn than anything else. As John's memory was gradually rehabilitated in those quarters that had condemned him, Cyril was willing to go along with it and to mollify his earlier criticisms. He even quoted extensively from John's writings on several occasions and referred to him as orthodox. John McGuckin, *Saint Cyril of Alexandria and the Christological Controversy: Its History, Theology, and Texts* (New York: Brill, 1994, repr. St. Vladimir's Seminary Press, 2004), 5–6.

4. The philosopher's name was Hypatia. The church historian Socrates states that "she fell victim to the political jealousy which prevailed at that time. For because she had frequent interviews with [Alexandria's political leader] Orestes, it was slanderously reported among the Christian populace that it was she who prevented Orestes from being reconciled to the bishop [Cyril]. Some of them therefore, carried away by a fierce and bigoted zeal, whose ringleader was a lector named Peter, waylaid her as she was returning home. Dragging her from her carriage, they took her to the church called Caesareum, where they completely stripped her, and then murdered her [by slicing her] with tiles. After tearing her body in pieces, they took her mangled limbs to a place called Cinaron, and there burnt them. This affair brought considerable opprobrium, not only upon Cyril but also upon the whole Alexandrian church. And surely nothing can be farther from the spirit of Christianity than the allowance of massacres, fights, and transactions of that sort" (NPNF ser. 2, 2:160, slightly adapted for clarity).

The story of Hypatia was written up as a serialized historical novel by Charles Kingsley (1853) in an attempt to undermine Victorian enthusiasm for the church fathers by making Cyril seem culpable for such a heinous crime. More recently, the atheist astronomer Carl Sagan attributed her murder to Cyril's wicked henchmen in his *Cosmos* (New York: Random House, 1980), 335–336. A modern scholarly treatment that likewise lays the blame for the incident at Cyril's feet is Maria Dzielska, *Hypatia of Alexandria* (Cambridge: Harvard University Press, 1995). Today there is even a journal of feminist philosophy called *Hypatia*. It appears this ancient woman has come to symbolize the oppression of noble free-thinkers by the powerful and ascendant Christian church. Charles William Mitchell's 1885 portrait of Hypatia, considered scandalous in its day, makes this symbolism quite clear.

5. For a defense of Cyril's actions in light of his historical situation, in which he is judged by his original context and not our modern values, see John A. McGuckin, "Cyril of Alexandria: Bishop and Pastor," in *The Theology of St Cyril of Alexandria: A Critical Appreciation*, Thomas G. Weinandy and Daniel A. Keating, eds. (London: T&T Clark, 2003), 205–211.

6. Augustine, *Letter 4*.5*. This letter was lost to history for centuries and was only rediscovered in 1975. Roland Teske, *Letters 211–270, 1*- 29*, The Works of Saint Augustine, part 2, vol. 4 (Hyde Park, NY: New City Press, 2005), 247.

7. Socrates Scholasticus, *Ecclesiastical History* 7.7 (NPNF ser. 2, 2:156).

8. *Patrologia Graeca*, vols. 68–77, of which the first seven volumes are exegetical. For an appreciation of Cyril's role as a biblical commentator, see Robert L. Wilken, "St. Cyril of Alexandria: The Mystery of Christ in the Bible," *Pro Ecclesia* (Fall 1995), 454–478. Wilken remarks, "Exegesis is an occasion to discuss Christ as taught in the church's creeds and worshipped in the church's liturgy. Christ is Cyril's true subject matter. Yet without the Bible there is no talk of Christ. Cyril knew no other way to interpret the words of the Bible than through Christ. His biblical writings are commentaries on Christ and only if one reads them in that spirit can one appreciate his significance as interpreter of the Bible" (478).

9. "Because the incarnation is the climactic work of God's self-revelation, the event becomes central to all Scripture." Steven A. McKinion, *Words, Imagery, and the Mystery of Christ: A Reconstruction of Cyril of Alexandria's Christology* (Leiden: Brill, 2000), 227.

10. When Cyril became bishop, he initiated policies designed to disadvantage the heretics and Jews living in Alexandria. In many of his comments about the Jewish people, Cyril speaks in deprecating ways that are rivaled only by John Chrysostom. "He knew no other way to interpret Christianity than in relation to Judaism, and Christian tradition knew no other way to view Judaism than as an inferior foreshadowing of Christ." Robert L. Wilken, *Judaism and the Early Christian Mind: A Study of Cyril of Alexandria's Exegesis and Theology* (New Haven, CT: Yale University Press, 1971; repr. Eugene, OR: Wipf & Stock, 2004), 227.

11. Nestorius, *First Letter to Celestine*. Edward R. Hardy, *Christology of the Later Fathers*, The Library of Christian Classics (Philadelphia: Westminster Press, 1954), 346–348.

12. J. N. D. Kelly, *Early Christian Doctrines* (New York: Harper & Brothers, 1959), 312.

13. Cyril of Alexandria, Epistle 4.4, 4.6. Lionel Wickham, *Cyril of Alexandria: Select Letters* (Oxford: Clarendon Press, 1983), 7–9.

14. *Epistle 11.1, to Pope Celestine.* McGuckin, *Saint Cyril of Alexandria and the Christological Controversy*, 276.

15. Ibid., 11.5. McGuckin, *Saint Cyril of Alexandria and the Christological Controversy*, 279.

16. See for example *Letters X, XXXIII, CLVI*, and *Sermons II, III, LI, LXII, LXXXII*, in NPNF ser. 2, vol. 12.

17. See *Letters XVII, XL, XLII, LXVI*, and *LXVII* (NPNF ser. 2, vol. 12).

18. Two important studies of this period are Peter Brown, *The Rise of Western Christendom: Triumph and Diversity A.D. 200–1000* (Oxford: Blackwell 1996, 2nd ed., 2003); and Richard Fletcher, *The Barbarian Conversion: From Paganism to Christianity* (New York: H. Holt and Co., 1998).

19. At first Cyril was reluctant to affirm the idea of "two natures" because of his insistence on unity. But he became sufficiently influenced by the Antiochene bishops to agree to a formula which allowed this terminology. Yet for Cyril, the two natures in no way sundered the hypostatic union. In Jesus Christ, there is a single person who possesses two natures. Cyril believed the Nestorians split apart the two natures to such an extent that unity was no longer maintained. Unfortunately, the terminology Cyril used was not always clear. Today the theological language has been clarified: "person" is the term for oneness in Christ, and "nature" is the term for twoness. See the discussion of Cyril's ambiguity in Norman Russell, "'Apostolic Man' and 'Luminary of the Church': The Enduring Influence of Cyril of Alexandria," in *The Theology of St Cyril of Alexandria: A Critical Appreciation*, 238–240.

20. McGuckin, *Saint Cyril of Alexandria and the Christological Controversy*, 193–195, or more broadly, see all of chapter 3.

21. I quote here from Bettenson and Maunder, *Documents of the Christian Church*, 56. The full Definition may be found in NPNF, ser. 2, 14:262–265 (left-hand column). It is also widely available online in various translations.

22. The Oriental Orthodox Churches are: the Armenian, the Coptic (including the British Orthodox), the Eritrean, the Syrian (including the Malankara church in India) and the Ethiopian communions. They are distinct from Eastern Orthodoxy (Greek, Russian, etc.) because of their non-acceptance of Chalcedon. They prefer to be called not "Monophysite," but "Miaphysite," to distinguish themselves from ancient heretical views.

23. This church was originally located in Persia (modern Iraq and Iran). From there it stretched to India and even into remote parts of China. Today there are Assyrian Churches all over the world, including North America and Europe; but the greatest numbers of Assyrian Christians are found in Iraq, Iran, Syria, and Lebanon.

24. Cyril uses the same verb here as in Jesus's cry on the cross, "My God, my God, why have you forsaken me?" In this section of the treatise, Cyril was responding to his opponents' contention that such an expression is not worthy of being uttered by the divine Logos, and so was only a cry bursting forth from the human nature of Jesus. But Cyril contends that the unity of Christ makes this a legitimate cry for the God-Man to utter as a single speaker. By describing the human race as "forsaken," Cyril shows that Christ on the cross has fully entered into our plight.

25. Cyril is not saying that everyone is now saved, but rather that in Christ a new freedom exists which makes salvation possible. All people will be raised from the dead because of what Christ has done; yet not all will go on to eternal life. For Cyril, Christ comes to dwell in the believer through the Holy Spirit, especially by means of baptism and the Lord's Supper. Of course, the exercise of faith, grounded in human freedom, is required at the outset to receive Christ. "Cyril teaches that a rightly directed faith is the primary means of reception of all that Christ brings, but that this faith is necessarily ordered to and demonstrated by works of obedience (or it is no faith at all). The place of human free will as co-worker in the receiving or rejecting of divine grace is firmly upheld at every point in the divine-human interaction. Yet the gift of God precedes all and is rightly seen as the source of all things, even of faith." Daniel A. Keating, *The Appropriation of Divine Life in Cyril of Alexandria* (Oxford: Oxford University Press, 2004), 118.

26. Here Cyril rejects once again the Antiochenes' claim that the cry "My God, my God, why have you forsaken me?" originated only with the manhood of Jesus, not the Logos.